T0257073

Praise for *Defensive Security Handbook*, 2nd ed.

Defensive Security Handbook is a must-read for anyone looking to build a strong security foundation. It provides invaluable insights and practical guidance for protecting your organization's infrastructure.

—*Matt Warner, CTO of Blumira*

If you're looking for soup-to-nuts security, this book contains all the recipes you'll need for a well-balanced information security program. Easily digestible and all-inclusive, the contents are perfect for beginners and seasoned security veterans alike. Zero fluff, all flavor.

—*Heather Balas, keynote speaker and senior engineering manager of security, Etsy*

The authors have translated the otherwise overwhelming topic of building effective and comprehensive security programs into bite-sized segments in an entertaining yet business-focused, informative manner.

—*Liz Wharton, attorney and founder, Silver Key Strategies*

This book offers essential insights for mastering defensive security measures. Perfect for both beginners and experts, it provides practical strategies for building an effective defensive security program. A highly recommended resource for anyone in the field.

—*Dave Kennedy (HackingDave), founder and chief hacking officer for Binary Defense and TrustedSec*

A book by practitioners for practitioners. It's not just a good read but a much-needed reference work for security professionals on all levels.

—*Wim Remes, operations manager, Spotit.be*

The first edition of this book was a comprehensive guide to assist defenders in securing their environments. The second edition of this book continues as one of the best resources for understanding blue team concepts in an accessible and actionable way. You will not be disappointed having this book on your shelf and will refer to it for years to come. Amanda, Lee, and William continue to create excellent content that is sorely needed in our industry.

—*Bryan Brake, "Brakeing Down Security" podcast*

SECOND EDITION

Defensive Security Handbook

Best Practices for Securing Infrastructure

*Amanda Berlin, Lee Brotherston,
and William F. Reyor III*

Beijing · Boston · Farnham · Sebastopol · Tokyo

Defensive Security Handbook

by Amanda Berlin, Lee Brotherston, and William F. Reyor III

Copyright © 2024 Amanda Berlin, Lee Brotherston, and William F. Reyor III. All rights reserved.

Published by O'Reilly Media, Inc., 1005 Gravenstein Highway North, Sebastopol, CA 95472.

O'Reilly books may be purchased for educational, business, or sales promotional use. Online editions are also available for most titles (*http://oreilly.com*). For more information, contact our corporate/institutional sales department: 800-998-9938 or *corporate@oreilly.com*.

Acquisitions Editors: Jennifer Pollock & Simina Calin
Development Editor: Shira Evans
Production Editor: Clare Laylock
Copyeditor: Rachel Head
Proofreader: Krsta Technology Solutions

Indexer: nSight, Inc.
Interior Designer: David Futato
Cover Designer: Karen Montgomery
Illustrator: Kate Dullea

April 2017:   First Edition
July 2024:   Second Edition

Revision History for the Second Edition

2024-06-26:   First Release

See *http://oreilly.com/catalog/errata.csp?isbn=9781098127183* for release details.

The O'Reilly logo is a registered trademark of O'Reilly Media, Inc. *Defensive Security Handbook*, the cover image, and related trade dress are trademarks of O'Reilly Media, Inc.

While the publisher and the authors have used good faith efforts to ensure that the information and instructions contained in this work are accurate, the publisher and the authors disclaim all responsibility for errors or omissions, including without limitation responsibility for damages resulting from the use of or reliance on this work. Use of the information and instructions contained in this work is at your own risk. If any code samples or other technology this work contains or describes is subject to open source licenses or the intellectual property rights of others, it is your responsibility to ensure that your use thereof complies with such licenses and/or rights.

978-1-098-12724-4

[LSI]

Table of Contents

Foreword to the First Edition

Spend any time in the information security world, and it will become quickly evident that most of the press and accolades go to those folks working on the offensive side of security. From finding new vulnerabilities, creating exploits, breaking into systems, bug bounties, the occasional cable TV show, and capture the flag contests, the red teams get all the glory. But there is more—much more—to the security world than just offense.

Being on the defensive side, the blue team, can seem a lonely, unappreciated battle. But doing defense is a vital, noble, and worthwhile pursuit. We defenders matter, greatly, to the future of our organizations and the jobs and livelihoods of our coworkers. When the bad guys win, people lose their jobs, organizations are distracted from their core goals, and the bad guys are often enriched to continue their nefarious pursuits. And, like something out of a cyberpunk novel, with the trend of the Internet of Things, soon actually lives may be at threat when the bad guys are successful.

So many of us got our start in the security world as tool engineers, running perhaps a firewall or intrusion detection system (IDS) platform for our employer. Though those skills are highly valued, moving beyond them to a more holistic view of defensive security can sometimes be a challenge without the right resources to bring a bigger-picture view. As we continue to experience a shortage of valuable information security defensive talent, we will need more folks than ever to continue to learn and grow into the defensive security role, and to do it well, they need a holistic view of the security landscape.

Another challenge we often face is that a great deal of the narrative around defenses, technology, threats, and thought leadership in the defensive security world comes from the vendors themselves, and their snazzy demos and marketing presentations. Though a lot can be learned from vendors in the space, as they are laser focused on the problems organizations are trying to solve, they also have a sometimes narrow view of the world. IT Security Vendors will often define the problem set as the problem they can solve with their technology, not necessarily the problem an organization actually has. Countering that view with a holistic view of defensive security is vital to helping organizations become as secure as they can be.

This is why I am so honored to write the foreword for the *Defensive Security Handbook*. The world of security is changing rapidly, and we need more folks on the defensive side, learning from the best practices and the hard-won lessons of those who came before. This book does a great job of laying out key principles and skills, and giving a broad overview of the complex and growing landscape of the defensive security side of the world. Amanda Berlin and Lee Brotherston have laid out an overview of the multifaceted world of defensive security. Certainly, whole books have been written on tiny segments of the topics covered, but this handbook does a marvelous job of giving a defensive security professional an overview of the myriad of skill sets necessary to be successful. This handbook is a great primer for those new to the world of information security defense, those who want to expand their skills into more areas, and even those who have many years in the industry and are looking to make sure they are covering all their bases.

I think you'll find this a valuable resource to keep nearby and reference throughout your career. Best of luck on your path, and remember to keep fighting the good fight. Even when it may seem lonely and tough, remember what you are doing matters, and there are many out there who can and will help. Amanda and Lee have done a great job sharing their experience; now it's up to us to learn from their experience.

— Andrew Kalat
Cohost of the Defensive Security Podcast
February 2017

Preface

Over the last decade, technology adoption has exploded worldwide and corporations have struggled to keep pace. Usability and revenue creation have been the key motivating factors, often ignoring the proactive design and security required for long-term stability. With the increase of breaking news hacks, record-breaking data leaks, and ransomware attacks, it is our job not only to scrape by with default installs but also to secure our data and assets to the best of our abilities. There will always be cases where you will walk into an environment that is a metaphorical train wreck with so many fires that you don't even know where to start. This book will give you what you need to create a solid and secure design for the majority of situations that you may encounter.

Modern attacks can occur for many different motivations and are perpetrated by people ranging from organized crime groups seeking to monetize breaches, through to hacktivists seeking to enact retribution on the organizations they deem to be immoral or counter to public interest. Whatever the motivation and whomever the attacker, a large number of attacks are organized and carried out by skilled individuals, often with funding.

This change in landscape has led to many organizations engaging in a game of InfoSec catch-up, often realizing that their information security program has either not received the executive backing that it required or simply never existed in the first place. These organizations are seeking to correct this and begin along the path to initiating or maturing their information security efforts. There is, however, a problem.

Information security is an industry that is currently undergoing a period of negative unemployment; that is, there are more open positions than there are candidates to fill those positions. Hiring people is hard, and hiring good people is harder. For those seeking employment, this can be an advantageous situation; however, it is a high risk for employers seeking to hire someone for an information security position as they would be instilling a certain amount of trust with possible high-dollar assets in a new hire.

For this reason, many companies that are only now embarking on their information security program have taken the route to promote someone from another role such as a system administrator or architect to an information security practitioner role. Another common practice is hiring a more junior information security professional into a role than would normally be the case and expecting the newly appointed employee to learn on the job. This situation is precisely what this book is intended to address.

A large number of issues encountered by companies with an immature information security program can be remedied, or at least vastly reduced, with some basic security hygiene. The knee-jerk reaction to the task of inheriting a new and immature security department can be to buy as many devices with pretty blinky LEDs as possible, in the hope that they will remedy issues. Some people would rather pay another company to set up an outsourcing agreement, which can be leveraged in order to assist. Both of these options require money. Many organizations that are new to information security do not have the budget to undertake either of these solutions to the problem—using the tools that are already in the environment may well be all you have.

Our Goal

Our goal is to not only make this a standard that can be applied to most enterprise networks but also be a little entertaining to read along the way. There are already deep-dive standards out there from a variety of government and private organizations that can drone on and on about the validity of one security measure or the next. We want this to be an informative dialog backed by real-life experiences in the industry. There will be good policy, best practices, code snippets, screenshots, walk-throughs, and snark all mixed in together. We want to reach out to the masses—the net admins who can't get approval to hire help; directors who want to know they aren't the only ones fighting the battles that we see day in and day out; and the people who are getting their hands dirty in the trenches and aren't even close to being ready to start down the path of reading whitepapers and RFCs.

Who This Book Is For

This book is designed to serve as a Security 101 handbook that is applicable to as many environments as possible, in order to drive maximum improvement in your security posture for the minimum financial spend. Types of positions that will be able to take away knowledge and actionable data from this include upper-level chief information officers (CIOs), directors, security analysts, systems administrators, and other technological roles.

Navigating the Book

We have deliberately written this so that you do not have to adopt an all-or-nothing approach. Each of the chapters can serve as a standalone body of knowledge for a particular area of interest, meaning that you can pick and choose which subjects work for you and your organization and ignore any that you feel may not apply. The aim is not to achieve compliance with a particular framework or compliance regime but to improve on the current situation in sensible, pragmatic, manageable chunks.

We have purposefully ordered this book to begin with the fundamentals of starting or redesigning an information security program. It will take you from the skeleton steps of program creation on a wild rollercoaster ride into the depths of more technical topics. Many people fail to realize that a large amount of work and implementation can be performed in an enterprise before any major capital is spent. A common problem faced in information security is not being able to get buy-in from C-level executives. A step in the right direction in getting a security budget would be to prove that you have completed due diligence in your work. A large portion of this book includes steps, tools, processes, and ideas to secure an environment with little to no capital.

After the skeleton steps of planning out the new and shiny security program, we move on to creating a base set of policies, standards, and procedures. Doing so early in the stages of your security program will give you a good starting point for growth and maturation. Using policies as a method to communicate expectations allows you to align people across your organization with regard to what is expected of them and their role.

We included user education early on in the book as it is never too early to start teaching employees what to watch out for (and using them as a key role in detection). However, depending on the current strength of your defenses, it should not be a major focus until a strong foundation has been formed. Attackers aren't going to bother with human interaction if they can just connect remotely without one.

The book then moves on to planning and dealing with breaches, disasters, compliance, and physical security, all of which combine the management and organizational side of information security with the physical tools and infrastructure needed to complete them. Being prepared in the case of any type of physical or technical emergency can mean the difference between a smooth and steady recovery or a complete company failure—and anything in between.

A good, solid ground-up design is just the beginning. Now that we've covered part of the design of the overall program, we start to get into more technical categories and security architecture, beginning with the two main categories of operating systems. Both Microsoft and Unix have their pros and cons, but in regards to Microsoft, some of what will be covered is installing the Enhanced Mitigation Experience Toolkit (EMET), Group Policy best practices, and Microsoft SQL security. For Unix, we will cover third-party updates and server/OS hardening, including disabling services, file permissions, host-based firewalls, disk partitions, and other access controls. Endpoint management also falls into this category. A common struggle that we see in corporations includes bring your own device (BYOD) practices and mobile device management (MDM). We will also go into managing and implementing endpoint encryption.

Two other important verticals that are often ignored (or not given as much love as they should be) are networking infrastructure and password management. While going over networking infrastructure, we will cover port security, disabling insecure technologies, device firmware, egress filtering, and more. We will cover segmentation, including implementing virtual local area networks (VLANs) with access control lists (ACLs) to ensure the network isn't flat, delegation of permissions, and Network Access Controls. We will then look into vulnerability scanning and remediation. While most enterprise vulnerability scanners are not free, we talk about them in this chapter to prove their worth by using them for a free trial period (to work toward the purchase of the entire product) or getting the most out of a full version already in the organization.

Many organizations have their own development team; however, traditional training for developers typically focuses on performance optimization, scalability, and interoperability. Secure coding practices have only been included in software development training in relatively recent years. We discuss techniques that can be used to enhance the current situation and reduce the risk often associated with in-house development.

Purple teaming, which is the combination of both offensive (red team) and defensive (blue team) security, can be difficult to implement depending on staffing and corporate policies. It is a relatively new concept that has gained a significant amount of attention over the last couple of years. Chapter 18 covers some basic penetration testing concepts, as well as social engineering and open source intelligence.

Finally, some of the most time-intensive security practices and devices are covered as we go through the intrusion detection system (IDS), the intrusion prevention system (IPS), the security operations center (SOC), logging, and monitoring. We have found that many organizations feel as though these technologies are a one-time install or setup procedure and you can walk away feeling protected. It is well worth the time, effort, and investment to have a continually in-progress configuration because your internal environment is always changing, as are the threats you should be concerned about. We won't be making any specific vendor recommendations; rather, we have opted to discuss overall solutions and concepts that should stand the test of time a lot better than a specific vendor recommendation for the current toolset.

Oh, and the Extra Mile (Chapter 23) ... that's the junk drawer where you will find our bits and pieces of configuration ideas and advice that didn't really have a home anywhere else.

Now that we have said all that, let's see what we can do about improving some things.

Conventions Used in This Book

The following typographical conventions are used in this book:

Italic
> Indicates new terms, URLs, email addresses, filenames, and file extensions.

`Constant width`
> Used for program listings, as well as within paragraphs to refer to program elements such as variable or function names, databases, data types, environment variables, statements, and keywords.

`Constant width bold`
> Shows commands or other text that should be typed literally by the user.

`Constant width italic`
> Shows text that should be replaced with user-supplied values or by values determined by context.

> This element signifies a general note.

> This element indicates a warning or caution.

O'Reilly Online Learning

For more than 40 years, *O'Reilly Media* has provided technology and business training, knowledge, and insight to help companies succeed.

Our unique network of experts and innovators share their knowledge and expertise through books, articles, and our online learning platform. O'Reilly's online learning platform gives you on-demand access to live training courses, in-depth learning paths, interactive coding environments, and a vast collection of text and video from O'Reilly and 200+ other publishers. For more information, visit *https://oreilly.com*.

How to Contact Us

Please address comments and questions concerning this book to the publisher:

O'Reilly Media, Inc.
1005 Gravenstein Highway North
Sebastopol, CA 95472
800-889-8969 (in the United States or Canada)
707-827-7019 (international or local)
707-829-0104 (fax)
support@oreilly.com
https://oreilly.com/about/contact.html

We have a web page for this book, where we list errata, examples, and any additional information. You can access this page at *https://oreil.ly/DefSecHandbook2e*.

For news and information about our books and courses, visit *https://oreilly.com*.

Find us on LinkedIn: *https://linkedin.com/company/oreilly-media*.

Watch us on YouTube: *https://youtube.com/oreillymedia*.

Acknowledgments

First of all, we would like to extend a big thank you to our tech reviewers: Chris Dotson, Rajat Dubey, and Swapnil Shevate.

Amanda

I have so many people to thank; the plus of writing your own book is being able to keep going and going and going and...you get the idea.

My coauthor Lee has been absolutely amazing. We both pulled some crazy long hours to get the first edition done. Reviewing each other's work and bouncing ideas off of each other makes for a good friendship and working partner. I couldn't have hoped for a better match.

My second coauthor Bill really helped a ton when we added him to the second edition. Writing books isn't always easy, especially with everything in life that happens. Bill had the expertise and experience to help Lee and I take the second edition across the finish line and was amazing to work with.

I want to give special recognition to my three wonderful boys, Michael, James, and Wyatt. They have started to grow into such independent and amazing people, and without their support and understanding of my long hours over these last couple of years, I wouldn't be where I am today.

My mom for her continued support and encouragement, and for cleaning my house when I travel.

Matt for being the best partner anyone could ever ask for. The teamwork, mutual respect and support, and all of the other aspects made it that much easier to write a second edition. <3

I want to thank the coworkers I've had over the years and all of the times you've been there for me, mistakes and all. The people whom I consider my mentors; some I've had my entire career, others since starting down the path of both information security and leadership. A special thanks to @_sn0ww for the help with content on physical security and social engineering, as well as Alan Burchill for his Group Policy knowledge and content. The information security community has helped me to continue to evolve daily while struggling with imposter syndrome and self-doubt on a daily basis. You've been there for me when I needed you, to lean on, learn from, teach, and relax. While there are too many of you to list, I've cherished our in-depth conversations over drinks, hangouts, Facebook, Twitter, basements, and every other platform out there.

Finally I would like to thank my arms for always being at my side, my legs for supporting me, my hips for not lying, and my fingers for always being able to count on them. Thanks for believing in me.

Lee

First of all, thank you to my wife, Kirsty, and our children Noah, Amy, and Dylan for being so supportive of everything that I do, having incredible patience, and affording me the time to work on this. Thank you. I love you, x x x.

Everyone who worked with us on the first edition, without whom we wouldn't be releasing a second edition: Courtney Allen for believing in us, endlessly kicking butt on our behalf, getting this whole project started in the first place; our technical editors, Chris Blow, Mark Boltz-Robinson, Alex Hamerstone, and Steven Mask; and Virginia Wilson for reading our transcript so so many times.

Everyone who has joined us from O'Reilly on the journey to a second edition, without whom we would not be releasing this: Clare Laylock and Shira Evans.

Amanda for all the hard work that she has put into both the first and second editions of this book, and to William F. Reyor for joining us on this second edition.

O'Reilly Media for their help and support.

Bea Hughes, for whom "blame" is perhaps a better word...I jest...sort of :)

There are also a number of other people who make up the exciting Venn Diagram of InfoSec community, colleagues, and friends whom I want to thank for helping me out with this project in terms of emotional support, mentoring, advice, caffeine, and alcohol. To avoid committing some kind of InfoSec name-ordering faux pas, I am going to list these in alphabetical order:

James Arlen, Frederic Dorré, Bill Gambardella, Nick Johnston, Alex Muentz, Brendan O'Connor, Allan Stojanovic, Wade W. Wilson, pretty much everyone in the Toronto InfoSec community, and the 487 other people that I have inevitably failed to mention.

Bill

I stand on the shoulders of giants, and I would be lost without each of the following people personally investing in me. First, Bree Skowera, for teaching me at my very first IT job (ACS/HCS) how to think in terms of complex systems to solve incredibly complex problems. You are a wizard woman, and you helped build a foundation in me that I rely on to this day to solve problems.

To Will, those early days when you were first released in 2008; and you were working to demonstrate you were in it to make a positive contribution to society; we spent many days and nights working together and building, first with MySBKs PC distribution program; and then later when we cofounded NESIT hackerspace and BSidesCT. It was in the downtimes you also shared your insights (and many examples) into how the hacker mindset works and where I should expect pivots. Knowing and learning from you made me better than my peers when it came to finding bad and I am grateful for knowing you.

To Nick Sorgio and Tyler Tom, you taught me what true excellence in Incident Response looks like at UTC/RTX, and I am immensely grateful for your wisdom.

To Andy Dennis, for always driving me toward being a better subject matter expert, delivering better, and building better relationships with my team, peers, and customers at Modus Create. It was through Andy that I learned what high-functioning development and DevOps teams look like. And it's a surprise to no one who's met him that he's done this with a level of optimism and positivity unrivaled by anyone I've ever met before.

To Amanda Berlin and Lee Brotherston, thank you for your friendship and the invitation to contribute as a coauthor to such an amazing project. To all of the excellent people we worked with at O'Reilly Media, including Shira Evans and Clare Laylock, to make this project possible, thank you for believing in us.

To my husband, Patrick Tassos, you have supported and stood by me no matter what over these last 24 years. You've always been my biggest advocate, and I am so lucky to have you; 143.

CHAPTER 1

Creating a Security Program

Humans are allergic to change. They love to say, "We've always done it this way." I try to fight that. That's why I have a clock on my wall that runs counter-clockwise.

—Grace Hopper, "The Wit and Wisdom of Grace Hopper" (1987)

Creating or improving upon a security program can be a daunting task. With so many facets to consider, the more initial thought and planning that is put into the creation of this program, the easier it will be to manage in the long run. In this chapter, we will cover the skeleton of a security program and initial administrative steps.

Do not fall into the habit of performing tasks, going through routines, or completing configuration with the mindset of "This is how we've always done it." That type of thinking will only hinder progress and harm your security posture as time goes on.

We recommend that when creating your program, you follow the steps outlined in this chapter in order. While we've attempted to group the remaining chapters accordingly, they can be followed as best fits your organization.

Laying the Groundwork

There's no need to reinvent the wheel when laying the initial groundwork for an information security program. There are a few standards that can be of great use, which we'll cover in Chapter 8. The National Institute of Standards and Technology (NIST) has a risk-based cybersecurity framework that covers many aspects of such a program. The NIST Cybersecurity Framework (CSF) 2.0 (*https://oreil.ly/p5k3B*) consists of six concurrent and continuous functions: *identify*, *protect*, *detect*, *respond*, *recover*, and *govern*. When considered together, these functions provide a high-level, strategic view of the lifecycle of an organization's management of cybersecurity risk.

Not only will a framework be a possible asset, but so will compliance standards. Although poorly implemented compliance standards can hinder the overall security of an organization, they can also provide a great starting point for a new program. We will cover compliance standards in more depth in Chapter 8. Of course, while resources like these can be a phenomenal value add, you must always keep in mind that every organization is different, and some aspects we cover may not be relevant to your case—there are recurring reminders of this throughout the book.

Establishing Teams

As with many other departments, there are virtues in having the correct staff on the correct teams with regard to security. Open cross-team communication should be a primary goal, as without it the security posture is severely weakened. While smaller organizations may combine several of the following teams (or not have some of them at all), this remains a good goal to populate a security department:

Executive team
> A chief information officer (CIO) or chief information security officer (CISO) will provide the leverage and authority needed for business-wide decisions and changes. An executive team will also be able to provide a long-term vision, communicate corporate risks, establish objectives, provide funding, and suggest milestones.

Risk team
> Many organizations already have a risk assessment team, and this may be a subset of that team. In the majority of organizations, security is not going to be the number one priority. This team will calculate risks surrounding many other areas of the business, from sales to marketing and financials. Security may not be something they are extremely familiar with. In this case, they can either be taught security basics on a case-by-case basis, or a security risk analyst can be added to the team. A risk framework such as NIST's Risk Management Framework (RMF) (*https://oreil.ly/wJ7W_*); the Operationally Critical Threat, Asset, and Vulnerability Evaluation (OCTAVE) framework; or the Committee of Sponsoring Organizations of the Treadway Commission (COSO) can assist with this.

Security team
> The security team will perform tasks to assess and strengthen the environment. The majority of this book is focused on this and the executive team. They are responsible for daily security operations, including managing assets, assessing threats and vulnerabilities, monitoring the environment for attacks and threats, managing risks, and providing training. In a large enough environment, this team can be broken up into a variety of subteams, such as network security, security operations, security engineering, application security, and offensive security.

Auditing team

It's always a good idea to have a system of checks and balances. This allows you not only to look for gaps in your security processes and controls but also to ensure the correct tasks and milestones are being covered. As with the risk team, the auditing team may be a subset of a larger group.

Again, it's entirely possible that due to factors like budget or staffing constraints, a small- to medium-sized business may combine one or all of these teams into one. In those cases, we definitely commiserate with you. As the company grows, and hopefully the security program also grows, the separate roles can be planned and adequately filled.

Determining Your Baseline Security Posture

The unknowns in any environment are going to be scary, but that shouldn't stop you from diving in. How will you know what level of success the program has had without knowing where it started? At the beginning of any new security program or any deep dive into an existing one, a baselining and discovery phase should be one of the first priorities for all teams. In this book, we will cover asset management several times in different ways. Establishing the baseline of the security of the organization is just another step in that management process. For this, you'll want to gather information on all of the following:

- Policies, procedures, and incident response playbooks
- Endpoints—desktops and servers, including implementation date and software version
- Licensing and software renewals, as well as Secure Sockets Layer (SSL) certificate expiration dates
- Internet footprint—domains, mail servers, demilitarized zone (DMZ) devices, cloud architecture
- Networking devices and information—routers, switches, access points, intrusion detection/prevention systems (IDSs/IPSs), and network traffic
- Logging and monitoring
- Ingress/egress points—ISP contacts, account numbers, and IP addresses
- External vendors, with or without remote access, and primary contacts
- Applications—any primary software applications either maintained by your company or used in any aspect as primary business functions

Assessing Threats and Risks

As mentioned previously, establishing a risk team or role is an essential part of creating an information security team. Without knowledge of the threats and risks your organization faces, it is difficult to custom-fit technologies and provide recommendations for a suitable defense. How threats and risks are assessed will be different for each and every organization. Each internal and external footprint is unique when combined with the individual infrastructure involved. Assessment therefore requires both a high-level overview and in-depth knowledge of assets.

You can find much more detailed information by researching governance, risk, and compliance (GRC). As we can't cover the entirety of GRC in this book, we'll go over a general risk framework. There are a handful of risk management frameworks out there, but in general, they can be summarized in five steps: *identify*, *assess*, *mitigate*, *monitor*, and *govern*.

Identify Scope, Assets, and Threats

Organizations should be concerned with a large number of potential threats and risks that will cross industry verticals. Focusing on industry trends and specific threats will allow the security program to be customized and prioritized to become more efficient. Many organizations have put very little thought into what threats and risks they face on a day-to-day basis, and they will continue to do so until they fall victim to them. Invaluable resources in this case are available through Information Sharing and Analysis Centers (ISACs), which are brought together by the National Council of ISACs (NCI) (*https://oreil.ly/-DVqI*) to share sector-specific information security guidelines. The NCI describes these (*https://oreil.ly/_xR7Q*) as follows: "ISACs collect, analyze and disseminate actionable threat information to their members and provide members with tools to mitigate risks and enhance resiliency."

Not only should industry-specific threats be identified, but so should overall trending threats, such as malware, ransomware, phishing, and remote exploits. Three very important resources to make note of are the OWASP Top 10 (*https://oreil.ly/ZAuaR*), the Center for Internet Security Critical Security Controls (CIS Controls) (*https://oreil.ly/RpT5m*), and the standards outlined by the Cloud Security Alliance (CSA) (*https://oreil.ly/Z-Re1*). The majority of the items on these lists will be covered in more depth in this book, but keeping up-to-date with them year to year should be a key part of any strategic plan.

Assess Risk and Impact

After the potential risks have been identified, assess these risks to determine if they apply to your particular environment. Tasks such as internal and external vulnerability scans, firewall rule audits, authentication/user permission assessments, and asset management and discovery will help you paint a better picture of your overall risk exposure.

During the assessment step, you'll want to analyze each identified risk to determine the likelihood of it negatively impacting the organization, how severe that impact might be, and what the attack would look like when executed. For example:

Threat: An attacker exploits a new vulnerability on a _____.

Vulnerability: Unpatched

Asset: Mail server

Consequence: Use remote code execution (RCE) to access and pivot to internal systems

Mitigate

Mitigation of risks is the meat and bones of why we're all here; it's also the purpose of the majority of this book. Options include avoiding, remediating, transferring, or accepting the risk. Here are some examples:

Risk avoidance
> Dave decides that storing Social Security numbers for customers is an unneeded process and discontinues the practice.

Risk remediation
> Alex starts turning off open ports, implementing stricter firewall rules, and patching endpoints.

Transferring of risk
> Ian outsources credit card processing to a third party instead of storing the data onsite.

Accepting risk
> Kate knows that a certain endpoint has no access to other endpoints and runs a third-party application. This application has a low-risk vulnerability that is required for it to function. While at this point in time the vulnerability cannot be remediated, the risk is currently low enough to accept.

You should only accept risk as a last resort. If a risk ever makes it to this point, request full documentation from the third-party vendors and the executive team, as well as documentation of processes that have been attempted prior to making this decision. Plan at least an annual review of any accepted risks to ensure they are revisited accordingly.

Monitor

Keep track of the risk over time with scheduled quarterly or yearly meetings. Throughout the year, many changes will take place that affect the amount and types of risk that you should consider. As a part of change monitoring or change control, determine if the current change being made is affecting risk in any way.

One way of tracking ongoing risk status is by using a risk register to document different scenarios, controls, and treatment plans. This can be combined with a vulnerability management program.

Govern

Governance in the context of risk management is a crucial step that ensures the continuous alignment of an organization's security practices with its overall goals and regulatory requirements. This process involves the establishment of policies, procedures, and controls that guide the decision-making process regarding the handling of risks. It serves as the framework within which all risk management activities operate, ensuring consistency, accountability, and compliance across the organization.

Effective governance involves the active participation of senior management and stakeholders to set clear risk management goals, define roles and responsibilities, and establish the criteria for risk acceptance and tolerance. It's about creating a culture of risk awareness where decision making is informed by a thorough understanding of risks and their potential impacts on the organization.

Key governance activities include:

Policy development and maintenance
Craft comprehensive policies that outline how risks are identified, assessed, mitigated, monitored, and reported. These policies should be regularly reviewed and updated to reflect the changing threat landscape and organizational priorities.

Regulatory compliance
Ensure that the organization's risk management practices comply with applicable laws, regulations, and industry standards. This includes keeping abreast of regulatory changes and adjusting policies and procedures accordingly.

Risk communication and reporting
Establish clear lines of communication to ensure that all levels of the organization are informed about risk management activities, findings, and decisions. Regular reporting to stakeholders, including executive leadership and the board of directors, ensures transparency and supports informed decision making.

Training and awareness

Develop and deliver training programs to enhance risk awareness among employees and ensure they understand their roles and responsibilities in mitigating risks. Promote a culture that values security and risk management as fundamental components of the organization's success.

Continuous improvement

Implement a feedback loop to learn from past incidents, audits, and assessments to continually improve the risk governance framework. This involves analyzing the effectiveness of risk management strategies, identifying areas for improvement, and adjusting practices to better meet organizational objectives.

By effectively governing its risk management processes, an organization can ensure that it not only protects its assets and minimizes losses but also optimizes its operational effectiveness and maintains trust with customers, partners, and regulators. Governance is the capstone of the risk management framework, bringing together the efforts of identifying, assessing, mitigating, and monitoring risks into a coherent, strategic approach that drives organizational resilience and success.

Prioritizing

Once threats and risks have been identified and assessed, they must be prioritized from highest to lowest risk percentage, to plan for remediation (with a concentration on ongoing protection). This doesn't always have to be an expensive venture, however. Many defensive mitigations can be performed at little or no cost to an organization. This enables many opportunities to start a security program without having a budget to do so. Performing the due diligence required to get the program off the ground for free should speak volumes to an executive team.

> Do not always take application, vendor, or third-party advice about prioritization. Every environment is different and should be treated as such. Prioritize tasks based on the bigger picture when all of the relevant information has been collected.

This book is not intended to be taken as a sequential list of security tasks to complete. Prioritization can differ greatly from environment to environment. Just remember, if the environment is already on fire and under attack, don't start by creating policies or reverse-engineering malware. As a fire marshal, you shouldn't be worried about looking for the arsonist and point of origin when you haven't put out the fire yet.

To determine the priority of some risks, you can use a risk matrix (*https://oreil.ly/nJdmK*), where the overall risk level is calculated by taking "Likelihood × Impact," as illustrated in Figure 1-1.

	1: Rare	2: Unlikely	3: Possible	4: Likely	5: Highly likely
5: Very severe	Medium 5	Medium high 10	High 15	Very high 20	Very high 25
4: Severe	Low 4	Medium 8	Medium high 12	High 16	Very high 20
3: Moderate	Low 3	Medium 6	Medium 9	Medium high 12	High 15
2: Minor	Low 2	Low 4	Medium 6	Medium 8	Medium high 10
1: Negligible	Low 1	Low 2	Low 3	Low 4	Medium 5

Figure 1-1. A risk matrix

Creating Milestones

Milestones will take you from where you are to where you want to be. They represent a general progression on the road to a secure environment. This is heading a little into project manager (PM) duties, but in many cases companies do not have dedicated PMs. Milestones can be broken up loosely into four lengths, or tiers:

Tier 1: Quick wins

> The earliest milestones to meet should be quick wins that can be accomplished in hours or days and address high vulnerabilities—one-off unused endpoints that can be eliminated, legacy devices that can be moved to a more secure network, and third-party patches all could fall under this category. We will mention many free solutions in this book, as the procurement process in some organizations can take a significant amount of time to complete.

Tier 2: This year

> Higher vulnerabilities that may require a change management process to address, create a change in process, or be communicated to a significant number of people might not end up in tier 1. Major network routing changes, user education implementation, and decommissioning shared accounts, services, and devices are all improvements that require little to no budget to accomplish, but they can take a little more time due to the need for planning and communication.

Tier 3: Next year

Vulnerabilities and changes that require a significant amount of planning or that rely on other fixes to be applied first fall into this tier. Transitioning entire business functions to a cloud service, domain upgrades, server and major infrastructure device replacements, implementing monitoring, and authentication changes are all good examples.

Tier 4: Long-term

It may take several years to accomplish some milestones, due to the length of a project, lack of budget, contract renewals, or the difficulty of the change. This might include items such as a network restructure, primary software replacement, or new datacenter builds.

It's helpful to tie milestones to critical controls and risks that have already been identified. Although starting with the higher risks and vulnerabilities is a good idea, they may not be easy fixes. In many cases, not only will these items take a significant amount of time and design to fix, but they may also require budget that is not available. All of these aspects need to be taken into account when planning each tier.

Use Cases, Tabletops, and Drills

Use cases are important for showcasing situations that may put critical infrastructure, sensitive data, or other assets at risk. Brainstorm with data owners and leaders to plan ahead about how to handle malicious attacks. It's best to come up with around three different use cases to focus on in the beginning and plan on building security mitigations and monitoring around them. Possible use cases include ransomware, distributed denial of service (DDoS) attacks, disgruntled employees, insider threats, and data exfiltration. After several use cases have been chosen they can be broken down, analyzed, and correlated to each step of any one of the security frameworks that are covered in this book, or additionally others that may end up being created after we're done writing. One example of a common framework used to map use cases is Lockheed Martin's Intrusion Kill Chain (aka Cyber Kill Chain (*https://oreil.ly/dk8JN*)).

As described in the Lockheed Martin whitepaper (*https://oreil.ly/btd1i*), the Intrusion Kill Chain is "a model for actionable intelligence when defenders align enterprise defensive capabilities to the specific processes an adversary undertakes to target that enterprise," and it is composed of seven steps:

1. Reconnaissance

Research, identification, and selection of targets, often represented as crawling Internet websites such as conference proceedings and mailing lists for email addresses, social relationships, or information on specific technologies.

2. Weaponization

Coupling a remote access trojan with an exploit into a deliverable payload, typically by means of an automated tool (weaponizer). Increasingly, client application data files such as Adobe Portable Document Format (PDF) or Microsoft Office documents serve as the weaponized deliverable.

3. Delivery

Transmission of the weapon to the targeted environment. The three most prevalent delivery vectors for weaponized payloads…are email attachments, websites, and USB removable media.

4. Exploitation

After the weapon is delivered to [the] victim host, exploitation triggers intruders' code. Most often, exploitation targets an application or operating system vulnerability, but it could also more simply exploit the users themselves or leverage an operating system feature that auto-executes code.

5. Installation

Installation of a remote access trojan or backdoor on the victim system allows the adversary to maintain persistence inside the environment.

6. Command and Control (C&C)

Typically, compromised hosts must beacon outbound to an Internet controller server to establish a C&C channel. APT malware especially requires manual interaction rather than conduct[ing] activity automatically. Once the C&C channel establishes, intruders have "hands on the keyboard" access inside the target environment.

7. Actions on Objectives

Only now, after progressing through the first six phases, can intruders take actions to achieve their original objectives. Typically, this objective is data exfiltration, which involves collecting, encrypting, and extracting information from the victim environment; violations of data integrity or availability are potential objectives as well. Alternatively, the intruders may only desire access to the initial victim box for use as a hop point to compromise additional systems and move laterally inside the network.

This whitepaper has a good amount of information that can be used for creating use cases as well.

Table 1-1 is an example of a step-by-step kill chain use case we've created for a ransomware attack without deploying expensive software or hardware for a company with time for implementing open source projects.

Table 1-1. Ransomware use case

Kill chain step	Malicious action	Defensive mitigation	Potential monitoring
Reconnaissance	An attacker obtains email addresses and information on technologies used and creates an organizational profile based on that information.	Create policies around sharing internal information on sites such as LinkedIn or using corporate email addresses for nonbusiness use. After any major breach is reported in the news, run a password reset. Even though they shouldn't, employees will reuse passwords for other services and sites.	Have corporate emails been seen in breaches elsewhere? How many emails are found with open source intelligence (OSINT)?
Weaponization	An attacker creates a malicious exploit to send to the victim or uses a current exploit.	Knowledge and awareness of threats currently being used by attackers will allow for better constructed and tuned mitigation steps.	N/A
Delivery	A user receives a phishing email.	Assess which attachment types are needed in the organization. File types such as *.js* can be extremely harmful and are rarely exchanged from external sources. Implement mailing block lists and graylists such as Spamhaus, DNSBL.info, or other Domain Name System (DNS) block lists to block known malicious mail servers.	Instill the idea of "trust but verify" in your users. Implement blocking of file types of a certain size known to be malicious and associated with ransomware (e.g., flag *.scr* files over 22 MB and *.js* files over 15 MB).
Exploitation	An endpoint downloads a JavaScript file or Word document with a malicious macro.	Disable macros and malicious filetypes via group policy. Ensure any endpoint protection is up-to-date and installed.	Monitor proxy logs for unexpected file retrievals (e.g., JavaScript is the first file fetched from that host, host is on a threat intelligence list, etc.). Use proxies or an intrusion detection system (IDS) (if clear text) to monitor for known deobfuscation strings.
Installation	The payload is executed on the end user's device. (Lucky, Cerber, and CryptoWall use the built-in Windows Crypto API to handle the encryption.)	Keep backups (that are not permanently attached) so that encrypted files can be restored easily. Depending on the OS, you can use "filesystem firewalls" such as the Little Snitch Network Monitor (*https://oreil.ly/_Vzv-*) to permit access to files on a per-process basis. That means that you can permit read access to MS Word but not IE, for example. There are experimental techniques that can be used to block crypto-based ransomware (e.g., Decryptonite (*https://oreil.ly/WETMn*)).	Watch for a large increase in Windows Crypto API activity over a short amount of time, excessive numbers of characters in a domain, or a low percentage of meaningful strings in a domain.

Kill chain step	Malicious action	Defensive mitigation	Potential monitoring
Command and control (C&C)	The ransomware contacts a C&C server on the internet to transmit the decryption key.	Implement DNS sinkholing and autoblock outbound connections to known malicious IP addresses using dynamic block lists (DBLs).	Monitor for connections to known C&C servers.
Actions and objectives	The malware starts encrypting the files on the hard disk, mapped network drives, and USB devices. Once completed, a splash screen, desktop image, website, or text file appears with instructions for the ransom.	Implement honey directories, so when the ransomware goes into C:\\$$ it sees another $$ directory, when it goes into C:\\$$\\$$ it sees another $$ directory, and so on.	Advanced file auditing can be enabled for alerting on an extreme increase in filesystem changes.

Many different defensive mitigations and specific detections can be added at each step of the kill chain for an overall decrease in risk at each layer.

Following the creation and implementation of security controls around use cases, tabletop exercises and drills can serve as proofs of concept and help you build up a collection of playbooks. A *tabletop exercise* is a meeting of key stakeholders and staff who walk step by step through the mitigation of some type of disaster, malfunction, attack, or other emergency in a low-stress scenario. A *drill* is when staff carry out as many of the processes, procedures, and mitigations that would be performed during one of the emergencies as possible.

While drills are limited in scope, they can be very useful to test specific controls for gaps and possible improvements. A disaster recovery (DR) plan can be carried out to some extent, backups can be tested with the restoration of files, and services can be failed over to secondary cluster members.

Tabletop exercises involve several key groups or members:

- During a tabletop exercise, there should be a moderator or facilitator who will deliver the scenario to be played out. This moderator can answer "what if" questions about the imaginary emergency, as well as leading discussion, pulling in additional resources as needed, and controlling the pace of the exercise. They should inform the participants that it is perfectly acceptable not to have answers to all questions during this exercise. The entire purpose of tabletops is to find the weaknesses in current processes so they can be mitigated prior to an actual incident.

- A diverse set of participants should be included, including representatives from finance, human resources (HR), legal, security (both physical and information), management, marketing, and any other key department that may be required. Participants should be willing to engage in the conversation, challenge themselves and others politely, and work within the parameters of the exercise.

- One member of the group should evaluate the overall performance of the exercise, as well as create an after-action report. This evaluator should take meticulous notes and follow along with any relevant runbook or playbook to ensure accuracy. While the evaluator will be the main notetaker, other groups and individuals may have specific knowledge and understanding of the situation. In this case, having each member provide the evaluator with their own notes at the conclusion of the tabletop is a good step.

Possible materials to use in the tabletop include:

- A handout to participants with a description of the scenario and room for notes
- A current runbook of how security situations are handled
- Policy and procedure manuals
- A list of tools and external services

Postexercise questions and actions include:

- What went well?
- What could have gone better?
- Are any services or processes missing that would have improved resolution time or accuracy?
- Are any steps unneeded or irrelevant?
- Identify and document issues for corrective action.
- Change the plan appropriately for next time.

Tabletop Templates

- Tabletop templates (*https://oreil.ly/V_YKS*).
- Microsoft's incident response playbooks (*https://oreil.ly/1U5iR*).
- The Federal Emergency Management Agency (FEMA) has a collection of scenarios, presentations, and tabletops that can be used as templates (*https://oreil.ly/cLR3P*).
- We also recommend reviewing the case studies provided in *The CERT Guide to Insider Threats* by Dawn Cappelli, Andrew Moore, and Randall Trzeciak (Addison-Wesley), which covers in depth the MERIT model of insider IT sabotage.

Expanding Your Team and Skillsets

Finding a dedicated, passionate, and intelligent team can be one of the most difficult aspects of any professional's life.

What can you and your team do to expand your knowledge and skillsets? Here are a few ideas:

- Encourage staff to set up a home lab, or provide a lab for them. Labs can be used for testing out real-world scenarios, as well as practicing skills and learning new ones. You can set one up at a relatively low cost by buying secondhand equipment or by utilizing various cloud offerings. The best way to learn for the majority of people is hands-on, and with a lab there is no risk introduced into a production environment.

- Compete in or create capture the flag competitions (CTFs). CTFs are challenging, and they can provide training and team building as well as improving communication skills. Most information security conferences have CTFs (*https://oreil.ly/ JAYD_*). If you're looking to expand a team, CTFs are also a wonderful place to find new talent. Not only will participants be showing off their level of knowledge, but you'll also be able to get an idea about their communication skills, how well they work with others in a team, and their willingness to help and teach others.

- Find or create a project. Identify a need and fill it. Whatever skillset you want to exercise, there will be a project out there that needs help. Documentation is needed on nearly all open source projects, or you can automate something in the enterprise.

- Attend, organize, volunteer, speak, sponsor, or train at an industry conference or local meetup. There are hundreds of them across the US, and they almost always need volunteers. Just attending a conference has its benefits, but truly immersing yourself will push you further to learn and experience more. Many careers have been started by having a simple conversation about a passion over lunch or a beer. Keep in mind, though, that while networking is a game changer in our industry, it's not a silver bullet for everyone. You can network all you want, but unless you are a desirable candidate it won't matter. A willingness and desire to learn, listen, and collaborate and the ability to think for yourself are all ideal traits in such a fast-paced industry.

- Participate in mentoring. Whether as a mentor or mentee, structured or unstructured, mentoring can be a valuable learning process both on and off the job.

Conclusion

Creating an information security program is no easy task. Many programs are broken or nonexistent, adding to the overall lack of security in the enterprise environment today. Use this book as a guide to work through the different areas and adapt them to a custom-tailored plan. Organizational skills, strong leadership, an understanding of the specific environment, and a good, knowledgeable, hard-working team will all be crucial to an effective program.

CHAPTER 2

Asset Management and Documentation

As a whole, asset management is often not considered an information security function. However, we have found that without mature asset management processes in place, your information security program can be jeopardized. Consider how you would deal with the following events without asset management (and if these give you anxiety, it's a great idea to add them to the list of tabletop exercises you regularly conduct):

1. Exposed public-facing systems that are outdated have been reported on social media.
2. Ransomware is spreading across your internal network by exploiting a known vulnerability.
3. A massive increase in cloud spending has been reported to you by the accounting department.
4. An employee reports their device was stolen.
5. A dump of all of your company's critical HR records has appeared online.

If your company lacks reliable asset information, each of those scenarios becomes significantly more difficult to resolve. This is because without details on ownership or system managers it's impossible to know who to contact to take appropriate action, such as patching the system to prevent further damage in scenario 1. Similarly, in the case of a ransomware attack, without an inventory of application versions installed on all enterprise assets, it's hard to determine which assets are affected and how to stop the spread of the ransomware.

In scenario 3, a lack of asset information could make it impossible to identify which systems are experiencing issues—especially in orchestrated containerized environments, where malicious actors can deploy cryptominers to exploit the systems. For a stolen employee device, without asset management processes and an accurate inventory it will be challenging to validate that the device was encrypted, remotely wipe it, or even provide its serial number to law enforcement.

And for the last scenario, the architecture of HR systems can be complex, especially in larger organizations. Without proper documentation and asset information, it may be impossible to understand how HR data flows across the enterprise, who has access to the data, and how the HR ecosystem is interconnected.

Having solid asset management processes, policies, and technologies in place is crucial for addressing information security incidents and preventing damage to the organization. While it is one of the most difficult verticals to cover, an environment cannot be protected to its fullest without proper asset management. It's impossible to protect unknown assets, which can be a significant disadvantage in troubleshooting or investigating security incidents. In many larger and older networks, it may not seem feasible to be completely aware of every device that's connected or every piece of software users may have installed; however, with the correct organization and security controls in place, the burden of asset management becomes manageable.

The purpose of this chapter is to assist you in creating a comprehensive plan. For those without any existing asset management practices, our goal is to guide you in establishing one from the ground up. If you already have a system in place, this chapter aims to help you evaluate your current processes, identify and address any gaps, and stimulate critical thinking. We will also discuss optimal methods for identifying assets, consolidating information, and documenting it for easy access and problem solving. Ultimately, the two key principles of asset management are maintaining a single source of truth and understanding that it is an ongoing process, not a one-time project.

What do we mean by "not a one-time project"? When initiating asset management practices and developing an inventory, you may start by conducting a thorough inventory exercise, which includes scanning resources, documenting them in detailed lists, and classifying them with various labels. However, if you don't incorporate a system to regularly update this information as part of your routine business operations, the data will rapidly become obsolete due to factors like server decommissioning, employee turnover, and the introduction of new applications to achieve your organization's goals. So, when we emphasize that asset management is an ongoing process, we mean that having up-to-date information readily available is crucial for managing your information security program and responding to incidents. This can only be achieved by integrating asset management into your IT lifecycle management practices.

Let's start by briefly explaining what we mean by asset management.

What Is Asset Management?

Asset management—specifically IT asset management—refers to the end-to-end tracking of IT assets, which includes all network-connected devices, the network infrastructure, cloud-based resources, and the identities or services utilizing these assets. From an information security standpoint, it is essential to continuously monitor the ownership, patch level, secure configuration (e.g., according to CIS benchmarks), vulnerability assessment status, and types of data (such as personally identifiable information, trade secrets, or legally protected information) contained within each asset, including equipment, accounts, or applications. But you can only do that if you know what you have to manage.

Developing a well-defined classification system that identifies what constitutes an asset is crucial. Once established, this system can be applied to the organization's resources and devices to accurately identify, label, and understand each asset's dependencies, criticality, and assigned responsibilities. As the discovery and inventory processes may produce extensive lists of assets, having a predetermined classification system is vital for determining the appropriate level of oversight and management for each asset. The criteria for collecting assets and the methods for managing them should be outlined in a specific process or policy, which serves as the foundation for effective asset management. This chapter will help you ensure you have a solid process in place.

Documentation

Thorough and accurate documentation is a crucial component of asset management. Documentation should be an ongoing process from the beginning, establishing clear objectives and directions while providing a continuous reference when needed.

Allocate ample time to develop the documentation, creating detailed descriptions of all security projects, complete with charts and statistics. This documentation can prove invaluable when presenting how the security budget was utilized by management. Another advantage of documentation is the knowledge gained by all involved parties during its creation. Potential security vulnerabilities or weaknesses may be identified in the process, with each mistake serving as a learning opportunity. Document any issues or errors to prevent their recurrence.

The extent of the documentation required depends on the size and scope of the environment, but the following sections provide a starting point. Keep in mind that assigning an owner and/or custodian to each asset or group is essential. The asset owner acts as the point of contact for their designated asset, while a custodian is responsible for managing the stored information. Assets should then be categorized into different levels of importance based on the value of their information and the potential cost to the company if the asset is compromised.

Establishing the Schema

Your decisions regarding asset management will vary depending on the size of your organization. For instance, managing IT assets for a startup with 10 employees differs vastly from managing assets for a Fortune 100 company. In the following sections, we will present multiple options for creating a satisfactory asset management process tailored to the size of your organization. To make it easier to understand, we will classify organizations into three categories: small businesses, midmarket enterprises, and large enterprises. For the purpose of classification, a small business is any organization with fewer than 100 employees, a midmarket enterprise has between 100 and 1,000 employees, and a large enterprise has more than 1,000 employees. With this classification, we are assuming the technology scope follows along with the employee count. Of course, this won't always be the case: there may be 10-person companies that are managing 10,000 devices, and 10,000-person companies managing 500. You can modify your custom solution based on those differences.

Data Storage Options

It is crucial to determine up front how you will store and manage the data associated with your assets. The method of data storage should be secure, easily accessible, and scalable according to your organization's needs. In this section, we will discuss different data storage options suitable for small businesses, midmarket enterprises, and large enterprises.

Small businesses

For small businesses with limited resources, using spreadsheets or simple database solutions can be the most practical approach to storing asset data. These tools are cost-effective and widely available, often included in office suites such as Microsoft Office or Google Workspace. They provide a familiar interface that makes them user-friendly, allowing even nontechnical staff to manage the asset inventory with ease.

Spreadsheets, for example, offer standard functionalities such as filtering, sorting, and basic calculations, which can be sufficient for managing a small inventory. Simple database solutions like Microsoft Access or FileMaker (gasp, yes, some organizations still use FileMaker) can provide more advanced features, including data validation, custom forms, and the ability to create basic reports.

However, it's important to keep in mind that when using spreadsheets (as in Figure 2-1) or simple database solutions for asset management, there are certain limitations that you may encounter:

- As your organization grows and you acquire more assets, managing and navigating a large spreadsheet or simple database can become challenging. This might lead to reduced efficiency, slower response times, and a higher chance of errors occurring.

- When multiple users update the same spreadsheet or database, inconsistencies, duplication, and data loss become real risks. There might not be built-in mechanisms to ensure users input data accurately and consistently or to prevent them from overwriting existing information.

- Basic tools often lack advanced security features, making it difficult to safeguard sensitive asset data from unauthorized access, modification, or deletion. Furthermore, version control and backup options might be limited or even nonexistent, which increases the risk of critical data being lost.

- Basic tools might not easily integrate with other systems, which can pose a challenge when trying to automate processes or centralize data across various platforms.

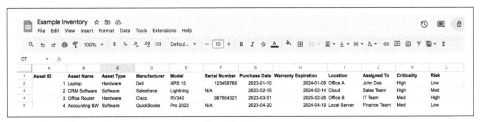

Figure 2-1. Example inventory using Google Sheets

You need to be aware of these limitations so that you can anticipate and address potential issues. By considering a transition to a more appropriate tool before these challenges escalate, you can ensure a seamless and efficient asset management process.

Midmarket enterprises

As the organization scales, it becomes necessary to adopt more sophisticated data storage solutions. Midmarket enterprises can benefit from using dedicated asset management software that provides additional features such as automation, reporting, and integrations with other systems. There are numerous asset management platforms available, both cloud-based and on-premises, which cater to different organizational requirements. When choosing a solution, consider factors such as ease of use, scalability, and the ability to integrate with your existing systems.

Large enterprises

Large enterprises require advanced and highly customizable data storage solutions to manage their extensive asset inventory. In this case, enterprise-level asset management platforms or custom-developed solutions are suitable options. These solutions offer robust data security, extensive reporting capabilities, and seamless integration with other enterprise systems, such as IT service management (ITSM), cybersecurity, and procurement platforms.

Regardless of the size of your organization, it is crucial to ensure that the chosen data storage method aligns with your organization's needs and facilitates efficient asset management. Moreover, it is essential to regularly review and update the stored data to maintain its accuracy and relevance, ensuring that your information security program remains effective and resilient.

Data Classification

Data classification is a critical component of any effective information security program. Systematically categorizing and labeling your data will enable you to better understand the value and sensitivity of the information your systems handle. This understanding will allow you to prioritize resources, implement appropriate security controls, and manage risks more effectively.

Creating a classification system

To better appreciate the importance of data classification, consider the analogy of a Dungeons & Dragons (D&D) adventure (for readers who hate D&D, we apologize, but this is only a few paragraphs, so please bear with us!).

In D&D, players navigate a complex fantasy world filled with various challenges, treasures, and encounters. Each player character possesses distinct abilities, skills, and attributes that help the party overcome obstacles and progress through the adventure. These abilities and attributes are clearly defined and categorized, allowing players to strategize effectively, allocate resources wisely, and maximize their chances of success.

Similarly, data classification serves as the foundational system for organizing an organization's digital information. Just as D&D characters' abilities and attributes are organized and categorized, data classification allows organizations to manage their digital assets effectively. By categorizing and labeling data based on its sensitivity and value, organizations can prioritize resources, allocate appropriate security controls, and minimize risks associated with unauthorized access or data breaches.

In our example, data classification is the "D&D character sheet" of information security, providing a structured framework for managing and protecting an organization's digital assets. Without proper classification, organizations are like a D&D party with characters that have undefined abilities and attributes, making it difficult to strategize, allocate resources efficiently, or implement effective security measures. By embracing data classification, organizations can improve their overall security posture, streamline operations, and ensure regulatory compliance.

Standing up an effective data classification system within your organization may seem like a mammoth task, but it's actually quite simple. You do this first by gathering your party. Just like when forming a D&D party, you'll want to figure out who should be part of your data classification quest. It could be you, the business owner, your tech-savvy sidekicks, or staff members who handle sensitive data regularly. Having the right team in place will help you ensure that your classification system stays on track and is consistently maintained.

Now it's time to create a simple classification system, much like organizing D&D characters' abilities and attributes. Don't worry about making it too complicated; just focus on the basics. Think about common categories like *public, internal, confidential,* and *highly confidential*; these should cover most of your business needs.

Next, explore to know your data, similar to discovering the challenges and treasures in a D&D adventure. Dive into customer information, financial records, employee details, and other sensitive information. Just as a D&D party interacts with characters from different realms, take the time to interview various departments within your business that you believe might process or store various types of data: accounting, marketing, HR, etc. This doesn't have to be complicated; just set up meetings with various department heads and prepare a few questions to gather information on how they use and store data, any regulatory requirements they must adhere to, and the potential risks associated with mishandling their data. While you could simply email these questions, we find that for the best results it's often more effective to schedule a face-to-face meeting, either in person or online. Questions you might ask include:

- What types of data does your department handle, process, or store?
- Can you identify any sensitive or confidential information your department deals with regularly?
- Are there any specific regulatory requirements or industry standards that your department must follow when handling data—for example, the Health Insurance Portability and Accountability Act (HIPAA), General Data Protection Regulation (GDPR), and Payment Card Industry Data Security Standard (PCI DSS)?
- Is there any type of audit system in place, and if so what are the findings?
- How is data currently stored, managed, and accessed within your department? Are there any security measures in place?
- Who is responsible for data management and security within your department?
- Have you experienced any data breaches, leaks, or incidents in the past? If so, how were they addressed?

- What data retention policies do you have in place, and how long is data typically stored?

- How is data shared within your department and with other departments or external parties? Are there any established protocols for data sharing and transfer?

- Are there any data classification or labeling practices already in use within your department?

- What potential risks or challenges do you foresee in handling data within your department, and how can they be mitigated?

Depending on your regulatory compliance requirements you may have additional questions you'll need to ask, but this is a solid foundation. And keep it light: you'll attract more bees with honey than with vinegar, as they say, and understanding what you're working with will allow you to classify your data more effectively. Each department may have unique perspectives on data sensitivity and importance, which will help you to create a more comprehensive and tailored data classification system that truly reflects the diverse data landscape within your business. This collaborative approach will not only help you classify your data more accurately but will also foster a shared sense of responsibility and ownership over data protection among your team members, much like in a cohesive D&D party facing challenges together. (Okay, D&D example done, thanks for sticking with us.)

A university advancement example

Here's a different example. Suppose a university's Department of Advancement is engaged in fundraising activities. To create a simple data classification system for this department, you could follow these steps:

1. Identify the types of data involved in fundraising activities. This could include donor information (names, contact details, and donation history), financial records (bank account details and transaction records), event data (attendee lists, event budgets, and sponsorship details), and internal communication (emails, meeting notes, and strategy documents).

2. Develop a basic classification system tailored to the department's needs. You might use categories such as:

   - Public information that is readily available to everyone, such as event announcements, press releases, or general fundraising updates

   - Private information that is intended for specific individuals but not for general distribution

   - Internal information that is not confidential but is intended for internal use only, like meeting notes or event planning documents

- Confidential or sensitive information that requires limited access, such as donor profiles, contact details, and donation histories
- Highly sensitive information with strict access controls, such as financial records, bank account details, and personally identifiable information (PII) of donors, that mandates regulatory compliance requirements

3. Assign responsibility to a designated staff member, like the department's data steward or director, to ensure that the classification system is consistently applied and maintained.

4. Train the department's staff on the data classification system, emphasizing the importance of protecting sensitive information and the consequences of mishandling data.

5. Implement security measures and access controls based on the classification levels, such as password protection for internal documents, encryption for confidential and highly confidential data, and secure channels for sharing sensitive information. Or heck, is the advancement department accepting credit cards? If so, you might need to classify much of their data and systems in scope for PCI DSS, right?

Without going through this exercise, having these conversations, and documenting the results, you might end up with large gaps of unprotected and unlabeled data.

Understanding Your Inventory Schema

A *schema* is a structured framework or plan that organizes, defines, and establishes relationships between data within a database, inventory, or information system. In asset management, a well-designed schema outlines the various fields, attributes, and categories related to each asset, as well as their relationships and hierarchy. This results in improved organization, understanding, and maintenance of the assets within the inventory. A well-crafted schema also ensures data consistency, accuracy, and usability, facilitating effective communication and collaboration among team members working with the inventory or database.

To effectively manage your assets and address potential security threats, it is crucial to develop a schema that incorporates security considerations. By including the criticality and risk in your inventory schema, you can properly categorize and prioritize your assets, ensuring focused and targeted security efforts. In this section, we will delve into the importance of defining criticality and risk within your schema and provide guidance on integrating these elements into your asset management process.

Criticality

Criticality refers to the importance of an asset to your organization's operations and overall goals. Identifying each asset's criticality allows you to prioritize resources and concentrate security efforts on the essential systems and data. To determine an asset's criticality, consider factors such as:

- The impact on business operations if the asset fails or is compromised (preferably measured in monetary terms; see *How to Measure Anything in Cybersecurity Risk* by Douglas W. Hubbard and Richard Seiersen [Wiley])
- The asset's role in supporting critical processes or services
- Regulatory and compliance requirements related to the asset
- The cost of replacing or recovering the asset in case of loss or damage

Assigning a criticality rating to each asset helps you create a prioritized inventory, enabling more efficient resource allocation and better decision making during incidents.

Risk

A risk assessment involves determining potential issues that could affect your assets, such as computers, software, data, and business processes. By understanding these risks, you can take steps to safeguard your assets. The risk assessment process typically includes several steps, including:

- Creating a list of assets (which you very well may be in the process of doing)
- Considering potential problems for each asset (e.g., cyberattacks, natural disasters, employee mistakes, system failures, etc.)
- Assessing the likelihood of a problem occurring (using past events or data from businesses in the same sector, possibly through an ISAC membership (*https://oreil.ly/zwe56*))
- Evaluating the impact if things go wrong (again, Hubbard and Seiersen's *How to Measure Anything in Cybersecurity Risk* is highly recommended for this)

It's worth noting that risk assessments and threat modeling may seem similar, but they have distinct differences. Threat modeling focuses on understanding who might want to attack your organization and how they could do it. While it shares similarities with risk assessments, threat modeling is more focused on the product development lifecycle's creation phase.

Stanford University provides an excellent example to illustrate this approach. It categorizes its data and systems into three distinct risk tiers—Low Risk, Moderate Risk, and High Risk (with and without protected health information, or PHI)—as shown in Figure 2-2 (along with definitions). The assigned risk level dictates the accessibility of the data and the necessary security measures required to safeguard it. You can use this simple methodology to effectively classify your assets, irrespective of the size or scope of your organization.

Stanford Service	Low Risk	Moderate Risk	High Risk: Non-PHI	High Risk: PHI
Audio and Video Conferencing: Zoom and WebEx, Microsoft Teams **IMPORTANT:** Teams is only approved for PHI data with Cardinal Key.	✓	✓	✓	✓
Backups: Backup and Recovery Service for Servers (BaRS)	✓	✓	✓	✓
Backups: CrashPlanPROe	✓	✓	✓	✓
Calendar: Office 365	✓	✓		
Cardinal Fax	✓	✓	✓	✓
Cardinal Print	✓	✓	✓	✓

Low Risk	Moderate Risk	High Risk
• Applications handling Low Risk Data • Online maps • University online catalog displaying academic course descriptions • Bus schedules	• Applications handling Moderate Risk Data • Human Resources application that stores salary information • Directory containing phone numbers, email addresses, and titles • University application that distributes information in the event of a campus emergency • Online application for student admissions	• Applications handling High Risk Data • Human Resources application that stores employee SSNs • Application that stores campus network node information • Application collecting personal information of donor, alumnus, or other individual • Application that processes credit card payments

Figure 2-2. Risk classifications and their definitions (Source: Stanford (https://oreil.ly/ XZzw4))

Connecting your asset inventory to security controls in this way has a tremendous positive impact on security because your efforts and focus are centered on what matters most (the most critical, the highest risk). Maintaining an asset inventory that incorporates risk and criticality ratings can significantly optimize security processes like patch management, vulnerability management, security monitoring, and data labeling. For example:

Patch management

An asset inventory containing risk and criticality ratings empowers you to prioritize patching based on the potential impact a vulnerability could pose to your organization. This strategy enables you to concentrate on addressing high-risk and critical assets first, safeguarding those assets against known threats and decreasing the overall likelihood of a successful attack.

Vulnerability management

Integrating risk and criticality ratings into your asset inventory allows for more effective prioritization of vulnerability remediation efforts. By honing in on high-risk and critical assets, you can focus your resources on the most significant vulnerabilities first, reducing the attack surface and the chances of exploitation.

Security monitoring

Maintaining an asset inventory with risk and criticality ratings optimizes security monitoring processes by highlighting high-risk and critical assets. This ensures that your security team is promptly alerted to any suspicious activity or potential threats involving these assets, facilitating a faster response to security events and minimizing potential damage.

Data labeling

Incorporating risk and criticality ratings into your asset inventory enables you to prioritize data labeling initiatives based on the data's sensitivity and importance. By directing your attention to high-risk and critical assets, you can guarantee that sensitive information is adequately safeguarded and that your organization fulfills its compliance requirements.

Incident response

When walking through playbooks during any type of incident, having risk and criticality ratings in your asset inventory enables you to directly correlate how certain incidents are handled based on the ratings assigned to the asset(s) involved. Defining different processes based on these ratings can enable you to obtain a resolution more efficiently and reduce your time to remediation.

Asset-specific fields

Collecting asset-specific data is important for strengthening your organization's security and making various security tasks easier. This relates back to our earlier observation that asset management is often not given enough importance as an information security function. Without well-developed asset management processes, your information security program is at risk.

Gathering specific information for different types of assets enables you to better understand the unique risks and needs associated with each asset. This leads to smarter decision making and ensures the right security measures are applied to each asset category.

Looking back at the scenarios mentioned at the start of the chapter, having reliable asset information is crucial for dealing with problems like outdated public-facing systems, ransomware attacks, and stolen employee devices. By including asset-specific fields in your asset management processes, you can effectively handle these challenges and lower the risks associated with not having enough asset information.

Equipment. Numerous automated scanning tools can offer a comprehensive summary of the equipment you're using, for example, providing details on the following:

- Networking equipment:
  — Hostname
  — Licensing details
  — Location
  — Management IP address
  — Software, hardware, and firmware versions
  — Location of configuration backup
  — Serial number
  — Warranty and support information
  — System owner(s)
- Network:
  — Location of network diagrams
  — Dynamic Host Configuration Protocol (DHCP)/DNS servers
  — Ingress/egress points, public IP addresses for the whole site
  — Internet service provider (ISP) account information and contacts
  — Performance baselines of network traffic over a day/week/month period
  — Default gateways
- Servers:
  — Applications and roles
  — Virtualization platform
  — Storage configuration (RAID/SAN)
  — Department or group that manages/supports the server
  — Hostname
  — Integrated Lights-Out (iLO)/baseboard management controller (BMC) address
  — IP address(es)
  — Whether remote access is allowed
  — Compliance requirements (i.e., is there PII or other sensitive data?)
  — OS version
  — Open ports
  — Performance baselines of CPU, memory, and disk

- — Warranty information
- — System owner
- Desktops:
  - — Hostname
  - — Make/model
  - — Hardware specification (CPU/RAM, etc.)
  - — Asset tag
  - — Assigned user
  - — Department
  - — Patch level

Users. In addition to documenting individual user accounts, it is crucial to maintain a record of the specific access each user has. This information can often be tracked through an identity and access management (IAM) solution (think Active or Open Directory) or a manual process. Consider including the following details in your user asset inventory:

- User's name and job
- Department
- Contact information
- Account creation/termination dates
- Multi-factor authentication (MFA) status (enabled or not?)
- Access rights and permissions:
  - — Database administrator accounts
  - — Domain/enterprise/schema (and other admin-level) accounts
  - — Root and administrator accounts
  - — Service accounts

In our experience, when managing user inventory information, the most effective approach typically involves utilizing an IAM system. Setting up scheduled reports within the IAM system lets you stay informed about newly added accounts and their corresponding access levels. This method allows for efficient monitoring and management of user access, ensuring your organization's security remains robust and up-to-date. This information can also often help with social engineering attacks against your HR or help desk staff: if someone claiming to be a certain user calls asking for a password reset or some other information that is commonly used in such an attack, having a correct phone number to call the user back at can foil the attempt.

For more information on identity proofing, take a look at NIST 800-63A (*https://oreil.ly/GmUt9*).

Applications. Software management, tracking, and documentation can be an intimidating process. It often spans more than just the technology team, with owners and licensing being managed in many different systems and departments. However, striving to document the following items as a starting point can make troubleshooting and environment design a much more informed process:

- Application owner
- App name and version
- Administrative users
- Dependencies and integration points (servers and appliances and third parties involved)
- Vendor support details and licensing information
- Data classification (e.g., confidential, internal, public)
- Type of authentication
- Workflow of data:
  — How data is created, processed, and stored within the application
  — Data transmission methods between systems or components (e.g., APIs, file transfers, etc.)
  — Any data retention policies or schedules for data deletion

Cloud assets. Many cloud providers have their own automated asset management and tracking systems built into their solutions by default. However, if you have assets spread over multiple providers or are using less advanced providers where you have to track your own items, you'll want to remember to document the following:

- Monitoring and logging:
  — Alerting configuration (where are alerts sent, and what is monitored?)
  — Log storage and retention details
  — Integration with any third-party monitoring tools (e.g., Blumira)

- Users and secrets:
  - Secret management solution details
  - Assigned roles or security policies
  - Any other accounts that are assigned roles
- Network infrastructure:
  - Virtual private cloud (VPC) configurations
  - Subnets, using Classless Inter-Domain Routing (CIDR) notation
  - Network security groups and associated rules
- Databases:
  - Database instances
  - Encryption settings
  - Backup and retention policies
  - Data classification (e.g., confidential, internal, public)
- Other resources:
  - Compute engine virtual machines (VMs)
  - Cloud storage buckets and blobs
  - App engine instances
- Policies:
  - IAM policy
  - Access context manager policy

Other. Additional information you should keep track of includes:

- Certificates and expiration dates
- Domains and expiration dates

Tracking certificates and domains separately can make sense, depending on the structure and needs of your organization. If your organization manages a large number of both, tracking them separately can provide better visibility and control. It allows you to focus on specific aspects of these assets and effectively manage renewals and updates. On the other hand, if your organization only manages a small number of certificates it may make more sense to track this information within your application or server inventory.

It's important to keep track of this information, especially in the case of domains, because domain and subdomain takeovers can lead to data breaches. In his Medium post "Subdomain Takeover and How the Things Evolved with Domain Verification" (*https://oreil.ly/TaHAv*), Gupta Bless provides a concise explanation of this, describing how attackers hijack subdomains of a target domain and host malicious content on them and how to identify, execute, and prevent this kind of attack using various tools and techniques.

 Maintaining consistency and organization in the documentation of your assets is just as crucial as the documentation itself. Adopting a uniform naming convention helps in locating assets and comprehending their roles, and potentially for automation as there will be a pattern to follow. For instance, names like the following can convey a significant amount of information in a consistent way:

- ORG1-DC1-R2B-RTR3 = Organization 1, Datacenter 1, Row 2, Rack B, Router 3
- SVC_ORG2-SQL10-SNOW = The service account for Organization 2, SQL Server 10, the Snow Application
- ORG3-FL1-JC-AP3 = Organization 3, Floor 1, JC Hall, Wireless Access Point 3

Asset Management Implementation Steps

The asset management process can be separated into four distinct steps: defining the lifecycle, information gathering, change tracking, and monitoring and reporting. Assets can be added to the environment at an alarming rate via scripted VM rollouts or business acquisitions, refreshed to new hardware or software versions, or removed altogether. There are several enterprise-level tools that assist in identifying data on systems. A solution should be implemented that will track an asset from as early as possible until its eventual decommissioning. For a more verbose explanation, check out the SANS Institute whitepaper "Information Classification Who, Why, and How" (*https://oreil.ly/pMptw*) by Sue Fowler.

Defining the Lifecycle

There are many lifecycle stages in between delivery and decommissioning: an asset may be moved, the person it's assigned to may no longer be employed by the company, it may require repair or replacement, or it may go inactive while its assigned user is on a leave of absence. Define the possible lifecycle events, and document them. Each department or person involved in each step should understand when and how assets are tracked at every point of their lifecycle. This helps ensure that any unplanned deviation from documented processes is caught.

The following is a map of a very basic asset management lifecycle:

Procure

The procurement stage of the lifecycle is where assets are initially added to be tracked. At this point, the initial device information, such as serial number, purchase order (PO) number, asset owner, criticality, and model name and number, can be added to the tracking system. Be aware that many organizations procure equipment in more than one area.

Deploy

When an asset is deployed by a sysadmin, network admin, help desk technician, or other employee, the location of the device can be updated and any automated software data population can be tested. Remember: prior to deploying an asset, you should reset the default password, scan it for viruses and vulnerabilities, or build it with a custom secure image (if applicable). Too often, assets arrive from vendors that are already infected or that shipped with outdated software that has security flaws.

Manage

The management lifecycle step may have many substeps, depending on the level of documentation and tracking that is decided upon. Items can be moved to storage, upgraded, replaced, or returned, or may change users, locations, or departments.

Decommission

Decommissioning assets is one of the most important steps of the lifecycle due to the inherent security risks regarding the disposal of potentially confidential data. When deciding on disposal options, different classifications of data can be tied to varying levels. There are many different ways to destroy data, and these have varying levels of security and cost. For example, for solid state drives (SSDs) the options include:

Staging for disposal

Secure erase commands: Utilize the SSD's built-in commands, such as the ATA Secure Erase command, which is designed to erase all data stored on the SSD. This method is effective and maintains the drive's residual value for reuse.

Encryption: Employ full-disk encryption as soon as the SSD is put into use. Once decommissioned, erasing the encryption keys renders the data unrecoverable, allowing for safe disposal or repurposing of the drive.

Physical disposal

> *Physical destruction:* While SSDs do not have platters like hard disk drives (HDDs), physical destruction methods such as shredding or incineration ensure the flash memory chips are completely destroyed, making data recovery impossible. This method is typically reserved for drives containing highly sensitive data, and it eliminates the possibility of reuse.

> *Dismantling:* Carefully dismantling the SSD to remove and destroy the memory chips can be an effective way to ensure data is destroyed. This method requires more effort and technical knowledge but can be a secure way to decommission SSDs.

Information Gathering

Information gathering can be a challenging and complex process, varying significantly from one environment to another. To overcome these hurdles, it's essential to have a reliable software package and well-planned processes that enable efficient asset discovery and management. For those on a tight budget, there are several cost-effective, open source alternatives available. For example, Netdisco (*https://oreil.ly/FEMmh*) is a user-friendly open source network management tool designed to help organizations effortlessly create and maintain an inventory of their network devices and assets. As a Simple Network Management Protocol (SNMP)–based L2/L3 tool, Netdisco is perfect for managing moderate to large networks. By automatically discovering and collecting information about devices connected to the network, it offers a centralized view of the network infrastructure, making asset management a simple task.

Besides using a tool like Netdisco, there are various manual techniques that can help with information gathering, such as checking the Address Resolution Protocol (ARP) cache, referring to DHCP records, employing Nmap for network exploration, using PowerShell in Windows environments, leveraging the SNMP, integrating data from vulnerability management software, and taking advantage of the Windows Management Interface (WMI). However, these methods can be more challenging and time-consuming, so it's best to consider these approaches as backup options unless you have a specific reason to gather inventory information this way.

Vulnerability management software

Data from a vulnerability scanner can be added to the asset management system. This assists in tracking risks and adding to the overall amount of useful information about assets. In addition to tracking risks, vulnerability scanners often provide detailed information about the assets themselves, such as operating systems, software versions, and network configurations. This information further enriches your asset management database, allowing you to make more informed decisions about resource allocation, maintenance, and lifecycle management. One open source example is OpenVAS (*https://oreil.ly/5TqXO*); while it can be complex to set up and configure, if you're on a shoestring budget it can give you visibility you won't be able to gather any other way.

Asset management software

osquery (*https://oreil.ly/9u_cG*) is an open source tool that enables you to query your organization's devices, both servers and endpoints, as if they were databases. Developed by Facebook, osquery provides real-time insights into your systems' security, compliance, and performance by allowing you to run SQL-like queries on operating system attributes. It covers Windows, macOS, and Linux and performs similarly to many commercial endpoint management solutions.

Imagine you're an IT administrator at a midsized company, and you've been tasked with auditing the software installed on employees' workstations to ensure compliance with licensing agreements and company policies. To accomplish this, you decide to use osquery to interrogate the endpoints and gather the necessary information.

First, you'll need to install and configure osquery on the targeted endpoint or deploy it across the organization using a centralized management solution. Once osquery is set up, you can run SQL-like queries to gather information about the software installed on the endpoint and the users who have been using it. For example, to list all installed software on a Windows machine, you could run the following query:

```
SELECT name, version, install_location,
       publisher
       FROM programs;
```

This query would return the name, version, install location, and publisher of all installed software on the endpoint.

Next, to find out which users have been using specific software, you could query the logged-in users and their associated processes. You can achieve this by joining the users and processes tables, filtering by the desired software executable name. For example, if you wanted to find users who have been using Microsoft Word, you could run a query like:

```
SELECT u.username, p.pid, p.name,
       p.cmdline
       FROM users u, processes p
       WHERE u.uid = p.uid AND p.name = 'winword.exe';
```

This query would return a list of usernames, process IDs, process names, and command-line arguments for all instances of Microsoft Word (*winword.exe*) running on the endpoint.

With the results of these queries, you can analyze the installed software on the endpoint and identify which users have been using specific applications. This information can be used to ensure compliance with licensing agreements, company policies, and security best practices. It can help you make informed decisions about software usage, allocation of resources, and potential security risks in your organization, in addition to providing real-time data about the inventory of your fleet of assets.

Asset management in the cloud(s)

It's increasingly uncommon for an organization to have no resources hosted in the cloud. Ideally, a well-architected environment using a security reference framework will have been established to tackle inventory challenges such as tagging resources. However, many professionals find themselves working in cloud environments they didn't create, which can pose significant inventory management challenges. To address these issues, it's crucial to be able to manage assets and gather information across various cloud platforms, such as Amazon Web Services (AWS), Google Cloud Platform (GCP), and Microsoft Azure. Each provider offers unique tools and services to facilitate this process. For example, AWS Config (*https://oreil.ly/V7hCi*) is an essential service for maintaining a foundational inventory of resources hosted in the AWS cloud. It enables you to record, monitor, and evaluate the configurations of AWS resources in your account. To begin collecting basic information, simply activate AWS Config, and it will record your resources' configurations in a central, user-friendly store. You can then query this data using standard SQL syntax, such as:

```
SELECT resourceId,
       resourceType,
       configuration.instanceType,
       configuration.placement.tenancy,
       configuration.imageId,
       availabilityZone,
       configuration.tags.Owner
       WHERE resourceType = 'AWS::EC2::Instance';
```

More information on the AWS Config schema is available on GitHub (*https://oreil.ly/LJah8*). You can also sort and filter data within the AWS Config WebUI with minimal SQL expertise.

Another approach to gathering crucial data from AWS involves using the CLI or a simple Python script. For example, using the *Boto3* library, you can create a Python script like *aws_cost.py* (*https://oreil.ly/1tkUN*) to collect a list of Amazon Elastic Compute Cloud (EC2) hosts and their associated monthly costs. If you have implemented a tagging schema (such as Owner, Risk, or Criticality), you can easily adapt the script for your specific use case. To execute the script, simply upload it to a cloud shell and then call it with a command like the following:

```
python3 aws_cost.py
```

It's worth noting that AWS Systems Manager can also gather extremely detailed inventory information. Systems Manager offers visibility and control of infrastructure on AWS and provides an interface for managing resources. However, most organizations tend to use Systems Manager for inventory management only if they're already using it for other operational management tasks.

Embracing infrastructure as code

Utilizing infrastructure as code (IaC) tools like Terraform offers a consistent approach to managing cloud infrastructure across providers. Terraform enables you to create and manage infrastructure resources through declarative configuration files. By managing your infrastructure as code, you can implement an approval process, version control, and continuous integration, ensuring that any infrastructure changes are validated and approved before being applied. This method not only streamlines information gathering but also improves visibility, security, and control over your cloud infrastructure.

Focusing on inventory and asset management, Terraform's significance lies in its ability to track the state of every created resource in its state file. This allows you to manipulate and extrapolate a comprehensive inventory of your infrastructure built using Terraform.

You can pull the state to your local machine:

```
terraform state pull > terraform.tfstate
```

And then you can parse the state file with JQ. For example, if you wanted a list of EC2 instances, you could do:

```
jq '.resources[] | select(.provider ==
        "provider[\"aws\"]" and .type == "aws_instance") |
        .instances[].attributes.id' terraform.tfstate
```

How much useful information you'll be able to extract using this approach depends on your proficiency with JQ. However, mastering JQ is a valuable skill as you delve deeper into extracting data from cloud providers. Both Linode (*https://oreil.ly/bBYOV*) and Digital Ocean (*https://oreil.ly/xMbXD*) offer helpful guides.

Change Tracking

Maintaining an up-to-date inventory necessitates tracking changes in hardware, software, and performance. Certain alterations can significantly impact the security risk associated with a device. Here are three examples demonstrating how untracked changes can introduce new security vulnerabilities to an environment:

- Jennifer manages a division that has recently launched a new service line. They collaborate with the marketing team and receive approval to purchase a domain and set up a WordPress site. Before making the site public, Jennifer installs WordPress on their machine and starts adding plug-ins. WordPress itself has a history of vulnerabilities, and plug-ins, which can be developed by anyone, may introduce risks ranging from privilege escalation to cross-site scripting (XSS). Implementing a change-tracking solution can help identify and alert Jennifer's team of any unapproved or unlicensed software additions.

- Ethan decides to leave the company and, before departing, uninstalls an expensive software application from their work laptop to retain the license key for personal use. When the laptop is repurposed, the new user will likely need the same software. An asset management solution should have a record of the software, including licensing keys, vendor contact information, and renewal dates. This information ensures a smooth transition for the new user and prevents potential security gaps.

- Noah leads the DevOps team for a company heavily reliant on AWS infrastructure. They use various EC2 instances for application servers, databases, and load balancers. To ensure security and compliance, it's essential for Noah's team to monitor and manage changes across all resources. One day, a team member launches a new EC2 instance for a microservice using an outdated Amazon Machine Image (AMI) with a known security vulnerability. This misconfiguration could expose the company's infrastructure to potential breaches. Fortunately, Noah's team has set up AWS Config to monitor their AWS resources, including new EC2 instances. AWS Config automatically detects the new instance, compares its AMI against a list of approved, secure AMIs, and triggers an alert when it identifies the vulnerable AMI. Noah and their team quickly replace the vulnerable EC2 instance with a secure one using the latest approved AMI. By using AWS Config for change tracking in their cloud infrastructure, they effectively mitigate risks and maintain a secure and compliant environment.

Monitoring and Reporting

Monitoring and reporting on assets provides notifications of upcoming software licensing renewals and hardware warranty expirations. Trends can be discovered with the right amount of information, taking the guesswork out of creating yearly budgets and equipment procurement plans. This information can also be used to assist in any equipment refresh processes.

A helpful security measure to implement is the monitoring and alerting of any unapproved devices. In a perfect world, an alert would fire when a device's MAC shows up that isn't located in the asset management tracking program. As mentioned at the beginning of this chapter, however, this level of control for assets can be extremely difficult in larger, more complex, and older environments.

Alerts may also be created for lack of certain software or system settings: for example, if an endpoint has no antivirus or management software installed, isn't encrypted, or has unauthorized software. More than likely, this will be done with some sort of endpoint monitoring software, but it can also be accomplished via a more manual route with some software. Microsoft Endpoint Configuration Manager (formerly System Center Configuration Manager) has the ability to report on installed software as well.

Asset Management Guidelines

In addition to the steps involved in implementing asset management, there is also a solid set of guidelines to keep in mind during the implementation process.

Automate

To effectively manage your assets, aim to automate as many steps as possible. Whenever anyone involved in the asset's chain of custody encounters a repetitive manual process, it's essential to ask, "Can this be automated?" By automating processes, you can pull authoritative information from reliable sources on numerous assets. For example, DNS can provide hostnames and IP addresses, DHCP can link MAC addresses to IP addresses, and vulnerability scanners might uncover previously unknown networks. Implementing barcodes early in the asset lifecycle can also significantly aid in automation.

Before delving into automation, though, it's crucial to establish a schema and implement tagging, as previously discussed. While it may require initial effort, automation ultimately saves time and energy and streamlines your processes, making your overall asset management experience much more efficient.

Establish a Single Source of Truth

With numerous methods available for gathering information about devices, such as DNS and DHCP records, wireless connections, MAC address tables, software licenses, and Nmap scans, it's crucial to select software that seamlessly integrates with your existing technologies. Having conflicting information spread across various locations, like spreadsheets and SharePoint, will hinder your ability to form a complete understanding of your current assets.

Whatever software or method you choose to use, ensure that it is established as the single source of truth for all asset-related information. Communicate this clearly throughout the organization, and address any deviations from the process right away. For example, you might want to create processes that ensure software installs, changes, support, etc., are not performed until an asset is correctly inventoried. By maintaining a unified source of information, you can enhance the overall efficiency of your asset management process.

Organize a Company-wide Team

Assets enter an organization through various channels. While the purchasing department is an obvious point of entry, third-party vendors may introduce their own equipment, and a BYOD (bring your own device) policy can further complicate the situation. To ensure comprehensive coverage, it can be helpful to form an asset management team including representatives of departments responsible for purchasing, receiving, support, communications, and maintenance, as well as system administrators.

Anticipating every possible scenario can be challenging, so it's essential to prepare for the unexpected. Establish a process to address undocumented devices discovered by help desk team members or other groups with access to the asset management software. When an undocumented device is found, not only should it be added to the inventory, but the root cause should also be investigated. Figure out if there are other assets entering the organization through different departments or via alternative means that have yet to be incorporated into the asset management process.

Find Executive Champions

The asset management team should also include one or more members of the executive staff to act as champions and assist with process and procedure changes that will cross through several departments. In larger organizations it can be difficult to ensure changes and additions to procedures are communicated to the correct individuals, while some smaller companies resist change. A well-thought-out and well-communicated directive from someone other than security or IT staff will greatly increase success. This executive member of the team will also be able to see the effects of proper asset management in the form of cost savings and avoidances.

Keep on Top of Software Licensing

When it comes to software license management, knowing what you are entitled to have deployed is often at least as important as knowing what you actually have deployed. More often than not, organizations fail software audits for overdeployment because they can't prove exactly what they have the right to have deployed. Ending up behind on software licensing can be a very expensive mistake. Having an up-to-date list of currently installed software is a vital safeguard against both overage fees or fines and paying for software that isn't being used.

Conclusion

Asset management is an ongoing process, and it can be complex—but with the right approach, it becomes manageable and (dare we say) rewarding. Embrace the principles of classification, organization, automation, and continuous monitoring to maintain an up-to-date and accurate inventory. By consolidating information about endpoints and infrastructure devices, you'll not only facilitate short-term troubleshooting but also ensure you can make informed decisions for long-term planning and procurement. Remember, successful asset management is not a one-time project but a cycle of continuous improvement and adaptation.

CHAPTER 3

Policies

Policies are one of the less glamorous areas of information security. They are, however, very useful and can form the cornerstone of security improvement work in your organization. In this chapter we will discuss why writing policies is a good idea, what they should contain, and the choice of language to use.

Why are policies so important? There are a range of reasons:

Consistency

Having clear policies in place should vastly reduce concerns about inconsistent approaches from day to day or between members of staff. A written set of policies reduces the need to make judgment calls, which can lead to inconsistent application of rules.

Distribution of knowledge

It's all well and good for *you* to know what the policy is with regard to not sharing passwords with others, but if the rest of the organization is unaware of that policy, then it's not providing you much benefit. Policy documents disseminate information for others to consume.

Setting expectations

Policies set rules and boundaries. When you have clearly defined rules, it becomes equally clear when someone breaks those rules. This enables appropriate action to be taken. Departments like HR find it difficult to reprimand someone because it "feels like" they may have done something wrong; identifying and dealing with contraventions is easier when the rules are well defined.

Regulatory compliance and audit

Many industries are regulated or pseudoregulated, and many have auditors. The existence of policies is a criterion common to nearly every regulatory compliance or auditing scheme. By having a set of policies, you've already ticked a box on the regulatory compliance or audit checklist.

Sets the tone

The policy set can be used to set the tone of a company's security posture. Even if the organization's approach to security isn't explicitly laid out in those policies, they give an overall feel.

Management endorsement

A management-endorsed policy, published within an organization's official document library, lends credibility to the policy set itself—and by extension, to the security team as well.

Policies are living documents. They should grow with an organization and reflect its current state. Making changes to policy should not be frowned upon; evolution of both the policies themselves and the associated documentation is a positive thing. A scheduled annual review and approval process for policies will allow you to ensure that they remain aligned with business objectives and the current environment.

Language

Policies should lay out what you, as an organization, wish to achieve in a series of *policy statements*. Details on specifically *how* this is achieved are outlined in procedure and standards documentation. For this reason, there is no need to get caught up with complexity and detail in your policies. Policy statements should be fairly simple and clear and use words like "do," "will," "must," and "shall." They should not be ambiguous or use words and phrases such as "should," "try," and "mostly."

For example, a good policy will include statements such as:

A unique User ID shall be assigned to every user.

as opposed to:

A unique User ID should be assigned to a user.

The use of "should" rather than "shall" gives the impression that this is a "nice to have," not a rule. If there are times when a policy can be overridden, then this should be stated as part of the policy statement. This is often achieved by using phrases such as "unless authorized by a manager." Care should be taken not to introduce ambiguity with such statements, however; for example, it must be clear what constitutes "a manager" in this case.

Documents should be designed to be read. There is no need to fill documents with excessively wordy statements or confusing legalese. Policy statements can be formatted as bullet points and typically consist of only one or a few sentences.

Document Contents

Policy documents should contain a few key features:

Version information
> At the very least, this should include a version number and an effective date for the document. This allows a user in possession of two versions of a document to quickly establish which version is current and which is out of date and no longer applicable.

Revision detail
> Providing a brief summary of what has changed since the last revision allows approvers and those already familiar with the policy to quickly understand changes and the new content.

Owner/approver
> Being clear about who owns and approves any particular document (e.g., the IT director) is useful for demonstrating that it has been accepted and agreed upon by the appropriate level of management; in addition, it serves to facilitate feedback and suggestions for updates in future revisions.

Roles and responsibilities
> Defining whose responsibility it is to implement, monitor, abide by, and update policies (e.g., security engineers, help desk technicians, developers, etc.) ensures that there is little room for ambiguity with regard to roles.

Executive sign-off
> Ensuring that executive sign-off is clearly marked on each document makes it clear to the reader that it is endorsed at the highest level and approved for immediate use.

Purpose/overview
> This section provides a brief overview of what the policy document covers. It's typically a single paragraph and is intended to allow readers to gauge whether they are looking at the correct policy document before they get to the point of reading every policy statement.

Scope

In all likelihood, the scope section will only be a couple of sentences and will be the same for most policy documents. This explains who the policy document applies to; for example, "This policy applies to all *<Company Name>* full-time employees, part-time employees, contractors, agents, and affiliates." Of course, there could be policies that apply only to a particular subset of readers for some reason, and in those cases the scope can be adjusted accordingly.

Policy statements

As discussed earlier, these are the guts of the document—they are the policies themselves.

Related documents

Cross-references to other relevant documents, such as standards, policies, and processes, allow the reader to quickly locate related information. For ease of reference during an audit, it is prudent to also include references to sections of any relevant regulatory compliance standards and legal requirements.

Consistent naming conventions, not only for the documents themselves but also for artifacts they reference, ensure that they are easy to understand and can be applied consistently across the organization.

Topics

For ease of reading, updating, and overall management, it's generally easier to produce a set of policy documents rather than a single monolithic document.

Deciding how to break the policies up is, of course, a matter of determining what is most appropriate for your organization. You may have a favorite security framework, such as ISO 27002, for example, from which you can draw inspiration. Similarly, aligning policy topics with a particular regulatory compliance regime may be more in line with your organization's objectives. In reality, there are many high-level similarities between many of the frameworks.

SANS (*https://oreil.ly/0xx1d*), for example, publishes a list of template policies that you can edit for your own needs. At the time of writing, its list of topics is as follows:

- Acceptable Encryption Policy
- Acceptable Use Policy
- Acquisition Assessment Policy
- Analog/ISDN Line Security Policy
- Anti-Virus Guidelines
- Artificial Intelligence Policy
- Automatically Forwarded Email Policy
- Bluetooth Baseline Requirements Policy
- Communications Equipment Policy
- Cyber Security Incident Communication Log

- Cyber Security Incident Form Checklist
- Cyber Security Incident Initial System Triage
- Cyber Security Incident Recovery
- Data Breach Response Policy
- Database Credentials Policy
- Dial In Access Policy
- Digital Signature Acceptance Policy
- Disaster Recovery Plan Policy
- DMZ Lab Security Policy
- Email Policy
- Email Retention Policy
- Employee Internet Use Monitoring and Filtering Policy
- End User Encryption Key Protection Plan
- Ethics Policy
- Extranet Policy
- Incident Handling—Chain of Custody Form
- Incident Handling Forms—Cyber Security Incident Containment
- Incident Handling Forms—Cyber Security Incident Response Contact Details
- Incident Handling Forms—Cyber Security Incident Response Incident Summary
- Information Logging Standard
- Intellectual Property Incident Handling Forms—Incident Communication Log
- Intellectual Property Incident Handling Forms—Incident Contact List
- Intellectual Property Incident Handling Forms—Incident Containment
- Intellectual Property Incident Handling Forms—Incident Form Checklist
- Intellectual Property Incident Handling Forms—Incident Identification
- Intellectual Property Incident Handling Forms—Incident Recovery
- Internet DMZ Equipment Policy
- Internet Usage Policy
- Lab Anti Virus Policy
- Lab Security Policy
- Mobile Device Encryption Policy
- Mobile Employee Endpoint Responsibility Policy
- Pandemic Response Planning Policy
- Password Construction Guidelines
- Password Protection Policy
- Personal Communication Devices and Voicemail Policy
- Remote Access Mobile Computing Storage
- Remote Access Policy
- Remote Access Tools Policy
- Removable Media Policy
- Risk Assessment Policy
- Router and Switch Security Policy
- Security Response Plan Policy
- Server Audit Policy
- Server Malware Protection Policy
- Server Security Policy
- Social Engineering Awareness Policy

- Software Installation Policy
- Technology Equipment Disposal Policy
- Virtual Private Network Policy
- Web Application Security Policy
- Wireless Communication Policy
- Wireless Communication Standard
- Workstation Security (For HIPAA) Policy

This is not an atypical list; however, many of the policies listed will not apply to your organization. This is completely fine.

Storage and Communication

Policies and procedures are meant to standardize communication as much as possible throughout the organization. To achieve this goal, policies must be easily accessible. There are many software packages that can not only provide a web interface for policies but also have built-in review, revision control, and approval processes. Using software with these features greatly simplifies things when there are a multitude of people and departments creating, editing, and approving policies.

Another good rule of thumb is to print out two copies of all policies after each review. The majority of them will be used in digital format, but there will be many policies that refer to and are in direct relation to downtime or disaster recovery procedures. In cases such as these, they may not be accessible via digital media, so having a backup in physical form is a good idea.

Conclusion

Policies are important tools used to express the direction of an organization from a security perspective, clearly articulating expectations and providing a level of consistency. They can also be used to explicitly state and enforce rules that have previously been ambiguous or inferred.

Policies are not set in stone forever—they are living documents that can (and should) grow and change in line with your organization.

CHAPTER 4

Standards and Procedures

Over time, organizations can accumulate a large amount of documentation. It can be helpful to organize this into a hierarchy, as illustrated in Figure 4-1. Standards and procedures are two sets of documentation that support the policies and bring them to life. In this chapter we will discuss what standards and procedures are, how they relate to policies, and what they should contain.

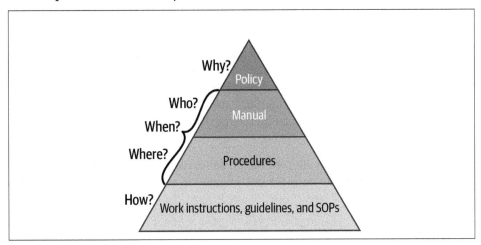

Figure 4-1. The documentation hierarchy

If we consider the policies of an organization to be the "why" we are trying to achieve, standards and procedures form the "what" and "how." Like policies, standards and procedures bring many advantages, including:

Consistency

Worries about the nuances of the implementation of policies at a technology level are removed when consistency is applied. Having a written set of standards and procedures ensures that the rules outlined in the policies can be applied equally across the organization.

Distribution of knowledge

As mentioned in the previous chapter, it's all well and good for *you* to know how to implement your policies in practice; however, if those elsewhere in the organization are unaware of this, they won't provide much benefit. Standards and procedures disseminate this information for others to consume. Organizations often make the mistake of relying on institutional or legacy knowledge, which over time can become almost impossible to communicate effectively to current employees. The original decision makers may have moved on from the company or switched roles, or they might not remember all the details or have the time to answer questions.

Setting expectations

Policies set rules and boundaries. However, they do not provide the detail required to consistently achieve those goals in the same way all the time. Standards and procedures do this by including a purpose and overview. (We'll cover these and other elements of these documents in the following sections.)

Regulatory compliance

As we discussed in Chapter 3, many industries are regulated or pseudoregulated, and regulatory compliance schemes almost universally require the existence of policies. In addition, they generally require the existence of standards and procedures to accompany the policies. So, having a set of standards and procedures enables you to tick a second box on the regulatory compliance checklist.

Management endorsement

Having a management-endorsed set of standards and procedures, as with policies, lends credibility to both the documentation set itself and, by extension, the security team.

Standards

Standards provide the "how" portion of a policy from a technology viewpoint, without specific procedural detail. For example, many policy statements include the requirement that access be authenticated by use of a password. A standard that provides more detail as to what constitutes a password should accompany this policy statement. For example, it will most likely cover topics such as complexity requirements, the process for changing a password, storage requirements, whether passwords can be reused, and so on.

Separating this detail into a separate document (and further separating out procedures, discussed in the following section) provides several advantages. For example:

Documents are easier to consume

A lightweight policy document is easier to navigate and less daunting to read than an all-encompassing policy document the size of a telephone directory. When policies, standards, and procedures are outlined separately, individuals can consult whichever one is best suited to providing the information they need, allowing them to find it faster.

Lack of repetition

Going back to the password example, if every policy that mentioned passwords had to provide complete details on how they are defined, used, and stored, this would amount to a lot of unnecessary repetition (and leave plenty of scope to introduce errors). Extracting this information into a single standards document avoids that; the high-level policies can be read easily, and if further clarification is needed the reader can refer to the appropriate accompanying standard.

Ease of maintenance

Related to the previous point is that a change in the standard need only be applied in one place for consistent application across the organization. If standards were rolled into the policy documentation, changes would need to take into account all instances of the affected statements. Forgetting to make the changes in just one or two places could have catastrophic consequences.

As with policies, the language used within standards documentation should be fairly simple and clear and use words like "do," "will," "must," and "shall." They should not be ambiguous or use words and phrases such as "should," "try," or "mostly."

Unlike policies, however, standards can be more specific and detailed in their guidance, for example, about the technologies in use. That said, they should remain free of specific procedural details, such as commands (that level of detail is included in the procedure documents, discussed next).

For instance, in Chapter 3 we used the example:

A unique User ID shall be assigned to a user.

The accompanying standards documentation would typically include statements such as:

A User ID is created in the format <first 6 chars of surname><first 2 chars of firstname>, unless this User ID is already in use, in which case…

A User ID shall only be created after HR approval.

A User ID shall only be created after Line Manager approval.

HR must review and approve user access rights, ensuring that they align with the user's role, prior to the User ID being provisioned.

A record of User ID creation and associated sign-off will be kept in...

A one-way hash function shall be used for the storage of user passwords. Acceptable hashing algorithms are...

These statements enhance, support, and provide more detail about the associated policy statement.

Like policies, standards should be designed to be read; there's no need to fill them with excessively wordy statements.

Procedures

Procedures take a similarly sized step further along the same trajectory as the step from policies to standards: they indicate how the standards, which offer guidance based on policies, are to be implemented at a technology-specific level.

Language is important here too, as ensuring that the procedures are applied consistently is the ultimate goal. Unlike with policies and standards, however, the level of detail in these documents will probably depend on corporate culture. For example, it is more appropriate in some organizations to provide an almost keypress-by-keypress level of detail for things like configuration changes. In others, prescribing which changes to make and allowing administrators to make a judgment call on how to apply them is more appropriate. In most environments, the latter is typically sufficient.

Let's revisit the last statement from the standards example:

A one-way hash function shall be used for the storage of user passwords. Acceptable hashing algorithms are...

The procedure documentation should explain how this is achieved on a specific platform. Because technology platforms differ and procedures are technology specific, it is entirely likely that there will need to be different platform-specific documents created to account for variations between technologies.

For example, to implement platform-specific documentation about FreeBSD on a FreeBSD system, the procedure statement might be something like:

To configure system passwords to use the SHA512 hashing algorithm, edit */etc/login.conf* and amend the `passwd_format` field to read:

```
:passwd_format=sha512:\
```

Whereas on a Linux platform the guidance would be:

> To configure system passwords to use the SHA512 hashing algorithm, execute the following command with root privileges:
>
> ```
> authconfig --passalgo=sha512 --update
> ```

Both are systems that have a Unix heritage, and both routes ultimately achieve the same goal. The precise method by which the goal is reached is clearly articulated for both, to ensure consistency of application across platforms and teams.

Technical writing at this level can be challenging as it can have a variety of audiences, so having the individuals that will be using these documents be a part of the review and approval process will be an integral part of making each one a success. Some good points to follow for procedure writing include:

- Write actions out in the order in which they happen.
- Use the active voice.
- Use good grammar.
- Explain your assumptions, and make sure your assumptions are valid.
- Write concisely. In technical writing, clarity and brevity are the goals.
- Use jargon and slang carefully, or not at all.

Document Contents

As with policies, documentation for standards and procedures should contain a few key features:

Version information
: At the very least, this should include a version number and an effective date for the document. This allows a user in possession of two versions of a document to quickly establish which version is current and which is out of date and no longer applicable.

Owner/approver
: Being clear about who owns and approves any particular document is useful for demonstrating that it has been accepted and agreed upon by the appropriate level of management; in addition, it serves to facilitate feedback and suggestions for updates in future revisions.

Purpose/overview
: This section provides a brief overview of what the document covers. It's typically a single paragraph and is intended to allow readers to gauge whether they are looking at the correct document before they get to the point of reading every statement.

Scope

This explains who the document applies to; for example, "This standard applies to all *<Company Name>* employees and affiliates." It can range from the entire company to a certain level of management or engineering or specific users of an application.

Statements

These describe the standards and procedures themselves. Ensure these statements are clear and concise and are reviewed on a regular basis for accuracy. The technologies in our environments are constantly changing, and the directions on how to manage them must keep pace.

Related documents

Cross-references to other relevant documents, such as standards, policies, and processes, allow the reader to quickly locate related information. For ease of reference during an audit, it is prudent to also include references to sections of any relevant regulatory compliance standards and legal requirements.

Consistent naming conventions should be used not only for the documents themselves but also for artifacts they reference, to ensure that they are easy to understand and can be applied consistently across the organization.

Conclusion

As a whole, policies, standards, and procedures offer a high-level administrative overview down to the specific technology and step-by-step implementation. While each has its own functions, they all must be written with the skill level of the reader in mind. A clear and concise set of documentation makes a huge difference in creating a standardized and well-understood environment.

CHAPTER 5
User Education

Security awareness is lacking in most organizations. The best approach to educate users about security is to find a way to demonstrate, with appropriate metrics, that you are successfully implementing change and producing a more secure line of defense. A large portion of the information security industry is focused on perimeter security, virtual private networks (VPNs), web application firewalls (WAFs), email filtering, etc. However, we are beginning to see a shift from strictly data-level protection to an increased focus on user-level security and reporting. The defense-in-depth mentality and view of security as a process must be filtered down and incorporated into user training.

Before you spend money on threat intel that may tell you how better to defend your specific sector, it's a good idea to start where everyone is being attacked. One of the largest threats today remains the targeting of our weakest link: people. According to the 2023 Verizon Data Breach Investigations Report (DBIR) (*https://oreil.ly/xTl_x*), "74% of all breaches include the human element, with people being involved either via Error, Privilege Misuse, Use of stolen credentials or Social Engineering. … The three primary ways in which attackers access an organization are stolen credentials, phishing and exploitation of vulnerabilities." (Verizon updated its metrics in 2024 to show that only 68% of breaches involved users, to separate out the difference in human error and human-targeted attacks.)

In this chapter we will demonstrate how to provide more value than the basic training offered in the majority of organizations.

Broken Processes

Experience and time in the industry have shown that the computer-based training (CBT) that many organizations require their employees to complete annually (or sometimes more often) is comparable in efficacy to a checkbox approach to governance, risk, and compliance. It is a broken process. Employees are required to complete and pass this training for continued employment, but once the training is over, the information covered is rapidly forgotten if no conscious effort is made to retain it. This is known as the *Ebbinghaus forgetting curve* (Figure 5-1), and it results in a large disconnect where it matters most—one of the largest proven gaps in security occurs when end users do not bring this information forward into their day-to-day working lives like they should.

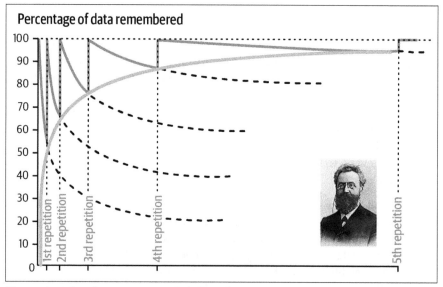

Figure 5-1. Graph representing the Ebbinghaus curve

Repetition based on active recall has been demonstrated as effective in other areas for avoiding this effect, and therefore it is the foundational design such awareness programs should be based on. Ebbinghaus hypothesized (*https://oreil.ly/UxO_B*) that basic training in mnemonic techniques can help overcome the difference in performance between individuals with faster and slower forgetting rates, asserting that "the best methods for increasing the strength of memory are: 1) Better memory representation (e.g., with mnemonic techniques); 2) Repetition based on active recall (especially spaced repetition)."

Bridging the Gap

There are significant additions and changes that can be made to transform user training into an effective and long-lasting security education.

Repetition and demonstration of real-life applicability is a proven, successful way to bridge the gap of compliance, teaching our users real-life skills and helping secure the infrastructure that we are responsible for protecting. This is best implemented with a comprehensive hands-on security phishing and awareness rewards program. A full program design will provide a level of depth and maturity that CBT does not. While CBT is a good value-add and can be used to reinforce real-life scenarios, relying on this as a primary means of security awareness training will not provide the required value or insight to the enterprise's often overlooked first line of defense: the end users themselves. By continually reinforcing the CBT with a custom-built awareness program, you increase the end users' skills and boost the organization's immunity to phishing and social engineering threat factors.

Building Your Own Program

Building a mature and strategic security awareness program from the ground up is achievable with executive support and cultural alignment. An awareness program need not equate to thousands of dollars spent on creating flashy presentations and brown-bag luncheons to draw crowds. Teaching by example and rewarding good behavior are what will improve users' awareness. As David Kennedy, founder and CEO of TrustedSec, put it (*https://oreil.ly/yMU16*): "The point has never been to make everyone experts in security, it has always been to arm the employees with basic knowledge so that in the event something out of the ordinary occurs, [they] may help notify the security team."

An important takeaway and key point to remember is that it is not the employees' responsibility to know the difference between a legitimate phish and spam, or to know that they should be hovering over links in emails and verifying them before clicking. It is our job to have a program that is open enough and makes it easy enough to encourage them to report abnormalities or when something is not quite right. The following are some guidelines to keep in mind when developing your security awareness program.

Establish Objectives

The design of an organization's security awareness program should be tailor-fit and reassessed periodically. With the constantly changing threat landscape, varying maturity of user understanding, and a progressing industry, the objectives should be thought of as moving targets; an objective of, say, one year of decreased malware removals on desktops may mature past that to increased reporting of phishing/vishing attacks the next. Take care not to establish too aggressive a set of objectives, as this can result in a failed or unrealistic program. Concentrating on one or two achievable objectives at the beginning of a new program will allow you to accomplish specific goals. You can then adjust the targets periodically to reflect the organization's and program's maturity.

Establish Baselines

Many organizations do not yet provide formal security awareness training, so establishing a baseline should begin with a live-fire exercise testing the skills and real-world knowledge of a good subset of your users. This will give you a realistic idea of where your security posture stands in relation to not only technical baselines but also cultural norms. It's important to know how users currently respond to threats and irregularities. Establishing an engagement with a certified and skilled penetration testing company can help you baseline these responses. By having a third party assess the skills of your users when confronted with professional phishing campaigns, for example, you will gain valuable data and insights.

Scope and Create Program Rules and Guidelines

When the user or employee is being treated essentially as a customer, rules and guidelines should be well thought out and strategized. Miscommunications will only impede the learning process, making succeeding with the program more difficult. Align the rules to be consistent with the organization's culture in order to achieve a higher adoption rate. Having input from people at different levels will enable you to define clear and concise program instructions and rules, making implementation easier.

You are taught in driver's education to wear your seat belt, adjust your mirrors, and look both ways at every intersection. This basic safety training is essential, but your first close call—or, even worse, real accident—provides you with real-world experience that your mind will fall back on each time you make a decision in the future. It's the same with security awareness: for example, experiencing a phishing attack is often what really gives employees pause when future emails show up that may look a little odd or out of place. Afterward, the training teaches them what could possibly be at risk when they click an illegitimate link. Setting up the attack to automatically redirect to a website that aligns with the program theme will create a connection between real-life events and the message being presented for education.

Provide Positive Reinforcement

An important aspect of such a program is letting users know that it's OK if they fall victim to the attack. This must be a consistent message throughout the educational materials. The more comfortable users feel reporting the incident, the more cooperation and adoption you will witness. Assure the users that it's better to gain experience from an internal training attempt than from a real phishing attack, and remind them that practice makes perfect. The training should include tips on what to look for and, equally importantly, how to report something that seems abnormal. Even with a great first line of defense and solid incident response procedures in place, it's crucial to secure the human element, which is sometimes the weakest security link—and a great detection asset.

Being able to reward good behavior is an essential part of the program as well. Employees should not feel ashamed about going to the right people for help, or afraid of being reprimanded for making a mistake. Gamification (applying game principles to a given situation) works well in many aspects of life, so why should this be any different? Make the program fun, and even with a small budget it may not just satisfy your expectations, but exceed them. Holding a gift card lottery or offering participants discounted services or other items to enforce the brand of the program can help reinforce your message and boost engagement.

Define Incident Response Processes

Incident response looks different in every organization. If you have a current proven method of incident response, you can use your newly created program as a case study for testing procedures and policies. This will allow you to flush out any inconsistencies, inefficiencies, or unplanned-for situations. Assessing each step of the process will give you the necessary information to add or change policies to fit the needs of the organization around certain types of attacks.

Obtaining Meaningful Metrics

> *Successful metrics programs include well-defined measurements and the necessary steps to obtain them.*
>
> —Bill Gardner and Valerie Thomas, *Building an Information Security Awareness Program* (Syngress)

As we mentioned in the previous section, an important part of an awareness program is establishing baseline metrics. Without these, you won't know how far your program has improved. Work toward long-term goals regarding the overall security of the organization. This will help you build appropriate metrics into the already forming security program to keep it on track.

Measurements

There is an abundance of measurements to take in a security awareness program. Depending on your program setup and your goals, they may have to be more tailor-fit, but here are some common totals to track:

- Emails sent
- Emails opened
- Links clicked
- Credentials harvested

- Reports of phishing attempts
- Emails not reported on
- Hits on training sites

Tracking Success Rate and Progress

Keeping track of click percentages, phishes reported, and incidents reported is a good start, and it is necessary for any complete metrics collection effort. However, charting your gains and losses with structured data over time will give your organization a deeper understanding of progress. Successful education and retained knowledge will be apparent with the increase or decrease of certain measurements and the achievement of goals set for particular metrics. Periodic assessment of shifts in metrics should be performed to assist in guiding the education program's goals and content, as well as other possible implementations or changes in the current environment's security structure.

Important Metrics

There's a difference between metrics and measures. Measures are concrete and quantitative and usually measure one thing (e.g., I have 10 bananas). Metrics describe a quality and require a measurement baseline (I have five more overripe bananas than I did yesterday).

The key metric you want to track is how much your security posture has improved with respect to your baseline. You should see increased reporting of suspicious activity on your network, less malware, fewer DNS queries to blocked sites, and a decrease in other activity that might lead an analyst to believe the possibility of a targeted attack has been blocked. The ability to link key metrics back to specific departments, buildings, or roles provides the information you need to scope more directed education.

Conclusion

User education can be a massive undertaking, but if done correctly it will provide a strong layer of defense and monitoring. It shouldn't be the first step toward creating a more secure environment, but it can greatly increase your level of protection once a strong baseline has been created. For the best results, remember to always use a carrot and not a stick.

CHAPTER 6

Incident Response

As the name suggests, incident response is the set of processes and procedures that are initiated once a security incident has been declared. In modern-day computing, however, incidents may range from a single compromised endpoint to complete network compromises resulting in massive data breaches. In addition, data breaches and enterprise-wide attacks are becoming more and more common, and thus incident response has grown in meaning beyond merely these processes and procedures to encompass an entire discipline within information security.

In this chapter we will discuss the various processes involved in incident response, tools and technology options, and the most common forms of technical analysis that you are likely to need to perform during an incident.

Processes

Incident response processes are an integral component of being able to react quickly in the event of an incident, identify a nonincident, operate efficiently during an incident, and improve after an incident. Having processes in place before an incident begins will pay dividends in the long run.

Pre-Incident Processes

The processes associated with incident response are not merely concerned with what happens during an incident. If there are no processes in place to recognize that an incident is taking place, that the incident response process should be initiated, and that those responsible for incident response should be notified, there is little point in having processes to deal with the incident, as they will never be called upon.

The pre-incident processes do not need to be complex; in fact, they should most definitely not be. The point of these processes is merely to determine if there is a potential incident and to initiate the incident response process—that's it!

Having been through multiple iterations of internal incident response, we can say that the most effective processes we have worked with do the following:

Leverage existing processes for dealing with events.

Most organizations deal with outages, configuration issues, user-reported issues, and other events. Don't try to set up a parallel set of processes, but leverage what's already there—in all likelihood, the same people who deal with these issues will be the first to hear of an incident anyway. Just modify or supplement the existing processes to include calling the incident response contact in the event of an expected incident, much like they already stipulate to call the on-call Unix person when a Linux host fails in the middle of the night.

Define what an incident is.

If you do not define what you class as an incident, you run the risk of either getting called about every support call or not getting called during a breach of 4 million data records. If it is not simple to define what an incident is, you can opt for wording like, "Once a manager has determined that an event is a security incident...." This way, you have at least defined that any event will have already progressed beyond triage by first-line support and someone experienced enough to make the determination has made a judgment call.

Incidents can also be defined and categorized using certain thresholds. For example, with a phishing email that is reported in your organization to be making it to email inboxes, if it gets to one user it could be a severity 3 and follow one process, but if it ended up in all users' inboxes, there will definitely be additional steps (and in multitude) involved in dealing with that same incident.

The result of a pre-incident process is nearly always to initiate the incident response process by declaring an incident and calling the contact for incident response.

 An incident that turns out to be nothing can always be downgraded again to a standard operations event. It's better to be called about a suspected incident that transpires to be nothing than to not be called for fear of a false positive.

It is in everyone's best interest to communicate clearly and early on. This not only saves time and effort later in fixing issues caused by miscommunications and hearsay but also allows those individuals responsible for fixing the incident more time to fully concentrate on the issue at hand. No downtime is too big (or too small) for proper communication to happen!

Incident Processes

The processes that take place during an incident, particularly from a technology perspective, cannot be too prescriptive. Incidents, like many operational problems, are far too varied and numerous to prescribe precise courses of action for all eventualities. However, there are some processes that are worth sticking to. These include:

Define an incident manager.
> This does not have to be the same person for every incident, but it should be someone who is senior enough to make decisions and empower others to complete tasks. The incident manager will run the response effort and make decisions.

Define internal communications.
> Communication between everyone working on the incident is key to avoiding duplication of work, promoting the sharing of information, and ensuring that everyone is working toward a common goal. We recommend that you:
>
> - Open a "war room." That is, use an office or meeting room to perform the role of center of operations for anyone in the same physical location. This is used as the central point for coordination of efforts.
>
> - Keep a conference/video call open in the war room. This allows people who are not at the physical location to check in, update those in the war room, and obtain feedback. If there is no physical war room, this will often serve as a virtual war room.
>
> - Hold regular update meetings. Regular updates allow people to move away, work in a more concentrated fashion, and report back regularly rather than feeling as if they are being overlooked and reporting back haphazardly. Typically, meeting every hour until the situation is well understood works well.
>
> - Allocate the task of communicating internally to stakeholders. Management will typically want to be kept abreast of a larger incident. However, sporadic communication from a number of people can send mixed messages and be frustrating for both management and the incident response team. Establishing a single point of communication between the two allows stakeholders to receive frequent, measured updates.

Define external communications.
> In many cases (but not all), some external communication may be required. Typically, this is because customers or other departments will be affected by the incident in some way. There may also be service-level agreements (SLAs) in contracts or certain regulations to take into account. This sort of communication should not be taken lightly, as it affects the public image of the organization and the internal technology department. If you are considering undertaking any external communications yourself, rather than allowing your corporate communication

or PR team to do it, we suggest you read Scott Roberts's blog post on the topic, "Crisis Communication for Incident Response" (*https://oreil.ly/9zC3p*).

Determine key goals.
By determining the goals that you wish to achieve in the event of an incident, you can ensure that all actions are taken with these goals in mind. By goals, we don't mean simply "fix it," but more specific objectives such as "preserve chain of custody for evidence" or "minimize downtime." In most cases, the priorities should be to remove the attacker's access, investigate to find any persistence that the attacker has established, and determine what has been damaged/stolen. This is discussed in more depth in Chapter 7.

Define high-level technology processes.
As mentioned previously, it's impossible to account for all eventualities, so being prescriptive with technology-based remedies may be difficult. However, there are some high-level processes that you may want to have in place. For example, there may be policies regarding taking snapshots of affected systems to preserve evidence, ensuring that staff stop logging in to affected systems, or a blackout on discussing incidents via email in case an attacker is reading internal email and will get a tip-off.

Plan for the long haul.
Many incidents are over in just a few hours, but many last substantially longer—often weeks. It can be tempting to pull in all available resources to help with an incident in the hopes of a timely conclusion, but if it becomes clear that this is not going to be the case, you should prepare for a longer-term course of action. Ensure people are sent away to get rest so that they can come in and cover the next shift, and keep those working fed and watered to prevent fatigue. Try not to burn everyone out, as this can be a game of endurance.

Document as much as possible.
In almost any incident, things can get very hectic. Do your best to remind all involved to keep as many notes and pieces of evidence as they can. These can be helpful later on, as it can be difficult to remember exactly what was done and when. You may also want to enable features such as logging command-line output to a local file; this will enhance any manual notes that are taken by giving a precise history of the commands that were run and the output.

Post-Incident Processes

Once an incident is over, it's valuable to hold a lessons-learned session (aka *postmortem*). This allows for feedback regarding what worked well and what worked less well, which can be used to update processes, determine training requirements, change infrastructure, and generally improve based on what you learned from the incident. This information can be captured in an *after action report* (AAR).

It is recommended that this session be held a short time after the incident closes. Give people a few days to reflect on what happened, gather some perspective, and recover, without leaving it so long that memories fade or become distorted. This session can also be used to update documentation, policies, procedures, and standards, allowing for updated tabletops and drills.

 Many people do not wish to manage incidents internally—at least, not beyond the initial triage point—and would rather bring in external subject matter experts as required. This is an option that works for many organizations. However, if this is the route that you decide to take, we recommend that you negotiate contracts, nondisclosure agreements, and service-level agreements *before* an incident happens. When you are elbow-deep in an incident is not the time to be negotiating with a potential supplier about when they can spare someone and what rates you will have to pay.

Tools and Technology

It would be easy to list a large number of technologies that are typically used by incident response professionals, especially in the field of digital forensics. However, inexperience in this area can make it easy to misinterpret results, either through lack of familiarity with the specific tools or lack of understanding of the complete context of what is happening.

Fully understanding the environment, knowing what the various logs mean, knowing what should and should not be present, and learning how to use the tools that are already available can vastly increase the chances of effectively managing an in-progress incident. Midincident is not the time to learn how to conduct a forensic investigation; that's better left to someone who has some prior experience in this field. That said, a high-level appreciation of what can happen during an incident can be achieved by reviewing some key topics. We'll also discuss some examples of tools that can be used to assess what is happening in an environment during an incident.

Log Analysis

The first port of call, as with any type of operational issue, is of course the humble logfile. Application and operating system logfiles can hold a wealth of information and provide valuable pointers to what has happened.

If logs are stored on the host that generated them, you should remain cognizant of the fact that if someone compromises that host, they can easily modify the logs to remove evidence of what is happening. If possible, the logs stored on your security information and event management (SIEM) platform should be consulted, rather than referring to logs on the target device. This not only reduces the chances of log tampering but also provides the ability to query logs across the whole environment at once, permitting a more holistic view of the situation. A SIEM also has the ability to show if a gap in logs has occurred.

When reviewing logs on a SIEM, it is likely that you'll need to use the SIEM's own log query tools and search language. You may also be able to use commands such as `curl` or customized scripts to access data via an API.

If the logs are not being accessed on a SIEM, it is recommended that you take a copy of them, if possible, and analyze them locally with your preferred tools. Personally, we opt for a combination of traditional Unix command-line tools such as `grep`, `awk`, `sed`, and `cut`, along with scripts written for specific use cases.

EDR/XDR/MDR/All the "Rs"

Endpoint detection and response (EDR), extended detection and response (XDR), and managed detection and response (MDR—the managed version of EDR/XDR) technologies represent a paradigm shift in how organizations approach the detection and investigation of and response to cyber threats. These tools go beyond traditional antivirus or firewall solutions by providing comprehensive visibility across all endpoints and networks, leveraging advanced analytics to detect threats more accurately and facilitating rapid response to incidents.

XDR/EDR platforms are crucial for incident responders due to their ability to continuously monitor and collect data from endpoints, network traffic, and other sources. This wealth of data enables more sophisticated analysis of potential security incidents, helping to identify patterns or anomalies that could indicate a compromise. Features and capabilities these platforms offer include:

Advanced threat detection
XDR/EDR platforms can detect advanced threats that traditional security measures might miss. This includes identifying zero-day exploits, polymorphic malware, and sophisticated attacker tactics, techniques, and procedures (TTPs).

Forensic capabilities
In the event of a security incident, XDR/EDR tools provide detailed forensic data that can help you trace the origin of an attack, understand its scope, and identify compromised systems. This data includes historical information about process executions, file modifications, network connections, and other relevant events on the endpoints.

Automated response and remediation

One of the key benefits of XDR/EDR solutions is their ability to not only detect threats but also respond to them automatically. This can include isolating infected endpoints from the network to prevent the spread of malware or executing predefined scripts to remediate identified threats, thereby reducing the window of opportunity for attackers.

Integration and orchestration

These platforms often integrate with other security tools such as SIEMs, threat intelligence platforms, and network security solutions. This integration allows for a more coordinated response to incidents and helps automate many aspects of the incident response process.

Incorporating XDR/EDR into an organization's security posture significantly enhances its ability to detect, investigate, and respond to cyber threats effectively. By providing comprehensive visibility across the digital environment and automating many aspects of the response process, they play a crucial role in modern incident response strategies.

Disk and File Analysis

Analysis of artifacts on storage devices can also provide clues as to what has happened during an incident. Typically, a disk image will yield more information than purely examining files, as this contains not only the files stored on the disk that are immediately visible but also potentially fragments of deleted files that remain on disk, chunks of data left in slack space, and files that have been hidden via rootkits. Using a disk image also ensures that you do not accidentally modify the original disk, which guarantees the integrity of the original should there be legal proceedings of some kind. Obtaining one traditionally involves taking a host down and using a tool such as dcfldd (*https://oreil.ly/IGNNK*) or a commercial equivalent to take an image of the disk, which is saved to another drive and then examined offline. Unfortunately, this causes downtime.

 In most virtualized and some cloud computing environments this is less of a problem because all the major vendors have various snapshot technologies that can be used to take an image of a guest operating system. However, these technologies will often compress disk images, removing unused space and losing much of this needed information.

Once you've obtained a disk image, you can use various commercial tools to analyze the filesystem to discover files of interest, construct timelines of events, and perform other related tasks. In the open source/free space, the old classics The Sleuth Kit (*https://oreil.ly/7DZvR*) and Autopsy (*https://oreil.ly/R0VQJ*) remain favorites.

If a simple recovery of files is all that is desired, PhotoRec (*https://oreil.ly/XSVqa*) is a simple-to-use tool that yields surprisingly good results. Despite the name, it is not limited to photos.

Memory Analysis

Code that is executing, including malicious code, is resident in RAM. If you can obtain a memory dump from a compromised host—that is, a file that contains a byte-for-byte copy of the RAM—you can perform an analysis to discover malicious code, memory hooks, and other indicators of what has happened. A popular tool to analyze these RAM dumps is the Volatility Framework (*https://oreil.ly/sl2VO*) (see the wiki on GitHub (*https://oreil.ly/NG1_x*) for more information).

The process for obtaining RAM dumps will vary from OS to OS, and this is a constantly changing field, so we recommend checking the Volatility documentation for the latest preferred method.

For virtualized platforms, however, there is no need to dump RAM using the OS, as the host can take an image of the virtual memory. Following are the three most common examples of how to achieve this:

QEMU

```
pmemsave 0 0x20000000 /tmp/dumpfile
```

Xen

```
sudo xm dump-core -L /tmp/dump-core-6 6
```

VMWare ESX

```
vim-cmd vmsvc/getallvms
vim-cmd vmsvc/get.summary vmid
vim-cmd vmsvc/snapshot.create vmid [Name] [Description]
  [includeMemory (1)] [quiesced]
```

PCAP Analysis

If you have any tools that sniff network traffic inline or via a span port or inline utilities IDS/IPS or network monitoring device, there is every chance that you could have sample packet capture (PCAP) files. PCAP files contain copies of data as it appeared on the network and allow an analyst to attempt to reconstruct what was happening on the network at a particular point in time.

A vast number of tools can be used to perform PCAP analysis; however, for a first pass at understanding what is contained in the traffic we recommend using IDS-like tools such as Snort (*https://snort.org*) or Zeek (*https://zeek.org*) (previously called Bro) that are configured to read from PCAP files, as opposed to a live network interface. This will catch obvious traffic that triggers their predefined signatures.

Some staple tools for conducting PCAP analysis include the following:

- tcpdump (*https://www.tcpdump.org*) produces header and summary information, hex dumps, and ASCII dumps of packets that are either sniffed from the wire or read from PCAP files. Because tcpdump is a command-line tool, it can be used with other tools such as sed and grep to quickly identify frequently occurring IP addresses, ports, and other details that can be used to spot abnormal traffic. tcpdump is also useful because it can apply filters to PCAP files and save the filtered output. These output files are themselves smaller PCAPs that can be fed into other tools that do not handle large PCAPs as gracefully as tcpdump does.

- Wireshark (*https://www.wireshark.org*) is the de facto tool for the analysis of PCAP data. It provides a full GUI that allows the user to perform functions such as filtering and tracking a single connection, protocol analysis, and graphing certain features of the observed network traffic. Wireshark does not, however, handle large files very well, so prefiltering with tcpdump is recommended.

- TShark (bundled with Wireshark) is a command-line version of Wireshark. It is not quite as intuitive or easy to use, but because it's terminal-based, it can be used in conjunction with other tools such as grep, awk, and sed to perform rapid analysis.

All-in-One Tools

If you are familiar with using live CDs such as Kali Linux in the penetration testing world, an approximate equivalent for incident response is CAINE (*https://www.caine-live.net*). CAINE is a collection of free/open source tools provided on a single live CD or USB thumb drive; it can be booted without prior installation for quick triage purposes.

Conclusion

Incident response is not a prescriptive process from beginning to end. However, there are some key areas that can be process driven, such as communication, roles and responsibilities, and high-level incident management. This allows incidents to be effectively controlled and managed without bogging down technical specialists with complex decision tree processes. NIST has a framework for handling incidents (*https://oreil.ly/xjJLD*) that can be a great asset to be familiar with as well.

Incident response is an area of information security that most hope they will never have to be involved with; however, when the occasion comes you will be glad that you have prepared.

CHAPTER 7

Disaster Recovery

The terms *disaster recovery* (DR) and *business continuity planning* (BCP) are often confused and treated as interchangeable. They are, however, two different (but related) practices. BCP pertains to the overall continuation of business via a number of contingencies and alternative plans. These plans can be executed based on the current situation and the tolerances of the business for outages and such. DR encompasses the set of processes and procedures that are used in order to reach the objectives of the business continuity plan.

BCP normally extends to the entire business, not just IT, including such areas as secondary offices and alternate banking systems, power sources, and utilities. DR is often more IT focused and looks at technologies such as backups and hot standbys.

Why are we talking about DR and BCP in a security book? The CIA triad (confidentiality, integrity, and availability) is considered key to nearly all aspects of information security, and BCP and DR are focused very heavily on preserving availability while maintaining confidentiality and integrity. For this reason, information security departments are often very involved in the BCP and DR planning stages.

In this chapter, we will discuss setting your objective criteria, strategies for achieving those objectives, and testing, recovery, and security considerations.

Setting Objectives

Objectives allow you to ensure that you are measurably meeting business requirements when creating a DR strategy and enable you to more easily make decisions regarding balancing time and budget considerations against uptime and recovery times.

Recovery Point Objective

The *recovery point objective* (RPO) is the point in time that you wish to recover to, and consequently, the maximum amount of data loss that an organization is willing to tolerate in the event of a disaster or disruption. That is, setting an RPO requires determining if you need to be able to recover data right up until seconds before the disaster struck, or if an hour before, the night before, or the week before is acceptable, for example. This does not take into account how long it takes to make this recovery, only the point in time from which you will be resuming once recovery has been made. There is a tendency to jump straight to seconds before the incident; however, the shorter the RPO, the higher the costs and complexity will invariably be.

Recovery Time Objective

The *recovery time objective* (RTO) is how long it takes to recover specific devices, applications, or business services, irrespective of the RPO. That is, after the disaster, how long can the delay acceptably be before you have recovered to the point determined by the RPO?

To illustrate with an example, if you operate a server that hosts your brochureware website, the primary goal is probably going to be rapidly returning the server to operational use. If the restored content is a day old, it's probably not as much of a problem as it would be if the system held financial transactions, for which the availability of recent transactions is important. In this case, an outage of an hour may be tolerable, with data no older than one day once recovered. In other words, the RPO would be one day and the RTO would be one hour.

It's worth noting that the RTO for a large organization with thousands of servers will be far longer than the RTO for a small company with a single server. Sure, even in a big organization you can restore a single server in an hour, but how long will restoring sections of or the whole infrastructure take?

There is often a temptation for someone from a technology department to set these times. However, they should be driven by the business owners of systems involved. There are a few reasons for this—for example:

- It's often hard to justify the cost of DR solutions, especially if you've never experienced a significant loss or downtime. Allowing the business to set requirements, and potentially reset them if the costs are too high, not only enables informed decisions regarding targets but also reduces the chances of unrealistic expectations on recovery times.

- IT people may understand the technologies involved but do not always have the correct perspective to make a determination as to what the business's priorities are in such a situation.
- The involvement of the business in the DR and BCP plans eases the process of discussing budgets and expectations for these solutions.

Recovery Strategies

A number of different strategies can be deployed in order to meet your organization's DR needs. Which is most appropriate will depend on the defined RTO and RPO and, as ever, cost.

Traditional Physical Backups

The most obvious strategy for recovering from a disaster is to take regular backups of all systems and to restore those backups to new equipment. The new equipment should be held at a dedicated DR facility or secondary office, located somewhere where the appropriate connectivity is available, and the servers can begin operating right away.

Historically, backups were often made to a tape-based medium such as digital linear tape (DLT) drives, which were physically shipped to another location. However, in recent years the cost of storage and network connectivity has dropped significantly, so backups can often be made to more readily available and reliable media, such as an archive file on a remote hard disk.

Backups tend to be made not continuously but rather as a batch job run overnight—and not necessarily every night. The RPO will therefore be, at best, the time of the most recent backup, which tends to be longer than with other strategies. We say "at best" because it's not uncommon for backups to fail, so in reality, the RPO is the time of your most recent working backup.

The RTO will vary depending on the speed of the backup media and the location of the backup media in relation to backup equipment. For example, if the backup media needs to be physically shipped to a location or if restoring would take days due to slow network and internet speeds, these considerations must be factored in.

Warm Standby

A warm standby is a secondary set of infrastructure, ideally identical to the primary, which is kept in approximate synchronization with the primary infrastructure. This infrastructure should be kept at a reasonable geographic distance from the primary in case of events such as earthquakes and flooding. In the event of a disaster, services will be manually "cut over" to the secondary infrastructure. The method of doing so varies, but it often involves repointing DNS entries from primary to secondary or altering routing tables to send traffic to the secondary infrastructure.

The secondary infrastructure is kept in sync via a combination of ensuring that configuration changes and patches are applied to both sets, and automated processes to keep files synchronized. Ideally the configuration and patching will happen in an automated fashion using management software; however, this is often not the case, and when differences occur they can cause problems.

The RPO is fairly short on a warm standby, typically determined by the frequency of filesystem synchronization processes. The RTO is however long the cut-over mechanism takes. For example, with a DNS change this is the amount of time required to make the change and for old records to expire in caches so that hosts start using the new system (so, you should ensure that the time-to-live (TTL) value of the DNS records is smaller than your RTO). With a routing change, the RTO is as long as it takes to make the routing change and, if using dynamic routing protocols, for routing table convergence to occur.

The main drawback of this system is that it relies on having an entire second infrastructure that is effectively doing nothing until such time as there is a disaster.

High Availability

A high-availability system is typically a model like a distributed cluster: that is, multiple devices in distributed locations, which share the load during normal production periods. During a disaster, one or more devices will be dropped from the pool, but the remaining devices will continue operating as normal. In addition, they will each process their share of the additional load from the device(s) that are no longer operational.

Due to the nature of high availability, it is typical that all devices in the cluster will be fully synchronized, or very close to it, and for this reason the RPO will be very short. Because many clustering technologies allow for devices to drop out of the cluster and other devices to automatically adjust and compensate, the RTO can also be lower than with many other solutions.

Although the RPO and RTO are both advantageous when using a high-availability system, there is a cost. The cluster needs to have enough capacity to compensate for some nodes dropping out in the event of a disaster and the remaining nodes handling the additional load. This means running hardware that is not fully utilized in order to have spare capacity. Also, additional investment in areas such as intersite/intercluster bandwidth will be required—keeping all devices synchronized to run a clustered solution requires sufficient bandwidth at a low enough latency, which places additional requirements on the infrastructure.

Alternate System

In some cases, using an alternate system is preferential to running a backup or secondary system in the traditional sense. For example, in the event that an internal voice over IP (VoIP) solution is rendered unavailable due to a disaster, the plan may not be to try to reinstantiate the VoIP infrastructure, but simply to switch to using cell phones until such time as the disaster is over.

This strategy does not always have an RPO per se, as recovery of the existing system is not part of the plan. That's why this type of approach is typically only taken with systems that do not hold data but provide a service, such as telephones. There is, however, a measurable RTO in terms of the amount of time it takes to switch over to using an alternate system.

System Function Reassignment

One approach that can prove to be cost-effective is *system function reassignment*. This is a hybrid of other solutions that involves the repurposing of noncritical systems to replace critical systems in the event of a disaster situation. It is not suitable for all environments, so you should give it careful consideration before deciding to use this strategy; if not all situations are considered or possible, you may get false testing results.

As an example of this approach, if you already run two datacenters, you might structure your environments so that for any production environment housed in one datacenter, its test, preproduction, or QA environment is housed in the other datacenter. In this scenario, you can have a near-production site ready, but not idle, at all times. In the event of a disaster, the environment in question will cease to operate as, for example, preproduction and will be promoted to a production environment.

This strategy requires that the two environments be separated by enough distance that a disaster affecting one will not affect the other. The state of the other environments should be tightly controlled so that any differences from production are known and they can be easily changed to match the production state prior to going live.

Cloud Native Disaster Recovery

Cloud native DR strategies leverage the capabilities of cloud computing to focus on minimizing both RTO and RPO through automation and orchestration. These strategies harness the power of cloud services to replicate and recover critical systems and data across different geographical locations in real time or near-real time.

Key components include:

Automated replication

Data and applications are continuously or at scheduled intervals replicated to one or more cloud regions. This ensures minimal data loss and quick restoration in the event of a disaster.

Infrastructure as code

IaC allows organizations to manage and provision their IT infrastructure through code. This capability is crucial for rapid deployment of resources in a DR scenario, ensuring that the recovery environment is a precise replica of the production environment.

Elasticity and scalability

Cloud environments can dynamically scale resources up or down based on demand. In a DR scenario, this means that resources can be scaled up quickly to handle the load, without the need for preprovisioned physical resources.

Multiregion deployment

By deploying critical systems and data across multiple cloud regions, organizations can ensure that a disaster in one region does not lead to a total system failure. Traffic can be rerouted to unaffected regions until the primary region is restored.

Orchestration and automation

Cloud native DR solutions often include orchestration tools that automate the failover and failback processes. This reduces human error and speeds up recovery times, ensuring business continuity with minimal manual intervention.

Advantages of cloud native DR include:

Cost-effectiveness

You only pay for the resources you use. In nondisaster times, you can minimize costs by running fewer instances and scaling up only when needed.

Agility

You can quickly adapt to changing requirements and scale your DR environment in real time as your business grows or your needs change.

Simplified management

Cloud providers offer tools and services that simplify the management of DR processes, including replication, monitoring, and testing of DR plans.

Dependencies

An important part of developing a strategy for DR and BCP is to understand the dependencies of all of the systems involved. For example, it doesn't matter that you can successfully bring up a file server in another location if the staff can't connect to it. Servers typically need a network connection, the associated routing and DNS entries, and access to authentication services such as Active Directory or Lightweight Directory Access Protocol (LDAP). Failure to determine the dependencies required for any particular system may lead to missing the RTO for that service.

For example, if you have an email server with an RTO of one hour but the network on which it depends has an RTO of three hours, irrespective of how quickly the email server is up and running, it may not resume operation in any meaningful sense until three hours have elapsed.

Mapping out dependencies such as this makes it much easier to identify unrealistic RTOs, or RTOs of other systems or services that need to be improved to meet given targets. Walking through tabletops and drills, as discussed in Chapter 1, will assist in discovering these dependencies.

Scenarios

When developing potential disaster plans, it's often useful to walk through a few high-level scenarios to get an understanding of how they impact your proposed plan. This exercise normally works most effectively with representatives from other IT teams who can assist in discussing the implications and dependencies of various decisions. Also consider creating, revising, and testing these in the tabletop exercises (as discussed in Chapter 1).

Here are a few broad categories of scenarios that are useful to consider (although which ones you choose to use will probably be dependent upon your own circumstances):

- Ransomware (everyone's favorite scenario) has begun encrypting your email server, and the attacker has been able to pivot into other internet-facing servers.
- A hardware failure has occurred in a mission-critical platform. Although this issue is isolated to a single platform, it's significant enough to cause a DR incident (for example, server hardware for the production environment of a key system might fail).
- You've lost an entire datacenter, potentially temporarily, such as during a power outage, or perhaps for a more prolonged period after a fire or earthquake.

- A pandemic has struck. Services may remain available, but physical access may not be possible, which in turn could prevent certain processes from taking place (such as physically changing backup tapes) and cause other issues (such as users working from home causing extra load on the VPN or other remote access services).

Invoking a Failover...and Back

It's all very well having a set of contingency plans in place and target times by which to achieve them, but if you don't know when you are in a disaster situation, there is little point to the plans. It's important to have a process in place to determine what is and is not a disaster, and when to invoke the plan.

There may be a few key, high-level scenarios in which the plan will obviously be put into action. For example, a fire in a datacenter is typically enough to invoke failing over to backup systems. However, care should be taken not to be too prescriptive, or else there's a risk of minor deviations from the situations outlined causing a failure to invoke the plan. Similarly, not being descriptive enough could cause an inexperienced administrator to invoke a DR plan needlessly. When in doubt, how do you determine when to invoke the plan? One of the most effective routes is to have a list of named individuals or roles who are authorized to determine when the organization is in a disaster situation and that the plan needs to be executed. The process for anyone who is not authorized to make this determination is to escalate to someone who can, who in turn will make the decision. This way, the alarm can be raised by anyone, but the ultimate decision to execute is left to someone suitably senior and responsible.

Of course, as well as failing over to contingency systems, there will need to be a process for switching back again after the disaster has ended. This is an often overlooked area of DR and BCP. Unlike with the initial failover procedure, in this case there is the advantage of being able to schedule the switch and take an appropriate amount of time to complete it. Nevertheless, this should be a carefully planned and executed process that is invoked, again, by an authorized person.

 Always remember to include details on the proper communication during potential outages, as these can be high-stress times. Again, no downtime is too big (or too small) for proper communication to happen!

Testing

Disaster recovery can be extremely complex, with many of the complexities and interdependencies not being entirely obvious until you are in a disaster situation. You might find that in order to complete a given task, you need a file that's on a server that is currently under several feet of water. For this reason, it is advisable—and, under some compliance regimes, mandatory—that regular DR tests be carried out. Of course, no one is suggesting that you actually flood a datacenter or set it on fire and attempt a recovery. Simply choose a scenario and verify that you can have the replacement systems brought up within the allotted RTO and RPO. This process should be completed without access to any systems or services located on infrastructure affected by the scenario you have chosen.

The test should be observed and notes taken on what worked well and what did not. Holding a post-test debrief with the key people involved, even if the test met all targets, is a valuable process that can yield very useful results (for example, with regard to what can be improved in preparation for the next time). Findings from the debrief should be minuted with clear action items for specific individuals in order to improve your plans and work toward a more efficient and seamless process. (A more in-depth look at this topic is provided in Chapter 1.)

Security Considerations

As with any process, there are security considerations involved with most plans. These can be summarized into a few key categories:

Data at rest
  Many contingency plans require that data from production systems be duplicated and retained at another site. This is true of both warm standbys and traditional backups, for example. It should always be remembered that this data will have controls placed on it in production in line with its value and sensitivity to the organization. For example, it may be encrypted, require two-factor authentication to access, or be restricted to a small group of people. If equal restrictions are not placed on the contingency systems, the original access controls are largely useless. After all, why would an attacker bother trying to defeat two-factor authentication or encryption on a production system when they can simply access a relatively unprotected copy of the same data from a backup system?

Data in transit
  In order to replicate data to a secondary system, it will probably have to be transmitted over a network. Data transmitted for the purposes of recovering from or preparing for a disaster should be treated as carefully as data transmitted for any other purpose. The appropriate authentication and encryption of data on the network should still be applied.

Patching and configuration management

It is often easy to fall into the trap of backup systems not being maintained in line with the production environment. This runs the risk of leaving poorly patched equipment or vulnerabilities in your environment for an attacker to leverage. In the event of a disaster, these vulnerabilities could be present on what has become your production system. Aside from the security issues, you cannot be sure that systems with differing configuration or patch levels will operate in the same way as their production counterparts. To avoid this, make sure that all configuration changes and patches are applied to both systems at the same time.

User access

During a disaster situation there is often a sense of "all hands to the pumps" in order to ensure that production environments are operationally capable as soon as possible. It should be considered that not all data can be accessed by just anybody, particularly if the data is subject to a regulatory compliance regime such as those that protect personally identifiable healthcare or financial data. Any plans should ensure the continued handling of these types of data in line with established processes and procedures.

Physical security

Often, the secondary site may not be physically identical to the primary site. Take, for example, a company for which the primary production environment is housed in a secure third-party facility's managed datacenter, and the secondary location makes use of unused office space in the headquarters. A lower standard of physical access control could place data or systems at risk should an attacker be willing to attempt to physically enter a building by force, subterfuge, or stealth.

Conclusion

There is no one-size-fits-all solution to DR, although there are several well-trodden routes that can be reused where appropriate. One of the most important aspects of DR planning is to work with the business to understand what their requirements are for your DR solution. Aligning your solution with their expectations makes it easier to measure success or failure.

CHAPTER 8

Industry Compliance Standards and Frameworks

Businesses may be required to conform to one or more regulatory compliance regimes, which are administered by a variety of governing bodies. Failure to comply with these standards can result in heavy fines or, in some cases, hinder the ability to conduct business (such as by preventing the capability of processing credit card transactions). Frameworks differ from regulatory compliance standards in that they are not required for a specific industry or type of data; they are more like guidelines.

The requirement to comply with one standard or the next does provide a few benefits to your organization. Certain standards leave significant room for interpretation, giving you the ability to tie security measures that should be implemented to a portion of that same standard. When compliance is involved, there are social, political, and legal components that can be leveraged to implement security controls and process changes that may not have been possible otherwise. It also may present the opportunity to piggyback off another department that has excess budget for a project.

As both standards and frameworks change frequently over time, in this chapter we'll just focus on explaining what each is used for, and some "gotchas" that some may have. Note that the majority of the standards discussed here are from the United States; international organizations have a whole different set of reporting requirements.

Industry Compliance Standards

It can be tempting to take the easy route of just "checking the boxes" when implementing the controls in a compliance list. However, compliance standards are a minimum guide at best, not a complete security standard. It's possible to be technically compliant with a standard and still not have a secured environment, just as it's possible (although less likely) not to be compliant but to be completely secure. Many standards leave room for imagination and can be interpreted in different ways, but following common best practices will usually lead to compliance as a side effect.

Most organizations will have a compliance officer, who may not be in the security department because the majority of regulatory standards are not based on the technology behind information security but aim to provide an overall solution to a greater problem. For example, HIPAA (discussed later in this section) is focused on the safety of patients and patient records, whether digital or physical.

Family Educational Rights and Privacy Act (FERPA)

FERPA is a federal law that protects the privacy of student education records in both public and private schools, as well as in higher education. As this law was enacted in 1974, it has no specific information related to technology, which leaves a large area open for interpretation in relation to the information security practices and protections that are required. It contains phrasing that should be interpreted as prohibiting the release or disclosure of any PII, directory information, or educational information of students to a third party.

PII can only be disclosed if the educational institution obtains the signature of the parent or student (if over 18 years of age) on a document specifically identifying the information to be disclosed, the reason for the disclosure, and the parties to whom the disclosure will be made.

Directory information is defined as "information contained in an education record of a student that would not generally be considered harmful or an invasion of privacy if disclosed"—for example, names, addresses, telephone numbers, and student ID numbers.

Educational records are defined as "records, files, documents, and other materials maintained by an educational agency or institution, or by a person acting for such agency or institution." This includes students' transcripts, GPAs, grades, Social Security numbers, and academic and psychological evaluations.

While there have been recorded requests for better cybersecurity recommendations and controls in many of the amendment comments over the years, it remains a very lax standard with regard to real information security requirements.

Gramm-Leach-Bliley Act (GLBA)

The Gramm-Leach-Bliley Act is a law that was passed in 1999 to reform and modernize the regulations affecting financial institutions. It is comprised of seven titles, and Title V (*https://oreil.ly/X_QH8*) contains two paragraphs on information security:

Title V – PRIVACY

Subtitle A - Disclosure of Nonpublic Personal Information

Section 501 – Protection of Nonpublic Personal Information

(a) PRIVACY OBLIGATION POLICY

It is the policy of the Congress that each financial institution has an affirmative and continuing obligation to respect the privacy of its customers and to protect the security and confidentiality of those customers' nonpublic personal information.

(b) FINANCIAL INSTITUTIONS SAFEGUARDS

In furtherance of the policy in subsection (a), each agency or authority described in section 505(a), shall establish appropriate standards for the financial institutions subject to their jurisdiction relating to administrative, technical, and physical safeguards

> (1) to insure the security and confidentiality of customer records and information
>
> (2) to protect against any anticipated threats or hazards to the security or integrity of such records; and
>
> (3) to protect against unauthorized access to or use of such records or information which could result in substantial harm or inconvenience to any customer.

To address the increase of widespread data breaches and cyberattacks, the Federal Trade Commission (FTC) amended the act in 2021 to include a much larger list of information security controls, such as:

- Access controls
- Audit trails
- Change management
- Cost
- Disposal procedures
- Encryption
- Multi-factor authentication
- Secure development practices
- "Sensitive" customer information
- System inventory
- System monitoring
- Third-party standards and frameworks
- Written risk assessment

GLBA compliance is mandatory for financial institutions including banks, mortgage brokers, real estate appraisers, debt collectors, insurance companies, and privacy companies. It also requires third-party service providers to comply with the privacy and security provisions relating to handling consumer personal data. Enforcement is carried out by various federal regulators, including the FTC, Federal Deposit Insurance Corporation (FDIC), Federal Reserve, Office of the Comptroller of the Currency (OCC), and others, depending on the financial institution. Violations can result in civil penalties of up to $100,000 each and remediation orders to correct any deficiencies.

Initially, the law left a large amount up to interpretation during implementation. The more recent amendment has provided greater guidance on best practices. For more information, we recommend consulting the Interagency Guidelines and the IT Examiners Handbook, both of which were created to assist with implementing security practices surrounding GLBA compliance.

Health Insurance Portability and Accountability Act (HIPAA)

HIPAA was enacted as law in 1996, establishing national standards for electronic healthcare records. It applies to any organization that stores or processes electronic protected health information (ePHI), healthcare providers, health plans, and clearinghouses. Thankfully, there's a little more definition regarding technology in the verbiage of this act compared to others we cover. There are more than 50 "implementation specifications," divided into administrative, physical, technical, and policies, procedures, and documentation requirements. Most of these involve having policies and procedures in place. Addressable specifications involve performing a "risk assessment" and then taking steps to mitigate the risks in a way that's appropriate for your organization. One of the largest HIPAA penalties (*https://oreil.ly/bRcsD*) against a small organization was levied not because an event occurred, but because the organization failed to address the possibility that it might. Loss of ePHI can cause significant harm to not only the patients whose data has been compromised but also the provider and individuals at fault, as they are required to report violations to the US Department of Health and Human Services (HHS) and the FTC. They are also the ones who will be on the receiving end of extremely large fines and possibly even jail time. HHS provides a breakdown of each portion of the security rule portion of HIPAA (*https://oreil.ly/8-Xls*) and assistance with the implementation of the security standards.

Payment Card Industry Data Security Standard (PCI DSS)

PCI DSS is a standard for organizations that store, process, or transmit credit cards and credit card data. PCI DSS compliance is required by the major card brands (MasterCard, Visa, Discover, American Express, and JCB) and is administered by the Payment Card Industry Security Standards Council (PCI SSC). This standard was created to increase security controls around cardholder data in an attempt to reduce credit card fraud. Failure to validate compliance can result in fines or other penalties, even including the removal of credit card processing capabilities.

PCI DSS regulates cardholder data (CHD). Cardholder data is any personally identifiable information associated with a person who has a credit or debit card. This includes the primary account number (PAN), cardholder name, expiration date, and service code. For current versions of this compliance standard, you can visit the PCI SSC website (*https://www.pcisecuritystandards.org*).

Sarbanes-Oxley (SOX) Act

The Sarbanes-Oxley Act is a law enacted in 2002 to set forth security requirements for all US public company boards, management, and public accounting firms. Portions also apply to privately held companies in regard to withholding or destroying information to impede any federal investigations. SOX has 11 sections and was created to ensure widespread corporate corruption and scandals such as Enron and WorldCom don't happen again. Many organizations that have SOX compliance requirements also abide by either the Committee of Sponsoring Organizations of the Treadway Commission (COSO) or Control Objectives for Information and Related Technologies (COBIT) frameworks, which we cover in the following section.

The two principal sections of the SOX Act that relate to security are Section 302 and Section 404:

- Section 302 is intended to safeguard against faulty financial reporting. As part of this, companies must safeguard their data responsibly so as to ensure that financial reports are not based upon faulty data, tampered data, or data that may be highly inaccurate.

- Section 404 requires the safeguards stated in Section 302 to be externally verifiable by independent auditors, so that independent auditors may disclose to shareholders and the public possible security breaches that affect company finances. Specifically, this section guarantees that the security of data cannot be hidden from auditors, and security breaches must be reported.

Frameworks

Frameworks are different from compliance standards in that adhering to them is not a requirement. They are industry- or technology-specific guidelines created to assist in organizing thoughts, practices, and implementations.

Center for Internet Security (CIS)

CIS not only has a framework for assisting with cyberattacks but also provides benchmarks, workforce development, and other resources such as whitepapers, publications, newsletters, and advisories. It offers in-depth system-hardening guidelines for specific operating systems and applications. Together with NIST, CIS provides frameworks for the purposes of securing critical infrastructure and other cross-framework and compliance references.

Cloud Control Matrix (CCM)

The CCM is a framework built specifically with cloud security in mind by the CSA. It assists in tying together specific cloud security concerns and practices with all major compliance standards and frameworks. The CSA also has some great workgroups for specific sectors using cloud solutions. At the time of writing, the CCM is composed of 197 control objectives that are structured in 17 domains covering all key aspects of cloud technology and is considered a de facto standard for cloud security assurance and compliance.

The Committee of Sponsoring Organizations of the Treadway Commission (COSO)

COSO is made up of five organizations: the American Accounting Association, American Institute of Certified Public Accountants, Financial Executives International, the Institute of Management Accountants, and the Institute of Internal Auditors. It aims to provide guidance on enterprise risk management, internal control, and fraud deterrence.

Control Objectives for Information and Related Technologies (COBIT)

COBIT is a high-level framework created by the Information Systems Audit and Control Association (ISACA) to assist organizations with creating secure documentation, implementation, and compliance. COBIT is subdivided into four domains—Plan and Organize, Acquire and Implement, Deliver and Support, and Monitor and Evaluate—and aims to align itself with other more detailed standards. While some frameworks are free, COBIT is available for purchase through its website.

ISO-27000 Series

The International Organization for Standardization (ISO) is an independent, nongovernmental international organization that has created over 20,000 sets of standards across a variety of industries including food services, technology, and agriculture. Out of these standards, the 27000 series (*https://oreil.ly/tA9jV*) (specifically 27001–27006) has been used for the topic of information security. For example:

ISO-27001
> Provides requirements for establishing, implementing, maintaining, and continuously improving an information security management system (ISMS).

ISO-27002
> Establishes guidelines and general principles for initiating, implementing, maintaining, and improving information security management within an organization.

ISO-27003

Provides ISMS implementation guidance.

ISO-27004

Provides guidance on the development and use of measures and measurement for the assessment of the effectiveness of an implemented ISMS and controls.

ISO-27005

Provides guidelines for information security risk management (ISRM) in an organization.

ISO-27006

Specifies requirements for bodies providing audit and certification of ISMSs.

ISO standards are also available for purchase only.

MITRE ATT&CK

The MITRE ATT&CK (*https://attack.mitre.org*) framework was created in 2013 in the context of MITRE's Fort Meade Experiment (FMX) research project to document common tactics, techniques, and procedures that adversaries used against Windows environments. It is updated biannually and now serves as a common reference that both offense and defense can use to improve defense and detection capabilities.

The ATT&CK framework is broken up into three matrices, including adversary techniques used in attacks against enterprise infrastructure (including cloud platforms), mobile devices, and industrial control systems. MITRE also provides numerous resources to assist in utilizing the information in the framework.

NIST Cybersecurity Framework (CSF)

The NIST operates as part of the US Department of Commerce, creating standards for many sections of US infrastructure. This framework was created with both industry and government participation, and it consists of standards, guidelines, and practices surrounding critical infrastructure security. The CSF uses common industry business drivers to guide and manage risks, protect information, and safeguard the people using a business's services. It has three main parts, all of which focus primarily on risk management: the Framework Core, the Framework Profiles, and the Framework Implementation Tiers. The Core describes a set of cybersecurity activities and outcomes in easy-to-understand language. Profiles are mostly used to identify and prioritize the improvements in the cybersecurity posture at an organization. Lastly, the Implementation Tiers assist organizations by providing context around managing cybersecurity risk.

Regulated Industries

As mentioned previously, some industries are more heavily regulated than others. This is largely dependent on the sensitivity of the data they handle and the likelihood of it being stolen and used for malicious purposes. There is a large black market for stolen data that is used for both credit and identity theft. You've already read about the different regulation types; however, it's important to be aware that certain sectors are regulated strictly—or at least, strict regulations are attempted—for legitimate reasons.

Financial

The financial industry includes thousands of institutions, such as banks, investment services, insurance companies, other credit and financing organizations, and the service providers that support them. They can vary widely in size and the amount of data processed, ranging from some of the world's largest global companies with thousands of employees and many billions of dollars in assets to community banks and credit unions with a small number of employees serving individual communities.

Some of the major risks the financial sector must be concerned with are account takeovers, third-party payment processor breaches, ATM skimming and other point of service (POS) vulnerabilities, mobile and internet banking exploitation, and supply chain infiltration. Studies have shown that this sector is one of the ones where outdated legacy systems are most commonly seen throughout organizations, giving would-be attackers an easy foothold once access has been gained.

Government

Governments (specifically, in this case, the United States government) have pretty much every type of data imaginable to protect. From the large three-letter-acronym agencies such as the NSA, FBI, IRS, and FDA to smaller local government offices that contract with their own IT person, this one sector covers an extremely broad landscape. Government organizations can also differ greatly from commercial businesses in terms of the length of the approval process for changes and upgrades, ability and willingness to adopt new technology, and overall atmosphere and attitudes of personnel—and in the fast-changing security landscape, this has been seen to hinder progress.

In addition to the compliance frameworks mentioned earlier, US government entities have other rules and regulations they may need to adhere to at different levels (federal, state, local, etc.). Some common examples include:

Cybersecurity Maturity Model Certification (CMMC)

The CMMC introduces a tiered approach to cybersecurity, pertinent especially for entities involved directly or indirectly in the defense supply chain. Understanding the CMMC requirements can help in vetting contractors and ensuring contracts are compliant with federal standards.

Department of Defense (DoD) Impact Levels

These are designed to assess the sensitivity of information and the level of security needed to protect it within cloud environments. While not all government entities may directly handle information at all DoD Impact Levels, awareness of these levels helps in making informed decisions when selecting cloud services providers.

Federal Risk and Authorization Management Program (FedRAMP)

FedRAMP is based on NIST SP 800-53 and has a set of controls that cloud service providers must adhere to, tailored to the federal government's needs.

Federal Information Security Management Act (FISMA)

Although FISMA is a federal mandate, it sets a precedent for information security practices that many governments can adopt to strengthen their own cybersecurity measures. FISMA is a comprehensive framework that covers various aspects of developing, documenting, and implementing an information security program.

Many other countries similarly have their own rules and regulations, but even if you've made it this far into a compliance chapter, you'd probably stop reading if we started in on "Afghanistan, Albania, Algeria…"; we'll leave that exploration as an exercise for the interested reader.

The breadth of information contained within government agencies means they are the subject of a constant stream of high-profile attacks by organized crime, hacktivists, and state-sponsored agents. The Office of Personnel Management (OPM) suffered a huge data breach in 2015, which shed some light on the department's lack of security. The attack was underway for an entire year, and an estimated 21.5 million records were stolen. Other data breaches have exposed voting records and information, USPS employee information, IRS tax return data, NSA exploits and attack tools used against foreign adversaries, and other highly sensitive and potentially harmful data.

Healthcare

The healthcare industry remains one of the least secured industries today, and just like the financial sector, it is riddled with out-of-date legacy devices. For a long time, the FDA had strict control over the OS revision and patch level for medical devices, restricting the ability to upgrade these devices and still maintain FDA approval. This, coupled with the rapid growth and underestimation of the inherent risk of large quantities of sensitive medical and patient data stored electronically, created a hugely complicated, insecure environment. While the FDA has relaxed its requirements to allow security patches to be applied, software vendors and organizations have yet to keep up and implement best practice security controls.

Both the HSS Office for Civil Rights (OCR) and attorneys general have the power to issue penalties for the failure to follow HIPAA guidelines and as the result of personal health information (PHI) breaches. Not only can they enforce financial penalties, but they can also bring criminal lawsuits. In the past several years (2016–2021) the Department of Health and Human Services recorded over $80 million in HIPAA settlement payments. There are several tiers (*https://oreil.ly/s13l0*) for both financial and criminal penalties:

- Financial:
  - Tier 1: Minimum fine of $100 per violation up to $50,000
  - Tier 2: Minimum fine of $1,000 per violation up to $50,000
  - Tier 3: Minimum fine of $10,000 per violation up to $50,000
  - Tier 4: Minimum fine of $50,000 per violation
- Criminal:
  - Tier 1: Reasonable cause or no knowledge of violation—Up to 1 year in prison
  - Tier 2: Obtaining PHI under false pretenses—Up to 5 years in prison
  - Tier 3: Obtaining PHI for personal gain or with malicious intent—Up to 10 years in prison

Like the government sector, healthcare has its own nuances. The Health Information Trust Alliance (HITRUST) Common Security Framework (CSF) is a widely recognized certification that provides an overarching compliance framework for protecting sensitive healthcare information; it integrates and harmonizes various healthcare regulations, standards, and best practices, including HIPAA, NIST, ISO, PCI DSS, and others, into a single, comprehensive framework.

Conclusion

While obtaining compliance might be a necessity no matter what industry you're in, ensure that it is not the end goal. If compliance is viewed as an end goal, an organization can lose sight of its overall security and the bigger picture. Working with well-defined frameworks and best practices while keeping a compliance standard in mind remains the most effective way to secure your infrastructure.

CHAPTER 9

Physical Security

The security team is responsible for identifying and analyzing possible threats and vulnerabilities and recommending appropriate countermeasures to increase the overall security of a department or the organization as a whole. Physical security is often a feature of regulatory compliance regimes and vendor assessment questionnaires, as well as materially impacting the security of the systems and data that you are tasked with protecting. For this reason, it's a good idea to have at least a high-level understanding of physical security approaches, even if (especially in larger organizations) it is often dealt with by the facilities department and thus beyond the remit of the information security team. Physical security should be included in any internal assessments, as well as being in scope for penetration tests.

The goal of physical security is to prevent an attacker from mitigating these controls. As is the case with other aspects of information security, physical security should be applied as defense in depth. It is commonly broken into two areas: physical and operational. The physical element covers controls like door locks and cameras, while the operational side covers employee access, visitor access, and training, to give a few examples.

In this chapter, you will learn how to manage both the physical and operational aspects of physical security within your environment.

Physical

First and foremost, physical security is about managing the physical properties of your environment.

Restrict Access

The most obvious aspect of physical security is restricting access to the premises, or portions of the premises. Physical access controls such as door locks and badge systems prevent unauthorized personnel from gaining access to secure areas where they might be able to steal, interfere with, disable, or otherwise harm systems and data. It is recommended that highly sensitive areas be protected with more than one security control, essentially implementing two-factor authentication for physical assets. Commonly used controls include PIN pads, locks, radio-frequency identification (RFID) badge readers, biometrics, and security guards.

In addition to physical controls in the building, some physical security precautions can also be taken at every user's desk. For example:

- Ensure that screens are locked whenever users are not at their desks.
- Use computer cable locks where appropriate.
- Enforce a clear desk policy, utilizing locking document storage.

Access to network jacks, telephony jacks, and other potentially sensitive connectors should be restricted where possible. In public or semipublic areas such as lobbies, jacks should not be exposed so that the general public, or visitors, can easily access them. As discussed in more depth in Chapter 14, where possible, jacks should not be left enabled unless equipment has been authorized for use via that specific jack or if they are secured by authentication. These precautions reduce the chance of a physical intruder being able to find a live jack without unplugging something and risking raising an alarm.

Printers and printer discard boxes and piles can be a treasure trove of interesting information. Sensitive documents should be stored in a locked receptacle prior to shredding, or be shredded right away.

Video Surveillance

Video surveillance or closed-circuit television (CCTV) cameras can be useful not only for enabling physical security teams to notice and record incidents of tampering or theft of equipment, but additionally when correlated with other evidence such as user logons and badge swipes. This video evidence can sometimes be used to confirm attribution. For example, the use of a particular user account does not necessarily incriminate the account owner, as the credentials could have been stolen. Video footage of the owner standing at the console is much harder to dispute.

Cameras will typically be located at major ingress and egress points, such as lobby areas and entrance doors to the building, and in particularly sensitive locations such as server rooms and wherever else a high risk has been identified. Cameras located in positions that enable them to capture the faces of people when they swipe a badge permit correlation of logs with badging systems to determine if stolen or borrowed badges are being used to hide the identity of a criminal. In order to ensure that cameras are not tampered with, they should be placed out of easy reach and preferably within a tamperproof physical enclosure. Figure 9-1 shows a good example of how *not* to place surveillance cameras.

Figure 9-1. Inefficient surveillance equipment placement

Authentication Maintenance

Can you see what is wrong with the security control in Figure 9-2?

Figure 9-2. We're just going to assume this key code is 3456 and leave it at that. (Thanks to @revrance for the image. RIP.)

This example illustrates the need to have audits and to not forget that even if something is functional, it may not be secure. Maintenance also includes dealing with changes in staff. In the event that a member of staff ceases to be a member of staff, they should surrender their badge, along with any keys. Depending on the staff member's previous access, the codes for any doors or other assets that are fitted with a physical PIN pad may also need to be changed.

Secure Media

Controls for physically securing media such as USB flash drives, removable hard drives, and CDs are intended to prevent unauthorized persons from gaining access to sensitive data on any type of media. Sensitive information is susceptible to unauthorized viewing, copying, or scanning if it is unprotected while it is on removable or portable media, printed out, or left on a desk.

If stored in an unsecured facility, backups that contain this data may easily be lost, stolen, or copied for malicious purposes. Periodically reviewing the storage facility's security enables the organization to address identified security issues in a timely manner, minimizing the potential risk.

Procedures and processes help protect data on media distributed to internal and/or external users. Without such procedures, data can be lost or stolen or used for fraudulent purposes. It is important that media be identified such that its classification status can be easily discernible. Media not identified as confidential may not be adequately protected, increasing the risk of it being lost or stolen.

Media may be lost or stolen if sent via a nontrackable method, such as regular mail. Use of secure couriers to deliver any media that contains sensitive data allows organizations to use their tracking systems to maintain inventory and data on the locations and status of shipments. Larger organizations may make use of internal courier services, which will need their own security briefing related to their specific role in the company.

Without a firm process for ensuring that all media movements are approved before the media is removed from secure areas, it may not be tracked or appropriately protected, and its location may be unknown, leading to an increased risk of loss or theft.

Datacenters

It is important to design physical security into the interior of a datacenter. There may be a variety of situations to plan for, ranging from having colocated equipment to contractors needing physical access to the room, but not the equipment. Use rackable equipment so that locking server racks can be utilized. While they can technically still be moved unless bolted to the floor, the lock on the cabinet itself provides an additional layer of protection. Keys for the racks should remain in a central location from which they can be checked out as needed and not left in the racks themselves or in the datacenter.

Other situations that may sound far-fetched but are related to both security and physical safety should be considered as well. Is it possible to access the room through an adjoining room's ceiling tiles? We hear the term "firewall" all the time in our industry, but in this case it means that the wall is from floor to ceiling: a physical firewall.

The National Fire Protection Association (NFPA) 221 Standard for High Challenge Firewalls, Firewalls, and Fire Barrier Walls defines a firewall as a wall separating buildings or subdividing a building to prevent the spread of fire while maintaining structural stability and offering fire resistance.

Remote offices are sometimes more difficult to secure, as important assets may not be in a dedicated datacenter but instead share space with assets from another department or be tucked away in a closet somewhere. Normally this equipment is not extremely important, but it is still a potential vector of attack. Equipment like office routers, switches, and maybe a read-only domain controller are all common assets to protect. It's often just not feasible to have an entire rack for such a small amount of equipment, but having it in a locked equipment enclosure is a great step to take.

Operational Aspects

In addition to the physical properties, there are various operational aspects to physical security.

Identifying Visitors and Contractors

Being able to differentiate visitors, staff, and contractors is important so that people can quickly determine the appropriate approximate level of trust that they can place in a person with whom they are not already familiar. This ability to quickly differentiate staff from visitors, for example, plays a key role in ensuring that sensitive data is not exposed. Here are a few aspects to keep in mind:

Visitor actions
> All visitors should be signed in and out of the premises and be escorted to and from the reception area, leaving a permanent record of when they were in the building and who they were visiting, in case this information is required at a later date. Not only should a sign-in/sign-out procedure be required, but any action involving technology, equipment, or potential information gathering should also require an employee verification of intent.

Contractor actions

As contractors by nature will have more access than a normal visitor would, they should be properly identified as well. Proper policy and guidelines should be set regarding identification and access, with a photo ID required and verified upon entry. As with permanent staff, appropriate vetting should take place. In the case of contractors, this typically means their agency attesting to having run background checks on all contractors on your behalf.

Badges

Visitors should be issued a badge that is easily distinguishable from a staff badge, typically displaying the word "visitor" and being a different color than a staff or contractor badge. Visitor badges should be restricted to only the duration of the visitor's stay and surrendered when they sign out. There are also badges that will automatically void after a certain time limit, as seen in Figure 9-3.

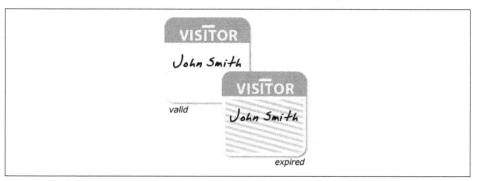

Figure 9-3. Over time, some badges will void themselves out

Badges are fairly simple to spoof with time and effort. Recon can be completed by someone malicious to attempt to re-create a legitimate badge.

Physical Security Training

Social engineering remains to this day a very effective way of accessing the inside of a network. It is within our nature to trust others, taking them at their word without verification. Employees should be trained not only on the digital aspects of social engineering but on the physical side as well, because these methods can be even trickier to detect. Criminals will often pose as internal personnel, contractors, or security engineers themselves in order to gain access to POS devices, server rooms, or some other endpoint.

Following are some scenarios and types of potential malicious activities to include in training:

Tailgating

Employees should be taught that while holding doors open for others is a normal polite response, they should not do this for badge, key, or other restricted access doors. This is an extremely effective way for an unauthorized person to gain access. Often this is one of the more difficult behaviors to address, as many companies have positive and people-friendly cultures. Adding signs to reinforce this idea (as seen in Figure 9-4) can be a helpful reminder.

Figure 9-4. Tailgating reminder sign

Badge cloning

RFID keys can easily be cloned with many different tools. One currently popular choice is a Flipper Zero (*https://flipperzero.one*). Others include BLEKey (*https://oreil.ly/xiDJl*) and Proxmark (*https://oreil.ly/C8M2E*) devices. As we've recommended elsewhere, highly sensitive areas should be protected with more than one method of authentication. Employees should not allow others to borrow, hold, or "test" their badges at any time.

Malicious media

While it is recommended that physical communication methods such as USB ports be restricted or disabled and controlled by an endpoint solution, this may not always be possible. In cases where USB ports are enabled and accessible by others, employees should be taught the dangers of this access. Not only can attackers stealthily insert a malicious USB device, but they might also drop them in public areas with tempting labels such as "Payroll projections 2016" or

"Executive Salary Q1," or ask for a document to be printed out. USB drives can be programmed with software to collect information or create reverse shells back to a waiting malicious device, among other attacks.

Restricted access and pretexts

Often, the time and effort to clone a badge isn't needed. It may be possible for an intruder to trick an employee into giving them access to a restricted area, using a predetermined persona and dialogue called a *pretext*. For example, they may try to fool personnel by dressing for the part (say, carrying a toolbox and dressed in workwear), and they could also be knowledgeable about the locations of devices. It is important that personnel are trained to follow procedures at all times.

Another trick criminals like to use is to send a "new" system with instructions for swapping it with a legitimate system and "returning" the legitimate system to a specified address. They may even provide a prepaid return postage label. Personnel should always verify with a manager or supplier that the device is legitimate, is expected, and comes from a trusted source before installing it or using it for business.

Conclusion

With the abundance of digital threats that we face every day, sometimes the old-school physical methods of protection get overlooked. It's important to keep in mind that the information security team should be actively working with whichever department is in control of physical security to provide feedback on current threats and gaps.

CHAPTER 10

Microsoft Windows Infrastructure

While it may be the bane of every security professional's existence, Microsoft Windows is being used in public and private infrastructures, both small and large, across the world. It is by far the most widely used operating system and also the most commonly misconfigured. Misconfigurations in Microsoft operating systems and software contribute to a huge number of security issues and compromises. The Exploit Database (*https://oreil.ly/Jd1A0*) currently lists over 10,000 exploits running under the Windows platform (compared to 8,000 when the first edition of this book was published).

Microsoft covers a staggering number of verticals, but in this chapter we'll stick to where it comes into play in the enterprise environment and the biggest bang for your buck in terms of security. We'll cover some quick wins such as moving away from older operating systems and turning off open file sharing, as well as in-depth best practices regarding Active Directory. Taking these few steps will significantly decrease your attack surface and increase your detection capabilities (and also might help you sleep better at night[1]).

Quick Wins

There are a few standard no-brainers that we should get out of the way at the beginning.

---

1 We're not doctors, no guarantee.

Upgrade

The first and most obvious quick win is upgrading endpoints to a supported operating system. While some corporations are still struggling to move off of Windows 7 and Windows XP (and, shockingly, even older operating systems), the threats keep piling up and the technology forges on. As shown in Figure 10-1, as of Q1 2024 unsupported Windows operating systems hold about 5% of the market share (with Windows 10, which has a market share of 67%, having an end of life in late 2025). Proportionally, this is less than when we published the first edition of this book (we'll take some credit), and we're excited to see that Windows XP has finally made it to <1%.

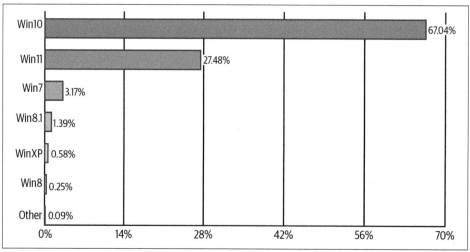

Figure 10-1. Windows desktop OS market share as of Q1 2024 (data from StatCounter)

What makes it that much harder for enterprise environments to make the switch is that many proprietary software packages for different industries were specifically written for XP, Server 2003, and other out-of-date OSs. Vulnerabilities like MS-08-067, an easy remote code execution bug, are still commonly found when these OS versions are present. Often, difficulties arise due to pesky vendor-controlled systems or other types of devices that leave you in the unfortunate position of not being able to apply updates. In cases like these, the devices should remain off the network as a matter of policy. If this is not feasible, the next most secure option is to have them on private virtual local area networks (VLANs) or an air-gapped network. We'll talk more about this in Chapter 15.

Another challenge is that security often takes a back seat when there is no real communication to stakeholders about the possibility of profit loss. When businesses cling to old technology, for whatever reason, their security risk goes up. The lack of support means that you are no longer protected from any new exploits, will not receive fixes for software bugs, and won't be able to take advantage of new features. Paying for prolonged support for defunct technology just delays the inevitable. Sometimes organizations are aware of the risks and still choose to maintain that technology; this can also be a valid choice, as long as communication has occurred about it so that there are no surprised faces when a more severe outage or breach happens.

Migrating off of a platform that has been in use for a long period of time has its own costs, in the form of software upgrades, data migration, and even possibly having to switch to new vendors. However, continuing to use unsupported and outdated software and equipment presents the inherent risk of data loss, network outages, breaches, and/or fines. It can be difficult to estimate the full cost of such an event prior to it actually happening.

Third-Party Patches

Surprisingly, another commonly overlooked protection is some type of software update platform. Windows Server Update Services (WSUS), System Center Configuration Manager (SCCM), and other third-party applications can keep the endpoints up-to-date with the latest security patches. Not only should you worry about regular Windows system patches, but there should also be a focus on outdated versions of commonly exploited software such as Java, Adobe Reader, Firefox, and other applications that are currently in use.

During the asset management process (discussed in Chapter 2), you will have determined what software exists in your environment. You should also ask yourself if it really needs to be there. Do all endpoints really need a PDF reader? (Hint: no, they don't.)

Open Shares

Open shares can cause all kinds of security problems. From saved credentials and trade secrets to PII and other sensitive data, file shares can house some extremely important assets. To search for open shares in your environment using Nmap, you can utilize the *smb-enum-shares.nse* (Nmap Scripting Engine) script. This script attempts to list shares on the target system and requires Server Message Block/ Common Internet File System (SMB/CIFS) networking to be accessible on the target. Here is a basic command to achieve this:

```
nmap -p445 --script smb-enum-shares.nse <target>
```

This can also be accomplished by using PowerShell:

```
# Read the list of server names/IPs from a text file
$servers = Get-Content -Path "C:\temp\servers.txt"
# Prompt for credentials
$cred = Get-Credential
# Enumerate shares on each server and select relevant properties
Get-WmiObject -Class Win32_Share -ComputerName $servers -Credential $cred |
    Select-Object PSComputerName, Name, Description, Path |
    Export-Csv -Path "C:\temp\sharereport.csv" -NoTypeInformation
```

Active Directory Domain Services

Active Directory Domain Services (AD DS) is a large part of the foundation of many infrastructure designs. It is a main building block and is relied upon for many things, including authentication, permissions, and asset identification. According to Microsoft (*https://oreil.ly/mO_du*):

> AD DS provides a distributed database that stores and manages information about network resources and application-specific data from directory-enabled applications. Administrators can use AD DS to organize elements of a network, such as users, computers, and other devices, into a hierarchical containment structure. The hierarchical containment structure includes the Active Directory forest, domains in the forest, and organizational units (OUs) in each domain.

While this hierarchical structure should not be solely relied upon for AD security, it can be used as an aid, allowing you to take a top-down approach to designing security. Being able to grow and adapt this structure as the organization grows and changes is essential to prevent the need for a complete restructure and redesign of the layout.

 Microsoft has recently renamed AD DS to Entra Domain Services, but in our experience they have renamed things so often that we're taking a stand. As the reader, you'll just need to replace "previous MS name" with "present-day MS name."

Forests

Per Microsoft (*https://oreil.ly/XdhYF*), "The forest acts as a security boundary for an organization and defines the scope of authority for administrators." While many organizations will have one forest with only one domain, others will have much larger footprints or may have acquired many smaller companies. This can make it difficult to balance the possibly large number of forests that may or may not have security access to other forests or domains (see Figure 10-2).

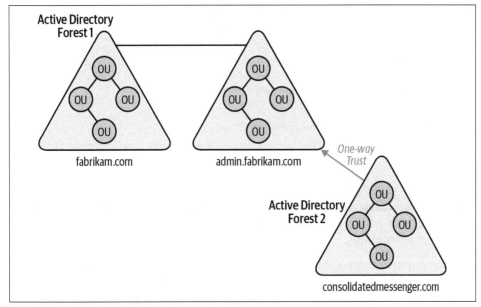

Figure 10-2. A forest can be a collection of domains or a single domain

Cross-domain and forest trusts, while helpful, can weaken the security between organizational containers, so they should be used only when the proper stakeholders have recognized the risk associated with them. The risks surrounding trusts lie in the ability to authenticate from one domain or forest to another. For example, a malicious user with administrative credentials who is located in a trusted forest could monitor network authentication requests from the trusting forest to obtain the security ID (SID) of a user who has full access to resources in the trusting forest, such as a domain or enterprise administrator. They could then use these credentials to access those resources themselves.

These risks can be mitigated with SID filtering and selective authentication (*https:// oreil.ly/FrPo_*) when the forests are completely on premises, and by using managed Azure AD DS in a hybrid environment (*https://oreil.ly/HFW_Y*). Controlling authentication in this way provides an extra layer of protection to shared resources by preventing them from being randomly accessed by any authenticated user in the trusted distributed user forests. Now, if one of these user forests is attacked and requires a rebuild, the entire trusting forest won't have to be rebuilt from the ground up.

Domains

Domains should never be considered a security boundary. Any domain account can query the Active Directory database (*ntds.dit*), which is located on every domain controller. This functionality exists to enable pulling down the entire structure with everything in it, from computer names to administrator roles to service accounts. The domain should be used purely as a structural container.

Domain Controllers

"What happens if someone steals one of my domain controllers?"

There is only one correct answer:

"You flatten and then rebuild the entire forest."

—Steve Riley, "Security Watch—Lock Up Your Domain Controllers" (*https://oreil.ly/ 2FkMf*)

Granted, there are other ways to perform an eviction, but rarely with 100% certainty that the attacker has been removed from the environment. Migration to Microsoft 365 cloud with MFA or performing the network eviction process (*https://oreil.ly/ S53IV*) are also options.

Domain controllers are the building blocks of AD DS; they house the Flexible Single Master Operation (FSMO) roles that control the different moving parts that make a domain work. They can be the keys to the castle and should be ferociously guarded.

FSMO roles are the seven special roles that domain controllers can be configured as: Primary Domain Controller (PDC) Emulator, Relative ID (RID) Master, Schema Master, Domain Naming Master, Infrastructure Master, Domain DNS Zone Master, and Forest DNS Zone Master. There is also a role called a Global Catalog (GC) that, while not an FSMO role, will still play a part in determining their placement.

The layout of a domain and how many forests there are will dictate where the FSMO roles are best placed. There are a few standard rules to abide by to ensure they're placed properly:

1. The PDC Emulator and RID Master roles should be on the same server, by themselves. The PDC Emulator is a large consumer of RIDs and is heavily utilized.

2. The Infrastructure Master should not be placed on a GC unless there is only one forest or unless every domain controller in the forest has a GC.

3. The Schema Master and Domain Naming Master should be on the same server, which should also be a GC.

By default, all roles are placed on the first promoted domain controller in the forest and can be migrated to additional domain controllers as they are created.

 At no point in time should a domain controller be a dual-purpose server, be easily accessible, or be treated like a standard workstation.

In datacenters, physical domain controllers should be installed in dedicated secure racks or cages that are separate from the general server population. When possible, domain controllers should be configured with Trusted Platform Module (TPM) chips, and all volumes in the domain controller servers should be protected with some type of drive encryption (*https://oreil.ly/Bx_Px*).

Remote domain controllers can be set up as read-only, with only certain parts of the AD structure being replicated. While it may be less likely that you would have an entire server rack dedicated to an offsite domain controller, there are other options you can take to secure it, such as using a small form factor server placed inside a locked cage, with the cage somehow bolted to the ground. While this may seem like overkill, many times we've seen domain controllers sitting in broom closets or break rooms.

Organizational Units

Organizational units (OUs) can be used for the purpose of delegating rights/permissions to perform certain actions to the objects located in it as well as implementing a well-thought-out structure for Group Policy Objects (discussed later in this chapter).

Groups

There are strict guidelines for what AD groups are and are not used for, because the nesting and assigning of groups can get quite messy. To properly prepare and implement these groups, you should adhere to the following practices:

- Place users into global groups.
- Place global groups into domain local groups.
- Place domain local groups on the access control lists of the data stored on the servers.

If there are multiple domains and universal groups are desired:

- Place global groups containing users into universal groups.
- Place universal groups into the domain local groups.
- Place domain local groups on the access control lists.

In addition to the security benefits of proper user nesting, following this standard can save you a significant amount of hassle. When users leave the organization for any reason and their accounts are subsequently deleted, you won't end up with unresolved SIDs all over the place. If you are working through the issue of cleaning this up in your organization, Microsoft has a wonderful tool called SIDWalk (*https://oreil.ly/S6NG-*) that can assist in removing old unresolved SIDs across the network.

Accounts

One of the largest hurdles companies can face is the massive number of user accounts that are members of the built-in Domain Admins group (or any other type of admin-level group). It is in the best interests of the security of the organization to do ample research on each application's access permissions. If you are lucky enough to be building a domain from the ground up this is significantly easier; performing it retro-actively involves significantly more work. Working with application analysts and ven-dors on file access, processes, and services will allow only the necessary permissions to be delegated at both an endpoint and a server level. This can be accomplished with a variety of tools, such as the Microsoft Sysinternals Suite, Wireshark, system logs, and application logs.

Many data stakeholders, server administrators, and other high-level access staff may request domain admin–level access because honestly, when it's used, the application being installed or the task being performed just works. There is no need to know exactly what files are being modified, what is being accessed, or what tasks are being completed when everything is allowed by default because you have the highest access available.

The use of service accounts is highly recommended. Service accounts are just that: accounts that are strictly used for controlling services and will never perform interac-tive logons. Use a standard naming convention for these accounts, such as "service-txvbserver-mssql," to facilitate monitoring and alerting.

The Local Administrator Password Solution (LAPS) (*https://oreil.ly/3TD_3*) is a free software from Microsoft that makes random password allocations to local adminis-trator accounts. This provides another added layer of security, making it difficult for an attacker to perform lateral movements from one device to the next.

 A second design flaw to stay away from (or move away from) is the use of shared user accounts. Shared accounts give zero accountabil-ity and can be a security auditing nightmare.

Group Policy Objects (GPOs)

Group Policy Objects are used to centrally manage hardware and software settings in a domain configuration. They are broken up into local and domain policies and can be applied to specific accounts or containers in a certain order to see differing results. Maintaining GPOs can be a full-time job in some domains. With the massive amount of available settings, it can become a hassle and extremely complicated to keep track of them.

This is one of the less glamorous jobs, and GPOs are sometimes just left alone as long as things are more or less working. However, knowing and being able to plot out the order of operations for GPO processing, as well as in-depth familiarity with each policy and setting, can not only improve the security of an organization but also speed up login times as well. While we won't go into detail on the actual design of the AD structure, there are many suitable resources you can consult for best practice structure guides, such as Alan Burchill's tutorial (*https://oreil.ly/Ht-b7*) on Group Policy Central.

Instead of starting from scratch and attempting to build a secure GPO by going through each individual setting, there are fully configured templates available for use. For example, NIST has a secure base set of GPOs (*https://oreil.ly/OgQdX*) available for download on its website; they contain settings such as standard password security requirements, disabling LM hashes for domain account passwords, disabling the local guest account, and preventing cached user credentials, as well as hundreds of other user and computer settings. A great first step for any organization would be to include these on any base image in the local policy. This will give the added benefit of a standard set of security settings if a computer is either taken off of the domain or somehow not added to it.

Going one step further, server and desktop administrators can be forced to follow proper process when performing new installs. While it is not possible to create a GPO linked to the default Computers or Users OU in Active Directory, it is possible to force all newly created accounts into a restricted OU. This gives you the ability to only allow certain functions, which will prompt the help desk or an administrator to move the account to the correct location later.

With a simple command running in an elevated PowerShell session, all of the computers that are joined to the domain will automatically end up in the OU of your choosing. This allows you to control the new default location of these accounts—for example:

```
redircmp "OU=MATTSTEAM,OU=ALLTHEHACKERS,DC=YAYBLUETEAM,DC=local"
```

Conclusion

There are countless configuration possibilities across all Microsoft products; our aim here was just to cover some of the low-hanging fruit and help prepare you to tackle the next hurdle in your environment. A great number of commonly scripted offensive attack scenarios can be mitigated by creating a structured and least-privileged Microsoft environment. For further reading, some of the best resources we can recommend related to Windows infrastructure are:

- Active Directory Security (*https://adsecurity.org*)

- Group Policy Central (*https://www.grouppolicy.biz*)

- Microsoft's "Best Practices for Securing Active Directory" (*https://oreil.ly/I5Vs6*)

While Microsoft products are extremely common in enterprise organizations, Windows is far from the only operating system that you need to consider. We will also cover Linux and macOS in later chapters, as well as some of the more specific Microsoft-related controls you can gain in cloud security.

CHAPTER 11

Unix Application Servers

Application servers are an obvious target for an attacker. They are often a central repository for all manner of data, be it authentication credentials, intellectual property, or financial data. Because they are typically so data rich, they are appealing to both financially motivated attackers looking for ways to monetize their attack and politically motivated attackers looking to steal, destroy, or corrupt data.

Of course, in a system architected to have many tiers, application servers may not contain data; however, they will still contain application code and are typically connected to other systems, such as databases. This means they serve as an ideal pivot point to other systems, which also places a target on the application servers.

For these reasons, we should seek to ensure that these servers are built both to perform their desired function to the required specification and to withstand an attack.

It is always recommended that the infrastructure surrounding an application be configured to defend the server from attack. However, ensuring that a server is as well defended as possible in its own right is also strongly advised. This way, in the event that any other defensive countermeasures fail or are bypassed—for example, by an attacker moving laterally within the infrastructure—the server is still defended as well as is sensibly possible.

The essentials for Windows-based platforms were covered in Chapter 10, so this chapter will focus on Unix platforms such as Linux, FreeBSD, and Solaris.

The topics covered in this chapter, Unix patch management and operating system hardening principles, are discussed in a deliberately general fashion. An in-depth discussion of securing Unix application servers, as with the topics of most of the chapters in this book, could fill a book itself. In order to remain agnostic to the flavor of Unix being used, the topics discussed are deliberately those that are common to most Unix flavors. If you wish to take further precautions and implement features that are common to only a specific few versions, it is certainly worth consulting guides that are specifically written for your operating system.

Keeping Up-to-Date

One of the most effective and yet often overlooked aspects of managing Unix servers is patch management. A large number of vulnerabilities in Unix environments occur either as a result of bugs in software that is installed on a system or bugs in the system itself. Thus, many vulnerabilities in an environment can be remediated simply by keeping a system patched and up-to-date.

Third-Party Software Updates

Unlike Microsoft environments, Unix-based environments typically use a system of package management to install the majority of third-party applications. Package management and update tools vary depending not only on which flavor of Unix you are running but also on which distribution you use. For example, Debian Linux and SUSE Linux use two different package management systems, and FreeBSD uses another.

Despite the differences, there are common themes surrounding the package management systems. Typically, each host will hold a repository of packages that are available to install on the system via local tools. The system administrator issues commands to the package management system to indicate that they wish to install, update, or remove packages. That system will then, depending on its configuration, either download and compile or download a binary of the desired package and its dependencies (libraries and other applications required to run the desired application) and then install them on the system.

In modern distributions, the various package management systems are so comprehensive that for many environments it would be unusual to require anything further. Deploying software via package management, as opposed to downloading it from elsewhere, is the preference unless there is a compelling reason to do otherwise. This greatly simplifies staying up-to-date and tracking dependencies.

Sometimes applications need to be installed outside of the package management system. This may be because the application is not included in the package management system, or because your organization has particular build and deployment requirements that require a custom build. If this is the case, it is recommended that someone be tasked with monitoring both the new releases of the application and its security mailing. Subscribing to these lists should provide notification of any vulnerabilities that have been discovered, as vulnerabilities in these applications will not be covered by updates addressed automatically by the package management system.

The same package management system can be used to perform upgrades. As the repository of available packages is updated, new versions of already installed packages appear in the package database. These new version numbers can be compared against the installed version numbers and a list of applications due for an upgrade to a new version can be compiled automatically, typically via a single command line. However, note that upgrading existing packages has been known to break some dependencies and setups. If possible, a "dry run" should be performed prior to any upgrades.

The simplicity of this approach means that unless a robust system of checking for and applying changes is in place for installed applications, the package management system should be used to provide an easy, automated method of updating all packages on Unix application servers. Not only does this remove the need to manually track each application installed on the application servers, along with all their associated dependencies, but it (typically) also means that the upgrade has already been tested and confirmed to work on that distribution. Of course, individual quirks between systems mean that you cannot be sure that everything will always work smoothly, so you should still have a testing process; however, you can enter into that process with a good degree of confidence.

To illustrate how this typically works, let's take a look at the Debian Linux method of patching. First, we can update the repository via a single command—in the case of Debian, apt-get with the argument update:

```
$ sudo apt-get update
Get:1 http://security.debian.org wheezy/updates Release.gpg [1,554 B]
Get:2 http://security.debian.org wheezy/updates Release [102 kB]
Get:3 http://security.debian.org wheezy/updates/main amd64 Packages [347 kB]
Get:4 http://ftp.us.debian.org wheezy Release.gpg [2,373 B]
Get:5 http://security.debian.org wheezy/updates/main Translation-en [202 kB]
Get:6 http://ftp.us.debian.org unstable Release.gpg [1,554 B]
Get:7 http://ftp.us.debian.org wheezy Release [191 kB]
Get:8 http://ftp.us.debian.org unstable Release [192 kB]
Get:9 http://ftp.us.debian.org wheezy/main amd64 Packages [5,838 kB]
Get:10 http://ftp.us.debian.org wheezy/main Translation-en [3,846 kB]
Get:11 http://ftp.us.debian.org unstable/main amd64 Packages/DiffIndex [27.9 kB]
Get:12 http://ftp.us.debian.org unstable/non-free amd64 Packages/DiffIndex [23B]
Get:13 http://ftp.us.debian.org unstable/contrib amd64 Packages/DiffIndex [102B]
Get:14 http://ftp.us.debian.org unstable/contrib Translation-en/DiffIndex [78B]
Get:15 http://ftp.us.debian.org unstable/main Translation-en/DiffIndex [27.9 kB]
Get:16 http://ftp.us.debian.org unstable/non-free Translation-en/DiffIndex [93B]
Get:17 http://ftp.us.debian.org unstable/contrib Translation-en [48.7 kB]
Get:18 http://ftp.us.debian.org unstable/main Translation-en [5,367 kB]
Get:19 http://ftp.us.debian.org unstable/non-free Translation-en [81.3 kB]
Get:20 http://ftp.us.debian.org unstable/main amd64 Packages [7,079 kB]
Get:21 http://ftp.us.debian.org unstable/non-free amd64 Packages [79.2 kB]
Get:22 http://ftp.us.debian.org unstable/contrib amd64 Packages [53.5 kB]
Fetched 23.5 MB in 13s (1,777 kB/s)
```

Now that the repository is up-to-date, we can use the `apt-get` command again, this time with the argument `upgrade`, to perform upgrades on any packages that have newer versions available than the one that is currently installed:

```
$ sudo apt-get upgrade
Reading package lists... Done
Building dependency tree
Reading state information... Done
The following packages will be upgraded:
  package-1 package-5
2 upgraded, 0 newly installed, 0 to remove and 256 not upgraded.
Need to get 4.0 MB of archives.
After this operation, 1,149 kB of additional disk space will be used.

Do you want to continue [Y/n]?
```

The output here tells us that the example packages "package-1" and "package-5" will be installed. If we select yes, the system will automatically build and install those packages.

Although this example uses Debian, the process is almost identical across most Unix systems and is covered in the base documentation for every system that we have seen.

Core Operating System Updates

Many, but not all, Unix systems have a delineation between the operating system and applications that are installed on it. As such, the method of keeping the operating system itself up-to-date will often differ from that of the applications. The exact method of upgrading will vary from OS to OS, but they typically fall into two broad buckets:

Binary update
Commercial operating systems particularly favor the method of applying a binary update—that is, distributing precompiled binary executables and libraries that are copied to disk, replacing the previous versions. Binary updates cannot make use of custom compiler options and make assumptions about dependencies, but they require less work in general and are fast to install.

Update from source
Many open source operating systems favor updates from source, meaning that they are compiled locally from a copy of the source code and previous versions on disk are replaced by these binaries. Updating from source takes more time and is more complex, but the operating system can include custom compiler optimizations and patches.

There's much debate over which system is better, and each has its pros and cons. For the purposes of this book, however, we will assume that you are sticking with the default of your operating system, as the majority of the arguments center on topics unrelated to security.

Updates to the operating system are typically less frequent than updates to third-party software. Additionally, they are more disruptive, typically requiring a reboot because they often involve an update to the kernel or other subsystems that only load at startup (unlike application updates, which can be instantiated via the restart of the appropriate daemon). Core operating system updates are advisable, though, as vulnerabilities are often found within both operating systems and applications.

As with any other patch of this nature, it is advisable to have a rollback plan in place when updating your OS. In the case of virtualized infrastructure, this can be achieved simply by taking a snapshot of the filesystem prior to upgrade; a failed upgrade can then be rolled back by reverting to the last snapshot. With physical infrastructure this can be more problematic, but most operating systems have mechanisms to cope with this issue, typically by storing copies of the old binaries and replacing them if required.

Patches to the OS are often required in order to close security gaps, so you should have a process defined to cope with this. As with applications, the effort required to upgrade the OS is lower the more up-to-date the system already is, so we recommend remaining as current as is reasonable, leaving only small increments to update at any one time.

Hardening a Unix Application Server

The next area to discuss is that of hardening the servers. This is the art of making the most secure configuration possible, without compromising the ability of the system to perform its primary business functions.

This can be a particularly difficult balancing act, as restricting access to users and processes must be tempered with the fact that the server must still perform its primary function properly and system administrators must still be able to access the system to perform their duties.

Disable Services

Every service (daemon) that runs is executing code on the server. If there is a vulnerability within that code, it is a potential weakness that can be leveraged by an attacker; it is also consuming resources in the form of RAM and CPU cycles.

Many operating systems ship with a number of services enabled by default, many of which you may not use. These services should be disabled to reduce the attack surface on your servers. Of course, you shouldn't just start disabling services with reckless abandon—before disabling a service, it is prudent to ascertain exactly what it does and determine if you require it.

There are a number of ways to determine which services are running on a Unix system, the easiest of which is to use the ps command to list running services. The exact argument syntax can vary between versions, but ps ax works on most systems and will list all currently running processes. To confirm the syntax on your operating system, check the manual page for ps using the command man ps.

Services should be disabled in startup scripts (rc or init, depending on the operating system) unless your system uses systemd, which we'll discuss momentarily. Using the kill command will merely stop the currently running service, which will start once more during a reboot. On Linux, the commands are typically one of rc-update, update-rc.d, or service. On BSD-based systems, you typically edit the file */etc/rc.conf*. For example, on several flavors of Linux the service command can be used to stop the sshd service as follows:

```
service sshd stop
```

To start sshd (one time), use:

```
service start sshd
```

And to disable it from starting after a reboot, use:

```
update-rc.d -f sshd remove
```

Some Linux distributions have moved toward using systemd as opposed to SysV startup scripts to manage services. systemd can also be used to perform other administrative functions with regard to services, such as reloading configuration and displaying dependency information. For example, to stop sshd (one time), use:

```
systemctl stop sshd
```

To enable sshd upon every reboot, use:

```
systemctl enable sshd
```

And to disable sshd upon further reboots, use:

```
systemctl disable sshd
```

Older Unix operating systems may use inetd or xinetd to manage services rather than rc or init scripts. (x)inetd is used to preserve system resources by being almost the only service running and starting other services on demand, rather than leaving them all running all of the time. In this case, services can be disabled by editing the *inetd.conf* or *xinetd.conf* files, typically located in the */etc/* directory.

Set File Permissions

Most Unix filesystems have a concept of *permissions*, indicating the level of access (read, write, and execute) different users and groups have to files and directories. Most also have the setuid (set user ID upon execution) permission, which allows a nonroot user to execute a file with the permissions of the owning user (typically root). This is because the normal operation of the file execution command, even by a nonroot user, requires root privileges, such as through the use of su or sudo.

Typically, an operating system will set adequate file permissions on the system files during installation. However, as you create files and directories, permissions will be set according to your umask settings. As a general rule, the umask on a system should only be made more restrictive than the default. Cases where a less restrictive umask is required should be infrequent enough that chmod (the command used to change access permissions) can be used to resolve the issue. You can view and edit your umask settings using the umask command; for further details, see the manual page (you can view this by typing man umask at the command prompt of almost any Unix system).

Incorrect file permissions can leave files readable (or worse) by users other than those who are intended to be able to see them. Many people wrongly believe that because a user has to be authenticated to log in to a host, leaving world- or group-readable files on disk is not a problem. However, they do not consider that services also run using their own user accounts.

Take, for example, a system running a web server such as Apache, nginx, or lighttpd. These web servers typically run under a user ID of their own, such as *www-data*. If files you create are readable by *www-data*, then, if configured to do so (accidentally or otherwise), the web server has permission to read those files and potentially serve them to a browser. By restricting filesystem-level access, you can prevent this from happening even if the web server is configured to read those files, as it will no longer have permission to open them.

In the Unix filesystem listing, there are 10 dashes (-), the last 9 of which correspond to *read*, *write*, and *execute* permissions for *owner, group*, and *other* (everyone). A dash indicates the permission is not set; a letter indicates that it is set. Other special characters appear less often; for example, an S signifies that the setuid flag has been set.

As an example, here the file *test* can be read and written to by the owner, *_www*, it can be read and executed by the group *staff*, and it can be read by everyone. This is denoted by the rw-, r-x, and r-- permissions in the directory listing, respectively:

```
$ ls -al test
-rw-r-xr--  1 _www  staff  1228 16 Apr 05:22 test
```

If we wish to ensure that *other* can no longer see this file, we can modify the permissions using the chmod command (o= sets the *other* permissions to nothing):

```
$ sudo chmod o= test
$ ls -la test
-rw-r-x---  1 _www  staff  1228 16 Apr 05:22 test
```

Note that the r representing the read permission for *other* is now a -.[1]

---

1 For further reading on this topic, consult the manual pages for the commands chmod, chgrp, chown, and ls.

Use Host-Based Firewalls

Many people think of firewalls as appliances located at strategic points around a network to allow and deny various types of connections. However, most Unix operating systems have local firewall software built in so that hosts can firewall themselves. By enabling and configuring this functionality, you can not only offer a server some additional protection, should the network firewalls fail to operate as expected, but also offer it protection against hosts on the local LAN that can communicate with the server directly.

Typical examples of firewall software in Unix systems include iptables/netfilter, ipchains, pf, ipf, and ipfw. Their configuration and use will vary from platform to platform, but the end goal is the same: to create a ruleset that permits all traffic required to successfully complete the server's tasks and any related administration of the server, and nothing else.

One point to note is that using a stateful firewall on a host will consume RAM and CPU cycles, to keep track of sessions and maintain a TCP state table. This is because not only does a stateful firewall permit and deny packets based on IP addresses and port numbers, but it also tracks features such as TCP handshake status in a state table. On a busy server, a simple packet filter (i.e., permitting and denying based on IP addresses, port numbers, protocols, etc., on a packet-by-packet basis) will consume way fewer resources but still allow an increased level of protection from unwanted connections.

Manage File Integrity

File integrity management tools monitor key files on the filesystem and alert the administrator in the event that they change. These tools can be used to ensure that key system files are not tampered with, for example, by a rootkit, and that files are not added to directories and configuration files are not modified without the administrator's permission (for example, via backdoors in web applications).

There are both commercial and free/open source tools for this purpose available through your preferred package management solution. Examples of open source tools that perform file integrity monitoring are Samhain and OSSEC. If you are looking to spend money to obtain extra features, like providing integration with your existing management systems, there are also a number of commercial tools available.

Alternatively, if you cannot for whatever reason install file integrity monitoring tools, many configuration management tools can be configured to report on modified configuration files on the filesystem as part of their normal operation. This is not their primary function and does not offer the same level of coverage, so it's not as robust as using a dedicated tool. However, if you are in a situation where you cannot deploy security tools but do have configuration management in place, this may be of some use.

Configure Separate Disk Partitions

Disk partitions within Unix can be used not only to distribute the filesystem across several physical or logical partitions but also to restrict certain types of actions depending on which partition they are taking place on. Configuration options can be placed on each mount point in */etc/fstab*.

When you edit */etc/fstab*, the changes will not take effect until the partition is remounted using the umount and/or mount command, or following a reboot.

There are some minor differences between different flavors of Unix with regard to the options, so consulting the manual page using man mount before using these options is recommended. Some of the most useful and common mount options, from a security perspective, are:

nodev

Do not interpret any character or block special devices. Typically, only the */dev/* mount point will contain these devices. This option should be used if no special devices are expected.

A character or block special device permits access to a file that has a backing device that isn't part of the filesystem it is contained on. A simple example is the "disk" objects on the */dev* filesystem. Executing character or block special devices from untrusted filesystems increases the opportunity for unprivileged users to attain unauthorized administrative access.

nosuid

Do not allow setuid execution. Attackers can use setuid binaries as a method of backdooring a system to quickly obtain root privileges from a standard user account. However, certain core system functions, such as su and sudo, will require setuid execution, so this option should be used carefully. setuid execution is probably not required outside of the system-installed *bin* and *sbin* directories. You can check for the location of setuid binaries using the following command:

```
sudo find / -perm -4000
```

Binaries that are specifically setuid root, as opposed to any setuid binary, can be located using the following variant:

```
sudo find / -user root -perm -4000
```

ro

Mount the filesystem read-only. If data does not need to be written or updated, this option may be used to prevent modification. This removes the ability for an attacker to modify files stored in this location, such as config files, static website content, and the like.

noexec

Prevents execution, of any type, from this mount point. This can be set on mount points used exclusively for data and document storage. It prevents an attacker from using this as a location to execute tools they may load onto a system and so can defeat certain classes of exploit.

Use chroot

chroot alters the apparent root directory of a running process and any child processes. The most important aspect of this is that the process inside the "chroot jail" cannot access files outside of its new apparent root directory, which is particularly useful in the case of ensuring that a poorly configured or exploited service cannot access anything more than it needs to.

There are two ways to initiate chroot:

- The process in question can use the chroot system call and chroot itself voluntarily. Typically, these processes will contain chroot options within their configuration files, most notably allowing the user to set the new apparent root directory.

- The chroot wrapper can be used on the command line when executing the command. Typically this will look something like:

  ```
  sudo chroot /chroot/dir/ /chroot/dir/bin/binary -args
  ```

For details on the specific chroot syntax for your flavor of Unix, consult the manual page (type man chroot at the command prompt of almost any Unix system).

It should be noted, however, that there is a common misconception that chroot offers some security features that it simply does not. Chroot jails are not impossible to break out of, especially if the process within the chroot jail is running with root privileges. Typically, processes that are specifically designed to use chroot will drop their root privileges as soon as possible so as to mitigate this risk. Additionally, chroot does not offer the process any protection from privileged users outside of the chroot jail on the same system.

Neither of these are reasons to abandon chroot, but they should be considered when designing use cases; keep in mind that a chroot jail is not an impenetrable fortress, just another method of restricting filesystem access.

Set Up Mandatory Access Control

There are various flavors of Unix that support mandatory access control (MAC), with some of the best-known being SELinux (*http://selinuxproject.org*), TrustedBSD (*http://www.trustedbsd.org*), and the grsecurity (*https://grsecurity.net*) patches. The method of configuration, granularity, and features of MAC vary across systems; however, the high-level concepts remain consistent.

MAC allows policies to be enforced that are far more granular in nature than those offered by traditional Unix filesystem permissions. The ability to read, write, and execute files is set in policies with fine-grained controls, allowing an individual user to be granted or denied access on a per-file basis rather than granting or denying access to files or directories based on the groups the user belongs to, for example.

Using MAC with a defined policy allows the owner of a system to enforce the principle of least privilege—that is, only permitting access to those files and functions that users require to perform their job, and nothing more. This limits their access and reduces the chances of accidental or deliberate abuse.

MAC can also be used with enforcement disabled—i.e., operating in a mode in which violations of policy are not blocked, but rather are logged—permitting a more granular level of logging of user activity. The reasons for this will be discussed in Chapter 20.

Conclusion

Keeping Unix application servers secure does not necessarily require the purchase of additional infrastructure or software. Unix operating systems on the whole are designed to have a large number of useful tools available to the user out of the box, with package management systems to provide supplemental open source tools.

A large number of vulnerabilities can be mitigated simply by keeping up-to-date with patches and ensuring that a sensible configuration is used.

CHAPTER 12

Endpoints

Endpoints—devices that an end user operates, such as a desktop, laptop, tablet, or cell phone—are becoming ever more popular targets for malicious individuals who are looking to compromise a network. With an increasingly mobile workforce and rapidly falling prices for storage, the amount of data that is either stored on endpoints or available to endpoints via the repositories that they access (i.e., shared drives) is growing more and more substantial by the day.

In what may appear (from a security perspective, at least) to be a counterintuitive response to this greater availability of data, demands are high for access to that data to be increasingly low-friction, often in the name of boosting the productivity or agility of the organization.

Endpoints are, of course, also the locations at which most people conduct activities such as web browsing, instant messaging, reading email, and clicking any random links or attachments that seem appealing to them at the time. The number of vectors available to attack endpoints is large, and enterprise networks are filled with targets for whom security is not necessarily the number one priority.

All of this has, unsurprisingly, led to endpoints being increasingly targeted not only by malware and ransomware but also by more precise spearphishing and hacking campaigns. In this chapter we will explore steps you can take on most endpoint devices to drastically reduce the chances of an endpoint being compromised, as well as to minimize the impact to your organization should this ever happen.

Keeping Up-to-Date

As with the server estate, ensuring that patches are installed on endpoints is critical to limiting the number of bugs, and thus vulnerabilities, on any one system. By minimizing the vulnerabilities on endpoints, you reduce the number of technology-based options open to an attacker, as well as their susceptibility to automated attacks by certain types of malware.

The method of patching will vary from platform to platform. It will also vary depending on the style of management used by an organization: the process may be quite different in an organization with a BYOD system of device selection and management and a more traditional setup where the employer provides the devices and manages their hardware, operating systems, and often applications.

Microsoft Windows

Ever since the launch of Windows 95, Microsoft has provided the Windows Update service, which has gone through a number of different incarnations but ultimately serves the purpose of distributing patches to endpoints in a semiautomated way. This service allows desktop PCs running Microsoft Windows to download updates and patches based on which version of the operating system is being run. However, it's mainly aimed at the consumer and BYOD markets and is fairly self-service, with the user being provided the opportunity to decline or defer updates and no visibility provided to system administrators with regard to the deployment status of various patches.

Microsoft has, in the past, provided what are effectively enterprise versions of this system in the form of Systems Management Server (SMS), Microsoft Operations Manager (MOM), and Windows Server Update Services (WSUS), to allow system administrators to deploy patches to workstations within the environment without relying on Windows Update or Microsoft Update. These systems are, however, no longer the standard.

At the time of writing, Microsoft recommends the use of Windows Update for Business (*https://oreil.ly/hWtc6*) for endpoints running Windows 10 and 11. You can use either Group Policy or mobile device management solutions to configure devices to use the Windows Update for Business service, as opposed to the consumer-style Windows Update service.

macOS

Modern macOS environments primarily leverage Mobile Device Management (MDM) solutions for central patch management. These systems provide comprehensive capabilities to enforce policies, deploy configurations, manage applications, and push updates to both macOS and iOS devices.

The Profile Manager tool (*https://oreil.ly/5SnJx*) distributed by Apple can be used to configure a number of configuration options for iOS and macOS devices in your estate. It is not a central management system per se, but it can be used to deploy policies.

For unmanaged devices—that is, devices for which you have not installed a configuration profile—the change of update server can be made manually using a command like the following:

```
sudo defaults write /Library/Preferences/com.apple.SoftwareUpdate
    CatalogURL http://my.update.server.tld:8088/index.sucatalog
```

It's worth remembering that, like other operating systems, macOS allows users with suitable privileges to install software outside of this ecosystem, and such software will not be automatically patched via a system such as this. In these cases, the onus may well be on the user to perform regular updates and to ensure that the system is functioning as expected.

One of the most popular methods of distributing third-party software to macOS hosts is homebrew (*http://brew.sh*). Users of this system can update their repository by running the command:

```
brew update
```

And then upgrade any packages that have been updated in the repository by running the command:

```
brew upgrade
```

It is essential for both managed and unmanaged devices to stay current with software updates to maintain security integrity. For managed devices, MDM solutions provide a centralized platform for automating updates. For unmanaged devices, educating users about the importance of regular software updates is crucial.

Unix Desktops

As is often the case, Unix desktops vary depending on the flavor of Unix in use, and between distributions within each flavor. However, the following high-level approaches can be researched for suitability, depending on the environment:

- Use similar management tools to those that may be used for Unix servers to run commands on desktops, causing the local package management software to perform the desired upgrades. Management tools such as Puppet (*https://oreil.ly/eqa-X*) and Ansible (*https://oreil.ly/BpWle*) can be used to centrally automate these tasks.

- Ensure that desktops are configured to run the automatic update and upgrade processes, if available, via a scheduled job (typically via cron).

- Entrust patching to the desktop owner.

Third-Party Updates

Not all software will be managed by the operating system's own update mechanisms. As mentioned previously, users with suitable privileges can install third-party software that is not covered by the central patch management systems described here. Thankfully, an ever-increasing number of applications are implementing automatic or semiautomatic update mechanisms to aid users with this process. The use of these automatic update systems is often more of a challenge with regard to user education than in terms of technology. Users should accept updates and thereby keep their applications patched and up-to-date; however, they should also be taught not to blindly click Accept on everything, as this will naturally expose them to several types of social engineering attacks (FakeAV malware, for example). It is recommended that users update their applications, but be aware of how to distinguish a valid update from a browser pop-up.

Applications that do not have an automatic update mechanism should be monitored for new releases, typically by subscription to mailing lists and such, with upgrades applied manually as new releases become available.

Keeping an inventory of applications installed within the environment is worthwhile. This way, in the event of an advisory being released for software, it is immediately apparent if you have a problem, how large it is, and how many desktops will need to be visited in order to mitigate it. This sort of information is typically kept in your asset register, as mentioned in Chapter 2.

Hardening Endpoints

As with servers (discussed in Chapters 10 and 11), *hardening* in the context of endpoints refers to the art of creating the most secure configuration possible, without compromising the ability of the system to perform its primary function. Patching, as mentioned previously, is the first critical step to hardening an endpoint, but there are other steps that should be taken in order to reduce the opportunity for compromise.

Disable Services

Every service (daemon) that runs is executing code on the endpoint. Not only is it consuming resources in the form of RAM and CPU cycles, but if there is a vulnerability within that code, it is also a potential weakness that can be leveraged by an attacker. A very well-known attack on a service was PrintNightmare (CVE-2021-34527) (*https://oreil.ly/c9Rjv*), which caused a massive number of organizations worldwide to disable the Windows Print Spooler service in 2021.

Many operating systems ship with a number of services enabled by default, many of which you may not use. These services should be disabled to reduce the attack surface on your endpoints. Of course, you shouldn't just start disabling services with reckless abandon—before disabling a service, it is prudent to ascertain exactly what it does and if it is required.

On Microsoft systems, there is a GUI-based administration tool within Control Panel that can be used to list, start, and stop services, either temporarily or permanently. There is also a command-line option to list running services:

```
sc query type= service
```

You can start or stop services from the command line too. For example, to stop the Task Scheduler—which, as it happens, you should *not* do!—you can type:

```
sc stop "Task Scheduler"
```

And to start it again, you can use:

```
sc start "Task Scheduler"
```

This only stops and starts a service for the duration that the endpoint is booted up, however. To permanently disable a service, you should use the following commands:

```
sc config "<servicename>" start= disabled
sc stop "<servicename>"
```

In addition to the built-in commands, there are other Microsoft tools that will provide a more in-depth view of services and their hooks into the operating system. Both Process Explorer and Process Monitor from the Sysinternals Suite can assist in research into service and process activities.

We discussed how to disable services on Unix-based operating systems in Chapter 11. macOS is based upon FreeBSD, a Unix system, and thus the `ps` and `kill` commands work in the same fashion as previously described. The preferred route is to use the `launchctl` command to control launchd, which can be invoked with the `list`, `stop`, or `start` arguments to list, stop, or start enabled services.

To disable a service, use the command:

```
launchctl disable <servicename>
```

It should be noted that there are a wide range of options when using `launchctl`, so it is recommended that you consult the command's manual page (`man launchctl`) before proceeding.

Use Desktop Firewalls

With an ever-growing mobile workforce, using desktop firewalls is becoming increasingly necessary. The days of having a workforce whose IT footprint is confined to the office environment are long gone for most organizations. The last time an employer gave one of us a desktop that was an actual desktop was back in 2002. Ever since then, irrespective of industry vertical or company size, our "desktops" have always been laptops, even if they remained permanently at a desk. This trend, together with increased acceptance of remote working, means that many users' main computing devices—the ones that probably hold a large volume of your corporate information— are at best being plugged into home networks along with partners', housemates', and children's devices, and at worst connecting to public WiFi hotspots in hotels and coffee shops.

Of course, a firewall is far from a panacea, but being able to block all ingress connections—and ideally, blocking egress connections also—is very beneficial when on an untrusted network. Ingress filtering blocks those attempting to connect to the endpoint. Blocking egress connections also allows applications that are unsafe to use on a shared network, such as those that use unencrypted protocols, to be blocked.

Windows systems have included a built-in firewall capability of one sort or another since Windows XP. We would hope that you are running something more recent than Windows XP, so we assume that this option is available to you. If you're running a Windows system that is older than XP, then you have quite a number of other problems to address, and your endpoints should not be connecting to public WiFi at all.

The location of the administration interface varies from version to version, but it is consistently within the Control Panel. In Windows 10 and 11, the interface is located in Control Panel→System and Security→Windows Firewall.

Since OS X Leopard, macOS has included an application firewall that, rather than operating on IP addresses and port numbers, allows you to configure settings based on an application. For example, you could specify that the web browser can make connections, but that the PDF reader cannot. The administrative interface is located in System Preferences→Security and Privacy→Firewall.

Linux-based desktops will almost without exception have a host-based firewall available to them, although this will vary between distributions. The default for Ubuntu, for example, is Uncomplicated Firewall, or `ufw` (for details on how to use `ufw`, consult the manual page, `man ufw`). Other Linux flavors and Unix systems might use any one of a range of firewalls; for details, consult the documentation for your specific distribution.

Implement Full-Disk Encryption

As we discussed in the previous section, today's workforce is becoming increasingly mobile due to the replacement of traditional desktop systems with laptops, which people carry around with them. This, of course, is accompanied by the risk of a laptop being stolen or left somewhere, which means that organizational data is also increasingly at risk.

This risk is compounded by the fact that evolving trends in the cost, capacity, and physical size of storage have led to large-capacity disks being commonplace in endpoint devices, meaning that members of staff can store large volumes of (often sensitive) data on their devices.

For these reasons, among many others, it is recommended to run a full-disk encryption solution to protect the hard disks or SSDs in employees' laptops and desktops. Modern hardware and operating systems are optimized for the use of full-disk encryption, so after the initial encryption of the drive, in most cases the performance overhead is not noticeable. Modern full-disk encryption implementations are also fairly transparent to the user, typically requiring only an additional boot-time password after initial encryption of the disk has taken place.

 It should be obvious, but for the sake of clarity, encrypting the storage on a laptop will (by design) render the data on it unreadable to anyone but the owner who is configured to decrypt the data. Thus, if you rely on the ability to perform disk forensics, for example, you should consider other solutions that include the option for centrally controlled keys to allow forensic examination by your team.

Current versions of most operating systems come with bundled full-disk encryption solutions that should serve perfectly well unless you have a requirement for centrally managed keys or the ability to use a specific configuration, such as altering the cryptographic characteristics.

Windows includes a tool called BitLocker, which can be found in Control Panel→System and Security→BitLocker Drive Encryption. Enabling BitLocker is simply a case of selecting the drive to encrypt, clicking "Turn on BitLocker," and following the onscreen prompts.

On macOS, there is a similar tool called FileVault. To enable FileVault, use the administrative interface located in System Preferences→Security & Privacy→FileVault; click "Turn On FileVault" and follow the onscreen prompts.

Full-disk encryption on Linux platforms is typically more difficult to accomplish after the installation of the operating system, so you should consult the documentation for your specific distribution. However, if you're installing a new system, this is often as simple as checking a box (this is certainly the case in recent versions of Ubuntu, for example).

Locked Screens, Sleeping, and Hibernating

Full-disk encryption works by leaving the filesystem on the disk encrypted at all times, with a key stored in memory. This key is then used by a driver for the disk, which reads encrypted data from the disk, decrypts its memory using the key, and then passes the decrypted data to the operating system and applications. The OS and applications are, for all intents and purposes, completely unaware that the data is encrypted on the drive.

This decryption key is itself encrypted on the drive but is decrypted using the passphrase entered by the user at encryption time, and again at each bootup. This allows for the key used to decrypt data on the disk to be substantially larger than the passphrases used by humans.

There is, however, one issue with this model: the key to decrypt the disk must remain in memory at all times. Memory is only cleared when the host is shut down; during normal operation, when displaying the lock screen, and when in sleep mode or hibernate mode, the memory is retained. This means that leaving a laptop on the lock screen will not necessarily protect it from an attacker.

This is no different from normal operation on a network, but users often expect that when a device's screen is locked or it's in sleep mode (for example, when it's left unattended in a hotel room), it is safe from a physical attacker. There are attacks that can be used to dump the memory over one of the ports on an endpoint, and from that memory dump the decryption key can be acquired.

Use Endpoint Protection Tools

Endpoint protection tools, such as antivirus software, are often a point of contention, especially with regard to their effectiveness versus potential new vulnerabilities that they may introduce into a system while performing their tasks. The issue is that at the same time they are fixing issues, they are themselves running additional code on a host that can, and does, contain bugs.

A general rule of thumb is that until you are suitably advanced in matters of security to make this determination for yourself, you are probably better off running the software than not. Antivirus, antimalware, and other endpoint protection tools are far from providing complete coverage, but they do catch low-hanging fruit and reduce the noise in the data that you are analyzing, which in turn makes it easier to spot other issues that could have been lost in the noise.

Mobile Device Management

Mobile device management (MDM) is the generic term used to describe a number of possible technologies that can be used to provide centralized management of mobile devices—typically smartphones as well as tablets and other mobile computing devices.

MDM is used to enforce policy on a device. It typically takes the form of a server running MDM software that has been configured on the device prior to delivery to the user. Examples of policies that can be enforced include:

- Enforce PIN/password
- Enforce VPN use
- Application installation
- Remote erase
- Enforce configuration options (ban or enforce the use of certain applications or configuration options)

Unlike with many other technologies mentioned in this book, there aren't really any prevalent open source MDM solutions that we can point to at the time of writing. There are, however, a number of commercial solutions. The largest differentiators between these solutions, other than cost, are which devices are supported and which sorts of policies you wish to enforce upon each device type. Before purchasing a solution, it's therefore advisable to understand what kinds of devices you need to support and what you would like to manage on them. This will instantly narrow down the number of contenders to evaluate.

Endpoint Visibility

Endpoint visibility tools allow the collection of key data on how an endpoint is operating. Details about open network connections, running processes, open files, and so on can be helpful for many purposes. For example, this information can often be used to detect compromised hosts, malware, or members of staff deliberately acting in a malicious way. When aggregated across the enterprise, it can be used not only for detection and blocking purposes but also potentially for reconstructing lateral movement and data exfiltration in the event of a larger compromise.

Endpoint visibility can be a potentially contentious topic, however, with regard to the expectation of privacy employees have within your organization. This often comes down to a number of factors: the organization itself, the industry vertical, the country in which you are located, and other cultural aspects. It's often wise to speak to human resources prior to deploying endpoint visibility tools in order to ensure that they are permissible under the contract of employment. Having staff trust the security team is crucial to being effective, and this small act can pay large dividends later on.

Various tools are available; for example, osquery (*https://osquery.io*) is a well-established and respected open source tool that supports Windows, macOS, and Linux out of the box, and Windows System Monitor (Sysmon) is valuable for the in-depth logging it adds to hosts (we'll talk more about this in Chapter 22).

Other Endpoints

In addition to endpoints with full operating systems, other devices should be considered as well—for example, Internet of Things (IoT) endpoints such as printers; cameras; and heating, ventilation, and air conditioning (HVAC) systems that interact with heating, cooling, and other infrastructure equipment.

Printers will ship with default passwords and may store Active Directory credentials on them for authenticating to LDAP to send scanned/printed documents to file shares. Printers are inherently insecure and can also often be coaxed into providing LM hashes. It is best to lock down logins that printers use as well as segmenting them as much as possible.

Supervisory control and data acquisition (SCADA) systems include devices that control industrial equipment such as remote telemetry units (RTUs), sensors, and actuators. These systems are not only known to be insecure, but they can also be extremely fragile when interacting with modern technology. The third-party vendors that supply or manage the systems may have security protocols specific to their devices, or they may have a backdoor into the system that has zero security. Any SCADA equipment should be treated just like any other part of the network; it should be documented, secured, and tested as a precautionary measure.

Other items to consider include:

- IP-enabled cameras
- IP-enabled thermostats
- Door locking systems
- IP telephony systems

Centralization

One of the goals of endpoint management is to centralize resources as much as possible. Central management consoles, central authentication systems, centralized logging, and centralized file stores all bring benefits such as economies of scale, ease of management, consistency of configuration, minimization of management overhead, and typically a simplified architecture. By aiming for a centralized infrastructure that makes sense for your organization, you'll make life easier both for yourself and for the end user.

Conclusion

Endpoints are the new go-to systems for attackers as remote and mobile workforces continue to grow and access to often-sensitive company data becomes more ubiquitous. Securing these endpoints is a must for any organization. There are several fairly simple steps you can take to vastly reduce the risk of compromise and to increase the chances of detection if it does occur. Patching, hardening, and using endpoint visibility tools are achievable goals for most organizations.

CHAPTER 13

Databases

At first, you might not see how important databases are for information security. But like asset management, databases help keep valuable data safe. Think about how tough it would be to handle these situations without good database security:

- Someone gains unauthorized access to sensitive customer data, harming both your clients and your company's reputation.

- An attacker uses SQL injection to disrupt an entire production database.

- An attacker steals and shares your company's private information, with the data leak resulting in serious financial and reputational loss.

- An employee with bad intentions changes or steals important data, damaging your organization's stability and trust.

Dealing with these issues gets much harder without a general knowledge of databases and strong database security. Databases are the main part of modern information systems because they're where we store, manage, and access structured data. Modern organizations create data faster than ever, and it's vital to store and process sensitive data securely.

In this chapter, we'll explore the fundamentals of databases and their significance in information security. We'll look at various types of databases—from relational and NoSQL databases to serverless and distributed systems—each with unique security needs. Our aim is to equip you with knowledge of common database management systems (DBMSs) and their security features and challenges, as well as key security strategies suitable for different data storage methods. While touching on the concept of distributed systems, our primary focus will be on understanding databases and effective measures to ensure their security.

Introduction to Databases and Their Importance in Information Security

Databases vary in their structure and management, each catering to distinct needs. For example, relational databases use a schema for data relationships with tables, columns, and rows. Relational database management systems (RDBMSs) are ideal for managing large datasets with complex relationships, where data integrity and security are crucial. Popular RDBMSs include MySQL, PostgreSQL, and Microsoft SQL Server. If you're generally new to database concepts, W3Schools (*https://www.w3schools.com/sql*) provides course material that can help you build foundational knowledge of relational databases.

NoSQL databases offer a flexible and scalable alternative, storing unstructured, semi-structured, or hierarchical data, and are frequently used in big data and real-time web applications. They include document stores, key-value stores, column-family stores, and graph databases like Neo4j. Careful consideration of security is crucial due to their complexity and unique data storage methods.

Database Implementations

Databases typically can be categorized into one of three implementations:

- *Self-managed databases*, like MySQL, PostgreSQL, and Microsoft SQL Server, require you to set up, configure, and maintain your own database server.

- *Cloud databases* are managed by cloud service providers and provide all the benefits of the cloud, such as scalability, flexibility, and reduced maintenance overhead. Cloud databases include services such as Amazon Relational Database Service (RDS), Google Cloud SQL, and Microsoft Azure SQL Database.

- *Serverless databases*, such as Amazon Aurora Serverless and Azure SQL Database, take the concept of cloud databases a step further and completely abstract away the database servers; they eliminate the need for traditional database servers, scaling automatically to workload demands. Serverless databases and functions have unique security challenges, and proper security measures are required to ensure data protection and cloud compliance.

In addition to these, distributed data storage and processing systems (such as Hadoop and its distributed filesystem, HDFS) are used to handle large-scale data storage and processing across distributed clusters. While these are crucial in big data scenarios, we'll focus on databases and their security challenges, as exploring the security of distributed systems is beyond this chapter's scope.

Microsoft Access is suitable for small-scale applications but not recommended for large-scale or enterprise environments due to limitations in security, performance, and scalability. Legacy Access integrations in enterprise applications via Open Database Connectivity (ODBC) connections should be evaluated and remediated, as they often have little to no protection.

Common Database Management Systems

A database can be thought of as a digital library filled with organized data, while a DBMS acts like the librarian who assists users in accessing, managing, and updating the content. The database serves as the repository for data, and the DBMS is the software application responsible for managing it.

In essence, a database is a structured collection of data, while a DBMS is the software that manages the data. Grasping this distinction is crucial.

MySQL and PostgreSQL are widely used open source RDBMSs, known for their reliability, scalability, and ease of use. Both are popular choices for web applications and support features such as materialized views, full-text search, and spatial data types. MySQL also offers JSON data type support, while PostgreSQL supports custom data types.

On the other hand, Microsoft SQL Server is a proprietary RDBMS developed by Microsoft. Providing many advanced features and tight integration with other Microsoft products and services, SQL Server is a common choice for organizations that are heavily invested in Microsoft technologies. As we will discuss later, its widespread use in enterprises makes it a frequent target.

MongoDB is a NoSQL document-oriented database designed for scalability, high availability, and rapid development. It is popular for big data and real-time applications and stores data in a flexible, JSON-like format called BSON (binary JSON).

Each DBMS comes with its own set of security features, making some more suitable for specific security requirements than others. When selecting a DBMS, it's essential to consider the unique security needs of your application or organization to ensure adequate data protection.

A Real-World Case Study: The Marriott Breach

In 2018, Marriott, a prominent hotel chain, experienced a massive data breach in the form of unauthorized access to the Starwood guest reservation database. President and CEO Arne Sorenson testified before the Senate that Marriott was first alerted by a notification from Guardium, a tool designed to monitor databases for unusual activity. The warning indicated that an administrator's credentials were being used to access a substantial amount of data.

After a thorough investigation, Marriott discovered that a threat actor was using malware and hacking tools like Mimikatz to obtain privileged user credentials. Eventually, they identified two large encrypted files that, once decrypted, were found to contain exported data from the guest reservation system relating to Marriott property guests, indicating that sensitive data had been compromised and exfiltrated.

Impact

While this example can be seen as highlighting the challenges of securing systems in acquired organizations, the fact is that Marriott acquired Starwood in 2016, meaning it had two years to fortify these systems between the time of the acquisition and the time of the breach. Consequently, Marriott faced severe repercussions, including lawsuits, regulatory investigations, and a $24 million fine (*https://oreil.ly/H4Ohl*) for failing to protect customer data.

Could better database security hygiene have made a difference?

Absolutely! In the following sections of this chapter, we will demonstrate how implementing data encryption, the principle of least privilege, timely patching and updates, strong authentication, privileged access management (PAM), network segmentation, and regular security audits could have prevented this incident.

Although the breach was traced back to a Chinese state-sponsored hacking group, the techniques employed were, in our view, traditional and effective methods commonly seen in data breaches. In fact, even though this is an older and much-cited example of a data breach, the attackers' tactics are so well documented in the resulting regulatory penalties and testimony that it will continue to serve as a useful case study in database control failures for years to come.

References

- UK Information Commissioner's Office Penalty Notice (*https://oreil.ly/bTI2p*)
- Transcript of Arne Sorenson's US Senate testimony (*https://oreil.ly/F6IZX*)

Database Security Threats and Vulnerabilities

In this section, we'll examine some of the numerous threats and vulnerabilities that miscreants may exploit to gain unauthorized access to, tamper with, or steal your prized data. Comprehending the potential risks will better prepare you to implement effective security measures to protect your organization's data from the persistent and devious adversaries ceaselessly searching for novel ways to bypass your defenses.

The common database security threats and vulnerabilities that we will address in this section include:

- Unauthorized access (brute force and other authentication attacks)
- SQL injection attacks
- Data leakage
- Insider threats and database manipulation

We'll also briefly consider the defense evasion tactics that attackers may employ to escape detection. At the end of this chapter, we'll walk through a hands-on exercise analyzing a database attack scenario.

Unauthorized Access

Unauthorized access is a significant concern in database security. Threat actors regularly attempt to bypass authentication mechanisms to gain entry into databases and access the sensitive data they contain, using tactics such as the following:

Brute force attacks
A brute force attack involves systematically attempting all possible password combinations to gain access to a database. While time-consuming, this method can be effective, especially when weak or shared passwords are used. Tools such as Hydra (*https://oreil.ly/hJifo*) and the Metasploit framework (*https://oreil.ly/ KwLbt*), or even a simple Python script (*https://oreil.ly/KYTO6*), can automate this process, making brute force attacks a prevalent threat to database security. These attacks are sometimes made easier by the fact that administrator user-names like *sa* tend not to be changed, giving attackers a starting point.

Credential stuffing attacks
Credential stuffing attacks occur when an attacker uses compromised credentials (usernames and passwords) from one data breach to gain unauthorized access to other databases or systems. This technique is often effective due to users' habit of reusing passwords across multiple platforms. For instance, a threat actor might identify a database administrator through a social media platform like LinkedIn and obtain their email address. The attacker can then search public breach data sources, such as DeHashed (*https://www.dehashed.com*), to find any leaked credentials associated with that email. The discovered credentials can in turn be used to attempt a credential stuffing attack against the databases under the administrator's responsibility.

Dictionary attacks

In a dictionary attack, the attacker employs a list of common words, phrases, or known passwords to crack user credentials, iterating through the list in hopes of finding a correct combination. This type of attack is less commonly used directly against a database and more commonly against hashes that the threat actor discovers. Some of the most common attack tools used for dictionary attacks are John the Ripper (*https://oreil.ly/cYeXJ*) and Hashcat (*https://oreil.ly/K_UzP*).

SQL Injection

SQL injection is a widespread and dangerous attack technique where a threat actor exploits vulnerabilities in an application's input validation and inserts malicious SQL code into a query. SQL injection attacks can be particularly harmful, as this malicious code may grant attackers access to sensitive information or enable them to execute administrative commands on the database server, potentially manipulating data or even destroying the database.

To understand SQL injection, consider a simple web application that allows users to log in using their email and password. The application might use the following SQL query to authenticate the user:

```
SELECT * FROM users WHERE email = 'user_email' AND password = 'user_password';
```

Here, `user_email` and `user_password` are values the user provides through the login form. If the application does not correctly sanitize and validate the user input, an attacker could provide malicious input such as:

```
user_email: admin@example.com' --user_password: anything
```

The double hyphen (`--`) used in this example is a comment delimiter in SQL (*https://oreil.ly/roanr*), effectively causing it to ignore the rest of the query. This allows the attacker to bypass the password check and log in as the admin user without knowing the correct password.

Expanding on this simple injection technique, consider the `xp_cmdshell` (*https://oreil.ly/KHtHF*) stored procedure built into Microsoft SQL Server, which allows users to execute operating system commands directly from a T-SQL script or a SQL query. Although it can be helpful for specific administrative tasks, it poses a significant security risk when used with SQL injection attacks.

For example, if an attacker injects the following SQL code through a vulnerable application:

```
'; EXEC xp_cmdshell 'dir C:\';
```

This will execute any system command specified. Ironically, even if `xp_cmdshell` is disabled, an attacker can use SQL injection to reenable it if the application database user is overprovisioned (i.e., has sysadmin-level database access) using the following command:

```
EXEC sp_configure 'show advanced options', 1;RECONFIGURE;
EXEC sp_configure 'xp_cmdshell', 1;RECONFIGURE;
```

This is a great example of why the principle of privilege, discussed later in this chapter, is so important—*don't give applications sysadmin-level access!*

Data Leakage

Data leakage involves unauthorized access, exposure, or transfer of sensitive data from an organization's systems. Several factors contribute to data leaks or "spills," including insecure data transmission, misconfigurations, poorly secured SQL backups, and the use of production data in test systems.

Here are three examples to illustrate these concepts further:

1. At FinServCo, a financial institution, Alyssa and their team have developed a custom application for managing client data. One day, Alyssa decides to work remotely from a local coffee shop. They connect to the public WiFi network and open Beekeeper Studio to review some data. Unfortunately, the developers overlooked implementing encryption for data transmission between the application and the database server. An attacker who is also connected to the same public WiFi network sniffs the network traffic using Wireshark (*https://www.wireshark.org*) and intercepts the data transmitted between Alyssa's laptop and the database server. As a result, the attacker gains access to the database credentials and sensitive client information such as account numbers, balances, and personal details.

2. A startup company, led by founders Jennifer and Ian, uses a cloud-based MongoDB database service to deploy a web application that manages customer orders. In the rush to meet the launch deadline, the development team inadvertently leaves the MongoDB (*https://oreil.ly/e0Hf7*) instance without authentication enabled and with its default configuration, which exposes it to public access on the internet. A competitor who regularly scans the internet for misconfigured databases discovers the startup's unprotected MongoDB instance and extracts the entire customer list, complete with contact details and purchase history. Armed with this valuable data, the competitor targets the startup's customer base with its own products and promotions, attempting to lure them away.

3. At EShopCo, an ecommerce company, Marcus is responsible for regularly backing up the database containing customer details, order history, and payment information to an on-premises file server. The company fails to encrypt the backups and does not restrict access to the file server. Will, a disgruntled employee with IT access, discovers the unencrypted backup files on the file server during a routine maintenance task. Seeing an opportunity to make some extra money, Will copies the backup files and sells the data on Tor, after which it is subsequently used to create fraudulent transactions.

As these examples suggest, data leakage and exfiltration pose significant risks to organizations. You must ensure your data is always protected, whether in transit or at rest. That means you need to build resilient systems that are secure even in the case of less than ideal access conditions—if you force TLS encryption or the use of a VPN or jump servers, for example, a user accessing the data over a public WiFi network becomes a nonissue.

Insider Threats

Insider threats arise when individuals with legitimate access to the system—such as employees, contractors, or partners—access or alter an organization's databases without the organization's authorization. These threats can be difficult to detect and address, since they often involve trusted individuals with the necessary permissions to access sensitive data.

Insider threats can be broadly classified as either malicious or inadvertent. Malicious threats arise when users intentionally exploit their access privileges for personal gain or other rotten purposes. In contrast, inadvertent threats stem from users unintentionally causing security incidents due to negligence, lack of training, or mistakes like succumbing to a phishing attack.

Addressing insider threats can be complex, warranting a more comprehensive discussion. We recommend *The CERT Guide to Insider Threats* by Dawn M. Cappelli, Andrew P. Moore, and Randall F. Trzeciak (Addison-Wesley), which thoroughly examines this critical security issue using a series of case studies.

Defense Evasion

Defense evasion is a critical aspect of cyberattacks. Attackers may use various techniques to avoid detection and bypass security measures used to protect database systems. By understanding these techniques, you can develop more effective security measures to protect your valuable data.

Obfuscating SQL code is a prime example. Threat actors often obfuscate their SQL code to make it more difficult for security tools and analysts to identify and understand malicious queries. Obfuscation techniques include using complex nesting, string concatenation, and encoding or encrypting data within the query. For instance, this example uses the `CHAR()` function to concatenate ASCII characters to create a message:

```
SELECT CHAR(72)+CHAR(101)+CHAR(108)+CHAR(108)+CHAR(111)+CHAR(32)+CHAR(87)+
CHAR(111)+CHAR(114)+CHAR(108)+CHAR(100)
```

Each character code corresponds to a specific letter or symbol, with ASCII code 72 corresponding to "H," and so on. This example just spells out "Hello World," but you can no doubt imagine more sinister applications of this technique. To dive deeper into the world of defense evasion, you can check out the entire Enterprise Tactic (*https://oreil.ly/3vn_a*) in the MITRE ATT&CK matrix.

Database Security Best Practices

As the previous section on database security threats illustrates, maintaining the integrity, confidentiality, and availability of data within databases has become a nonnegotiable priority. The importance of database security cannot be understated, as these reservoirs of information often contain an organization's most valuable and sensitive assets.

Database security practices vary depending on the type and size of the databases in question. However, there are fundamental principles and best practices that remain constant across the board. These practices (outlined in the following sections) lay the groundwork for an effective database security strategy, irrespective of the specific database technology or architecture in use.

The objective of these best practices is twofold: to protect the data itself from threats ranging from unauthorized access to data corruption and to ensure regulatory compliance (which is vital as many industries now enforce stringent data protection standards). A well-rounded understanding of these practices is important for anyone involved in information security, from database administrators to CISOs.

Data Encryption

While it won't prevent all attacks, data/database encryption is an effective way to keep your data safe. It's a method of turning data into a format that can't be read without the right decryption key or algorithm. In terms of databases, there are two main types of data encryption: at rest and in transit.

Encryption of data at rest refers to securing data that is stored on a disk, often in a database. This type of encryption keeps your data safe if the storage media or the physical server gets compromised. It's a critical defense against threats like data theft or unauthorized access to hardware, and most modern DBMSs support it. When using this security measure, you need to manage and secure your encryption keys carefully. If an attacker gets hold of these keys, they can decrypt and access your data.

Encryption of data in transit protects your data when it's being transferred over a network, like when it's being queried from a client application or during replication between database servers. The most common method of data-in-transit encryption is through Secure Sockets Layer/Transport Layer Security (SSL/TLS) protocols, which create an encrypted connection between the two endpoints.

It's important to note that encryption imposes a performance overhead on your database systems, as extra computational resources are required to encrypt and decrypt the data. However, the benefits of protecting sensitive data often outweigh this cost, and modern processors have hardware acceleration for encryption and decryption.

Another encryption method worth mentioning is transparent data encryption (TDE) (*https://oreil.ly/wGmbu*). TDE automatically encrypts the data before writing it to the disk and automatically decrypts it when read from the disk. This process is transparent to the applications using the database. TDE protects against the threat of malicious activity at the storage level.

Implementing database encryption: A practical example with Bree

As an IT director for a local municipality, Bree is responsible for a vast array of data, including but not limited to sensitive citizen information (names, addresses, Social Security numbers), property records, tax data, internal operational data, and emergency response plans. This data is stored across various databases, including MySQL for structured relational data, MongoDB for document-oriented storage, and Microsoft SQL Server for enterprise-level applications.

Bree knows that they need to implement strong encryption mechanisms to protect this sensitive data. Here's an approach they could follow:

1. *Assess the data and databases.*
   Bree starts by identifying the types of data they need to protect and the databases where this data is stored. They categorize the data based on sensitivity and prioritize the databases that store highly sensitive data for immediate encryption.

2. *Choose the encryption methods.*
   For data at rest, Bree decides to implement AES-256 encryption, a highly secure encryption standard, on the MySQL (*https://oreil.ly/1VreQ*) and SQL Server (*https://oreil.ly/hJn1J*) databases. MongoDB (*https://oreil.ly/l0t8p*), on the other hand, offers native encryption at rest as part of its enterprise version. Bree ensures this feature is enabled to protect the unstructured data stored in MongoDB.

   For data in transit, Bree implements SSL/TLS on all connections to the databases, ensuring that data is encrypted when moving across the network.

3. Manage encryption keys.

Bree generates strong encryption keys for AES-256 encryption. To securely manage these keys, they decide to use HashiCorp Vault (*https://oreil.ly/jiFSu*), an on-premises software-based key management solution. Vault allows them to store, manage, and tightly control access to tokens, passwords, certificates, and encryption keys in a virtual, secure, and isolated environment.

This system also provides Bree with capabilities to handle leasing, key revocation, key rolling, and auditing. Through the use of these features, Bree can rotate the keys regularly, reducing the risk of them being compromised. Furthermore, Vault's detailed audit logs offer Bree the visibility needed to monitor and track key usage, which is crucial for identifying any unauthorized access attempts.

4. Implement transparent data encryption.

For the SQL Server database, which holds some of the municipality's most sensitive data, Bree decides to go a step further and implement TDE. This provides an additional layer of security, ensuring that the data remains encrypted on the server's hard drive and is only decrypted when read into memory.

5. Perform regular audits and updates.

Finally, Bree ensures that regular audits are carried out to verify the effectiveness of the encryption and to identify any potential vulnerabilities. They make sure to keep the encryption software and protocols up-to-date, increasing their odds of withstanding the latest security threats.

By following these steps, Bree successfully implements a comprehensive encryption strategy for the municipality's databases. This ensures that the sensitive data they are charged with protecting is securely encrypted, reducing the risk of a data breach and guaranteeing compliance with data protection regulations.

Authentication and Authorization Mechanisms

Authentication and authorization are also critical components of any database security strategy. They play a vital role in maintaining the *principle of least privilege*—a key concept in information security that ensures users are granted only enough access rights to perform their tasks, but no more.

Authentication

In the context of a MySQL database, *authentication* is the process by which an application proves its identity to the database. This typically involves the use of a database connection string, which includes the username, password, and other details necessary to establish a connection.

A connection string may look like this:

```
Server=PoliceDB;Database=myCrimincalDataBase;Uid=Sergeant;Pwd=D0nutD1spatcher!;
```

When the application tries to establish a connection, it uses the connection string to present its credentials to the MySQL database. MySQL checks the provided username and password against its list of permitted users. If the credentials match, the database confirms the application's identity and allows the connection.

However, since the connection string contains sensitive information, it's important to protect it. One effective method is to use a *secret manager*, a tool that helps you manage and access sensitive information like connection strings, API keys, and other secrets. By storing the connection string in a secret manager, you can reduce the risk of exposure and enhance the security of your application.

In addition to requiring a username and password, MySQL also offers SSL/TLS encryption for these connections. This means that not only does the application need to provide the correct username and password, but it must also present a valid SSL/TLS certificate. This helps to ensure that the application is indeed what it claims to be and prevents unauthorized parties from intercepting the connection. Importantly, there are situations where it may be acceptable not to enable SSL/TLS encryption at the database level, including when databases and application servers are on the same local network (behind a firewall), for purely local connections on the same physical server, or where a load balancer on the same network segment is terminating the SSL/TLS connection.

Authorization

Authorization, which follows successful authentication, determines what actions the authenticated user can perform. Different users can be assigned different roles in a MySQL database, each with a specific set of permissions. An ordinary user might only have the ability to read data from certain tables (SELECT permission), while an admin user could have the ability to modify (UPDATE, DELETE) or even create new (CREATE) tables.

By enforcing the principle of least privilege through proper authorization, you can limit potential damage from both external and internal threats. Consider the SQL injection example mentioned earlier in this chapter. If a web application's database user is overprovisioned (i.e., given sysadmin-level access), an attacker could exploit this through a SQL injection vulnerability, enabling them to execute system commands via xp_cmdshell. If, however, the application's database user has been correctly provisioned, the attacker will not have the necessary permissions to execute these commands, thus limiting their potential impact.

Both authentication and authorization are important for maintaining database security. They ensure that only authorized individuals can access your databases and that they can only perform actions that they are specifically allowed to do.

Secure Database Configuration and Hardening

Database configuration and hardening are crucial components of a comprehensive information security strategy. Databases, with their myriad features designed for data storage and retrieval, may harbor unnecessary functionalities that could potentially be exploited if left enabled or misconfigured. By applying secure configuration practices and implementing robust hardening measures, these risks can be significantly mitigated.

A cornerstone of secure database configuration is the *principle of least functionality*. This principle dictates that any database functionality not essential to your application should be disabled or removed. This approach effectively restricts potential attack surfaces. For instance, MySQL features like the FILE privilege, which enables MySQL to read and write files on the server, can pose a security risk if left unnecessarily enabled.

Applying patches and updates promptly is also critical. Database vendors routinely release updates to address known security vulnerabilities. Failure to install these updates in a timely manner leaves your database vulnerable to these known threats.

An integral part of the hardening process is the creation of written configuration standards. These standards serve as a baseline for ensuring database security across the organization and provide numerous benefits, including consistency, accountability, efficiency, knowledge transfer, and compliance assistance. When crafting the standards, it's imperative to include details on all facets of database security, such as account management, permission settings, network configurations, encryption practices, and backup procedures.

When hardening your database, established guidelines like the Security Technical Implementation Guides (STIGs) and CIS Benchmarks are invaluable resources. They provide a comprehensive framework for securing databases, tackling specific security vulnerabilities, and minimizing potential attack vectors.

Hardening measures should include:

- Forcing the use of strong passwords and changing them regularly, along with implementing account lockout policies to mitigate brute force attacks.
- Following the principle of least privilege, ensuring that database accounts have only the permissions necessary to perform their designated tasks.

- Monitoring database activity to detect any suspicious behavior (e.g., in a SIEM/XDR). Recall from our earlier discussion of the Marriott breach that it was the logging and monitoring they had in place that enabled them to detect the intrusion.

- Implementing encryption for data at rest and in transit, and ensuring the use of hashing and salts (discussed in the upcoming hands-on exercise) to protect sensitive data like passwords.

- Regularly backing up databases and having a recovery plan in place to mitigate the effects of data loss incidents.

- Using firewalls to control inbound and outbound traffic. If possible, isolate your database in a secure network segment. Note that effective outbound firewall rules can prevent an attacker that successfully executed an injection attack from establishing command and control of the server.

- Keeping your database software up-to-date by applying patches and updates as soon as they're available. This reduces the risk of vulnerabilities being exploited.

Remember, securing a database isn't a one-and-done task; it's a continuous process demanding regular auditing, monitoring, and updating. Also, written configuration standards need to be treated as living documents, evolving to address emerging threats and organizational needs. By adhering to secure database configuration practices, referencing guidelines like the STIGs and CIS Benchmarks, and adopting hardening measures, you can greatly reduce the risk of a data breach and ensure the protection of your databases.

Database Management in the Cloud

Transitioning database management to the cloud shifts several security responsibilities from your hands to your cloud service provider's. While the provider ensures the security *of* the cloud, including the infrastructure, hardware, software, and networking components, you, as the customer, are tasked with handling security *in* the cloud. Your responsibilities in this shared model include data protection, managing access controls, and configuring security settings. This marks a significant departure from on-premises databases, where the organization shoulders all aspects of security.

In a cloud environment, databases can be accessed from anywhere across the globe via the internet. This global accessibility underscores the importance of effective access control. Cloud IAM systems can be intricate, requiring meticulous configuration to guarantee that only authorized personnel gain access. Ensuring the accuracy of IAM policies at all times becomes paramount.

While the underlying principles of database security remain consistent across on-premises and cloud environments, the strategies and tools used for securing databases in the cloud vary significantly. It's imperative to understand these differences to fortify your data protection measures in the cloud effectively. To aid you in this endeavor, we've dedicated an entire chapter to securing cloud infrastructure (Chapter 14).

Hands-on Exercise: Implementing Encryption in a MySQL Database (Operation Lockdown)

Imagine you've just been assigned the role of lead database administrator at an up-and-coming tech startup. The company recently secured its first round of funding and is onboarding its first major client. The stakes are high, and the responsibility for securing the company's MySQL database rests on your shoulders. Let's walk through how you might accomplish this:

1. Grab a coffee, clear your workspace, and open up your MySQL shell. Your workspace is your command center, and MySQL is your faithful aide in this mission.

2. For this exercise, we encourage you to set up an Ubuntu VM and install MySQL on it. You can do this by:

   a. Installing a Hypervisor, like Hyper-V (*https://oreil.ly/ou8PV*), VirtualBox (*https://www.virtualbox.org*), or VMware Workstation Player (*https://oreil.ly/a2Ked*)

   b. Downloading and installing Ubuntu (*https://www.osboxes.org/ubuntu*) as a VM

   c. Installing MySQL within the Ubuntu VM using a command like:

   ```
   sudo apt install mysql-server, mysql-client
   ```

3. Create a secure repository for your data. You'll create a Users table with the following fields: ID, username, password, and email. Here are the steps:

   a. Connect to the local MySQL server by running:

   ```
   mysql -u root -p <password>
   ```

   b. Create the database:

   ```
   CREATE DATABASE lockdown;
   ```

   c. Use the database:

   ```
   USE lockdown;
   ```

   d. Create the Users table:

   ```
   CREATE TABLE Users (
       ID INT PRIMARY KEY,
       username VARCHAR(30),
       password VARCHAR(100),
       email VARCHAR(50)
   );
   ```

4. To encrypt the passwords, you'll use OpenSSL, a full-featured open source toolkit implementing SSL/TLS, to generate SHA256 hashes (you won't be storing plaintext passwords—that would be a rookie mistake). Try it out:

```
echo -n 'password' | openssl dgst -sha256
```

Did you get 5e884898da28047151d0e56f8dc6292773603d0d6aabbdd62a11ef7 21d1542d8? (You should have.)

5. With the encryption method in place, you can begin to populate your database. You start with a test user, using the hashed password from the previous step:

```
INSERT INTO Users (ID, username, password, email)
    VALUES (1, 'testUser', 'hashedPassword', 'testuser@example.com');
```

(Remember to replace 'hashedPassword' with the hash you generated.)

6. Now, run a quick check to verify the data:

```
SELECT * FROM Users;
```

The password should appear as a hash—a testament to your encryption efforts!

The aim of this exercise is to familiarize you with one aspect of database security—specifically, the hashing of passwords, a fundamental component of data encryption. Hashing is a one-way process that obscures stored passwords, making them less vulnerable in the event of a database breach. However, it's important to note that this is only the tip of the iceberg when it comes to database encryption.

Also note that hashing isn't the same as encryption; the latter is a two-way function that permits data to be decoded back to its original form, provided you have the correct key. It's typically employed to safeguard data at rest and in transit, as discussed earlier in this chapter. This exercise, while educational, doesn't cover key management, which is a critical facet of any encryption strategy.

Furthermore, our exercise concentrates on password protection, but comprehensive database encryption should extend to all sensitive data, including personal details, financial information, and more. The hashing method used here is also quite basic. Real-world applications typically incorporate a *salt*—a unique value added to each password prehashing to safeguard against specific types of attacks.

Conclusion

Database security is a multilayered affair. Encryption and hashing are just pieces of a larger puzzle that includes secure configurations, access control, monitoring, and regular updates. The exercise we presented at the end of this chapter is a step in the right direction, but remember that a comprehensive, effective approach to database security requires a broad understanding and the application of various protective measures.

CHAPTER 14

Cloud Infrastructure

Think about the last time you saved a picture on your phone, worked on a document on your MacBook, or pushed code to GitHub. When you did these things, your data zipped off into a vast, interconnected network of servers and storage systems that we collectively call "the cloud." That term is used everywhere today, but what is it, exactly?

In essence, *the cloud* refers to a global network of remote servers that are hosted on the internet rather than on a local device or personal computer. These servers are designed to store, manage, and process data, providing you and your business with a wide range of services and applications accessible from anywhere with a stable internet connection.

The cloud has revolutionized the way we store, access, and share information, providing benefits like scalability, flexibility, and cost efficiency. Major tech companies such as Google, Microsoft, and Amazon have become leading providers, offering a wide array of storage, compute, and application development solutions.

As more and more data is stored in the cloud, ensuring that all the ways we use the cloud are secure has become more important than ever. Cloud security involves implementing technical controls and policies to protect everything from data to applications to infrastructure. It's not dissimilar to a castle defense with multiple layers of security.

In this chapter, we'll briefly explore the different types of cloud services and the unique security considerations for each. We'll discuss the shared responsibility model and the importance of maintaining clarity about who is responsible for securing each cloud component. We'll also examine best practices and emerging technologies that can help strengthen the security of your cloud environment so you stay ahead of the threats.

As we embark on this journey through our analogies of digital fortresses and cyber-punk cities, I like to keep in mind the words of William Gibson in the introduction to *Neuromancer*: "Hang in there, friend; it can only get stranger." By embracing and adapting to the new, we can navigate the complexities of securing data in the cloud era and build resilient systems that remain secure into the future.

Types of Cloud Services and Their Security Implications

When we talk about the cloud, we're not dealing with a one-size-fits-all solution. The cloud is as diverse as a busy metropolis like Chiba City, offering a variety of services for different needs. There are three core types of services you should know about: *SaaS*, *PaaS*, and *IaaS*. For newcomers this can sound a bit like a techy alphabet soup, so let's clear it up and establish some basic vocabulary so that we're speaking the same language. We'll also look at who has responsibility for the security of each type of service.

Software as a Service (SaaS)

First up, we have software as a service, or SaaS. If you're not working in IT, this is probably the type of service you're most familiar with. Ever use Google Docs, Hub-Spot, Slack, or Microsoft 365? Congratulations, you've used SaaS. A simplistic explanation might be that these are apps that you access via the internet, instead of downloading them to your device.

Responsibility-wise, the SaaS provider generally takes care of most of the heavy lifting: they're responsible for the security of the software itself. But you're not off the hook entirely; you still need to manage the access controls, ensuring only the right people have access to the data in these apps or services.

Platform as a Service (PaaS)

Next up is the platform as a service, or PaaS. This is kind of like a digital sandbox, providing a platform where developers can build, test, and deploy their own applications. Heroku, Google App Engine, and AWS Elastic Beanstalk are examples of PaaS.

The OS and everything beneath it are abstracted away and are the responsibility of the hosting provider. Security is a team effort: the provider is responsible for securing the underlying platform, and the security of your apps (source code) and data is your responsibility.

Infrastructure as a Service (IaaS)

Finally, there is infrastructure as a service, or IaaS. This refers to a cloud provider leasing out physical or virtual servers, storage, and networking resources. It's like renting a plot of land to build a digital skyscraper. Amazon Elastic Compute Cloud (EC2) and Microsoft Azure VMs are examples of IaaS.

With IaaS, you take on more of the security responsibilities. You need to secure everything from your data to the operating systems and apps running on your slice of the cloud.

The Shared Responsibility Model

As the previous sections highlighted, depending on the type of cloud service you're using, the security considerations will vary. You're part of a security team now, whether you're ensuring access controls for your SaaS apps, securing your apps on a PaaS platform, or locking down your digital skyscraper in IaaS. But don't worry; you're not alone in this. This partnership is commonly referred to as the *shared responsibility model*. While exact definitions can vary between providers, this model defines who's in charge of what aspects of the service, kind of like a chore chart for cloud security.

Your provider will often take care of the physical infrastructure, network, and operating system–level security, while you're in charge of securing your data, access to it, and sometimes parts of the application stack. In general, the provider ensures that the "house" is secure, but you're responsible for what happens inside that house. Let's look at how some of the major cloud providers approach this:

- Amazon Web Services (AWS) (*https://oreil.ly/UXdJ2*) emphasizes that while they're in charge of "security of the cloud," you're responsible for "security in the cloud." For example, AWS secures the infrastructure that runs all the services offered in the AWS Cloud, while you're in charge of anything you put in the cloud or connect to the cloud.

- Microsoft Azure (*https://oreil.ly/IXU1v*) uses a similar model, but it specifies responsibilities based on the type of cloud service you're using. For instance, if you're using Azure's IaaS, you're in charge of the data, endpoints, account, and access management, while Azure takes care of the physical hosts, networks, and datacenters.

- Similarly, with Google Cloud Platform (GCP) (*https://oreil.ly/Ct3Bz*), responsibilities are defined based on the kind of service you're using and the workload you're running. Google is always responsible for the underlying network and infrastructure, and you are responsible for how you configure and use the platform and how you protect and manage your data.

Common Cloud Security Mistakes and How to Avoid Them

Now that we've established the different types of cloud services and their security considerations, let's look at some common mistakes people make when securing their cloud resources. These mistakes can turn your digital fortress into a house of cards, but don't worry—we're here to help you prevent them.

Misconfigurations

One of the biggest and most common mistakes is misconfiguration. It's like leaving your front door wide open while you're away—it sounds silly, but it happens more often than you'd think. This can include everything from misconfigured firewall rules to storage buckets inadvertently set to public access, and with IAM, which is an increasingly complicated endeavor (especially in complex cloud deployments), it can be devilishly easy to misconfigure a role or service in a way that leads to a service compromise or privilege escalation.

Let's consider an infamous real-world example that helps illustrate the gravity of this issue: the Capital One data breach of 2019 (*https://oreil.ly/GJLau*). In this case, a misconfiguration in a web application firewall, a type of security measure deployed by Capital One, allowed an external actor with insider knowledge to gain unauthorized access to vast amounts of the organization's data. And this wasn't just any data—it included PII and financial information for over 100 million Capital One customers.

The specific misconfiguration in question was within an AWS cloud server used by Capital One. A bad actor exploited a server-side request forgery (SSRF) vulnerability, which allowed them to send requests to the WAF while posing as a trusted server. The data exfiltration was possible because the permissions (role assignment) provided to the WAF service were too broad and allowed it to retrieve sensitive information. In other words, the WAF service was overpermissioned—and if you've read Chapter 13, you might have started to get an idea of how critical it is to avoid this error, including for service accounts. This is one more example of how violations of the principle of least privilege can return later to bite the system maintainer.

 The concept of least privilege actually predates *Neuromancer* (published in 1984) by almost a decade (see "Least Privilege and More" (*https://oreil.ly/sYDAv*) by Fred Schneider), and we see it formalized in the US Department of Defense's Trusted Computer System Evaluation Criteria (*https://oreil.ly/1rB05*) (also known as the Orange Book, for fans of the movie *Hackers* (*https://oreil.ly/8gmtl*)).

At this point you're probably wondering, "How do we keep ourselves from leaving that front door open?" The key is in regular audits of your cloud configurations and clever use of automated tools. These tools can spot potential misconfigurations and raise the alarm before they turn into real issues—and if you can configure them in such a way that they prevent misconfigurations in the first place, you'll be way ahead of the game.

Let's say you're mainly using AWS. Your first port of call should be AWS Config and conformance packs (*https://oreil.ly/U_JWv*), but you might also consider using AWS Control Tower (*https://oreil.ly/oA7sg*) to provision your accounts and infrastructure. If Microsoft Azure is the base of your operations, then Microsoft Defender for Cloud (*https://oreil.ly/q_MO2*) should be on your radar. GCP users can rely on Security Command Center (*https://oreil.ly/CHsqW*). Each of these services can help you spot and fix common misconfigurations. For those using other cloud environments, like Digital Ocean, or wanting to bridge the gap with existing vulnerability management processes, Tenable Nessus (*https://oreil.ly/BJHpm*) (and also Tenable Cloud Security) can fit the bill by integrating scanning for vulnerabilities in the cloud into workflows you're already using for on-premises environments and systems.

Another preventative approach from a process perspective is adopting a process/procedure to make all changes to your cloud environment through infrastructure as code (a way of managing and setting up your cloud resources using YAML (*https://oreil.ly/8BH3Y*), in the case of Terraform (*https://www.terraform.io*), rather than manually tinkering with hardware or systems via a GUI or CLI). The security benefit comes when you combine IaC with a well-thought-out pipeline that requires both code scanning and reviewer approval.

There are huge security wins to be had by pairing IaC with a source control management system like GitHub, Bitbucket, or GitLab, because you get a complete log of all modifications made to your environment. It also becomes pretty simple to implement a pull request automation system so that changes can be scheduled and reviewed before they're deployed. Atlantis (*https://www.runatlantis.io*) is a tool that helps you do just that, and it works natively with most source control management systems.

If you've already embraced making all cloud changes via a continuous integration and continuous delivery (CI/CD) pipeline, then a solution like Atlantis may feel like a step backward. In that case, consider maturing your review and quality assurance process by following the DevSecOps maturity model (*https://oreil.ly/xwinS*) instead of adding another piece of tech to your stack—security is a journey, and there's always work to be done.

Inadequate Credential and Secrets Management

In the cloud, a credential is more than just a username and password—it's your passport, your lifeline. It's your ticket to access cloud resources and data. So, if you're sloppy with your credentials, it's like you've hidden the keys to your kingdom under the doormat. Not exactly the smartest move.

Let's look at some of the ways we get careless with our credentials. First, we've got weak passwords—the digital equivalent of using 123456 as your PIN. Then there's the age-old practice of sharing credentials, a move as risky as handing out copies of your house keys. And let's not forget about failing to revoke access when an employee exits your organization—it's like letting your ex keep a set of keys to your place post-breakup.

So, what's the prevention strategy? First, you need strong password policies. No *password123* nonsense. Think long, complex, and unique. If you aren't already mandating that your users use a secure password vault, that's prework you'll want to address first. We recommend looking at 1Password (*https://1password.com*) or Bitwarden (*https://bitwarden.com*), or, at minimum, using KeePass (*https://keepass.info*). If you're already using a SIEM and have visibility into file open events, you can do some fuzzy validation by creating queries that look for *notepad.exe* or other text editors opening files like *passwords.txt*. In Splunk, as Search Processing Language (SPL), that might look like this:

```
index=<your_index> \
sourcetype=<your_sourcetype> \
(process_name=notepad.exe OR process_name=<other_text_editor>) \
file_name=passwords.txt
```

Next, you should implement MFA, first for your root or admin-level accounts and then for all user accounts. From an AWS policy perspective, that would look like this:

```
{
  "Version": "2012-10-17",
  "Statement": [
    {
      "Sid": "DenyNonMFAAccess",
      "Effect": "Deny",
      "Action": "*",
      "Resource": "*",
      "Condition": {
        "BoolIfExists": {
          "aws:MultiFactorAuthPresent": "false"
        }
      }
    },
    {
      "Sid": "AllowMFAAuthentication",
      "Effect": "Allow",
      "Action": "iam:CreateVirtualMFADevice",
      "Resource": "arn:aws:iam::*:mfa/${aws:username}"
    },
    {
      "Sid": "AllowMFATokenAssignment",
      "Effect": "Allow",
      "Action": [
        "iam:EnableMFADevice",
```

```
        "iam:ListMFADevices",
        "iam:ListVirtualMFADevices"
      ],
      "Resource": "*"
    }
  ]
}
```

For additional information on AWS and MFA enforcement, be sure to check out Amazon's documentation (*https://oreil.ly/wCAGE*).

Finally, you should develop a solid offboarding process. This ensures that when someone leaves the team, their access is cut off right away—like changing the locks once a roommate moves out. If you're using a centralized directory like Microsoft Active Directory or Google Apps for single sign-on to the cloud, this is much less of a burden and can be almost entirely automated, assuming you can leverage an identity provider (IdP) and System for Cross-Domain Identity Management (SCIM)–type mechanism for automated provisioning/deprovisioning.

Now that we've covered general credentials, let's focus on something we haven't dug into yet: secrets and secret management. Secrets are the hidden treasures that are commonly found sprinkled in source code by assessors and threat actors. This isn't a good thing, because when someone finds a secret they can gain access to whatever resources that secret or credential has access to—and due to overpermissioning, that's often a lot more than it should be. But let's take a step back. What are secrets, anyway?

A secret is a specific kind of a credential, like an encryption key, API key, or database password (connection string), that provides an elevated level of access or privileges, typically to support the functioning of an application. When it comes to mishandling secrets, there are a few bad habits that need to be broken right away.

Let's break these down into a quick top three:

1. Hardcoding secrets directly into source code
2. Not periodically rotating all secrets
3. Storing secrets insecurely

When developers create applications, during the development process it's very common to simply hardcode a secret/key/credential during testing and leave it that way. This is bad because it means anyone who has access to the source code repository has access to that secret or credential. To combat this problem, as well as the dangers of stale or insecurely stored secrets, you have to provide development teams with a process to prevent these practices from occurring. This is best accomplished by adopting a vault solution and best practices to identify and avoid secret mismanagement in the first place. We'll talk more about this later, when we cover cloud security best practices.

Overpermissioned Cloud Resources

A common mistake in cloud security (and information security in general) is granting users or services more permissions than they actually need. It's similar to giving a stranger in your home free rein to go anywhere they like, including your private study. This can lead to potential security risks, as you may inadvertently be allowing these overpermissioned accounts to access sensitive data or perform unauthorized actions within your cloud environment.

You can prevent this issue by observing the principle of least privilege. As described in the previous chapter, the principle of least privilege advocates for granting users and services only the permissions necessary to perform their designated tasks, and nothing more. By adhering to this principle, you ensure that each entity has the minimum required access privileges, reducing the attack surface and limiting potential damage.

But how do you do this in practice? Here are a few guidelines:

1. Regularly review the permissions you've given to users, groups, and services within your cloud environment, checking for any that seem over the top or simply unnecessary. The aim is to grant only the bare minimum access required for each task— no more, no less. If you're using AWS, you'll find a gold mine of information in your AWS CloudTrail logs, which a SIEM can help you sift through. A post (*https://oreil.ly/wy2tX*) by Volker Rath on the AWS Security Blog describes a behavior-based detection approach to identifying abnormalities within AWS; this approach can easily be applied to Azure and GCP as well by applying the same tactics to activity logs (*https://oreil.ly/zSzC4*) or audit logs (*https://oreil.ly/IKS7K*) (Azure) or Cloud Audit logs (*https://oreil.ly/ffbVK*) (GCP). The most important thing here is that you're tracking what's happening and who's making permission changes on an ongoing basis and aren't falling asleep at the wheel.

2. When you create groups or roles for a job function, scope them to only what a person in that job function requires to accomplish their job. Then, rather than assigning individual permissions to a user, assign them the relevant role. We call this *role-based access control*, or RBAC for short. It prevents permission creep and makes it much easier to adjust permissions if a user changes jobs within your organization.

3. Create a change control process for provisioning new users and bolster it with alerting, especially in the case of any new privileged permission being assigned to a user. Establishing this process is essential to maintain the security and integrity of your system. It ensures that new users are granted appropriate access privileges and prevents unauthorized access or overpermissioned accounts.

Poor Security Hygiene

When we talk about security hygiene, we're talking about covering the basics and doing the minimum required to demonstrate due care. Failing to do the basics has historically resulted in legal findings citing "a lack of reasonable security." In California's 2016 Data Breach Report (*https://oreil.ly/6pdEA*) this was codified by specifically stating that failing to implement the CIS Controls as a minimum demonstrates lack of due care; so, for simplicity's sake we'll frame this discussion around CIS standards.

Poor security hygiene encompasses actions or omissions that significantly jeopardize system security and integrity. These mistakes can include neglecting software patching, disregarding data backups and DR, using weak passwords, sharing sensitive information without discretion, and ignoring established security benchmarks. These are not advanced concepts exclusive to cloud experts; rather, they are fundamental security principles that apply to everyone.

Let's discuss prevention in the context of the CIS Critical Security Controls (*https://oreil.ly/hPYeo*), which address key areas such as inventory management, data protection (including backup and disaster recovery), secure configuration, account and access control, vulnerability management, audit log management, network infrastructure management and defense, incident response processes, and penetration testing. By focusing on these core security controls, including backup and disaster recovery, you can establish a strong foundation for securing your cloud environment.

Adhering to the CIS Controls provides a comprehensive framework that addresses various aspects of system security, aiming to prevent poor security practices that can jeopardize system security and integrity. Remember this is a *minimum* security standard, so start here if you have nothing; if you already have security practices in place, then you'll want to focus on a maturity model or something like the NIST Cybersecurity Framework (*https://oreil.ly/HfVHp*), depending on your regulatory obligations, because just doing the minimum means you can do better.

The CIS Controls:

Emphasize continuous vulnerability management and secure configuration.
> By implementing these controls, you can use vulnerability data to drive the establishment of strong patch management processes that don't let things fall through the cracks. This ensures that software and systems are regularly updated with security patches, reducing the risk of exploitation through known vulnerabilities. The way it works is by adopting a "trust but verify" model, rolling out a patch management solution, and then doing a validating vulnerability scan at intervals (say, once a week) to make sure those systems really are patched and free of known vulnerabilities.

Cover data protection and data recovery, highlighting the importance of implementing regular data backups and establishing comprehensive disaster recovery plans.

These controls ensure that critical data is backed up regularly so that you can effectively recover from data loss incidents (say, ransomware attacks) and minimize the impact of disruptions. When you adopt validating technology, such as AWS Config and conformance packs and similar for other cloud platforms, you'll be alerted when disk volumes or S3 buckets aren't encrypted, so you can go address those issues.

Address account management and access control, emphasizing the need for strong authentication mechanisms and proper password policies.

When following these controls, you can enforce the use of strong passwords, implement MFA, and enforce password expiration and complexity requirements. This mitigates the risk of unauthorized access resulting from weak passwords, which, according to MITRE (T1078) (*https://oreil.ly/EXERA*), is one of the most common ways cloud services are breached. This is best achieved by adopting RBAC tied to job function, as described earlier, and mandating that all authentication happens via single sign-on with compulsory MFA.

Emphasize secure configuration and access control management.

By implementing secure configurations and enforcing access controls, you can restrict access to sensitive information and prevent indiscriminate sharing. These controls help protect sensitive data from unauthorized access and mitigate the risks associated with inadvertent or malicious sharing. Remember when we talked about tagging back in Chapter 2? This is one of the areas where that prework can really save you a lot of headaches; if you tag specific resources like EC2 hosts, buckets, etc., appropriately, you'll know where sensitive data is stored and you will be able to more easily validate that access controls tied to those resources are enforcing the principles of least privilege and need-to-know.

Provide established security benchmarks and guidelines for you to follow.

By following these benchmarks, you can align your security practices with industry-accepted standards and best practices. This will shore up your security posture and reduce the likelihood of common security mistakes turning into catastrophic breaches.

Now, here's the best part: AWS, Azure, and GCP offer native services that help with the implementation and management of the CIS Benchmarks for their respective cloud platforms. In AWS, you can use Config and conformance packs. Microsoft Azure provides Azure Policy, which includes built-in policy definitions aligned with the CIS Benchmarks. Finally, GCP offers the Cloud Security Command Center, which provides security and compliance visibility across your GCP environment (it assesses compliance against the CIS Benchmarks).

Remember, you don't have to align with the CIS Controls; there are plenty of other frameworks out there. However, as we mentioned previously, if you currently don't have anything at all in place, this is one of the easiest frameworks to wrap your head around.

Failing to Understand the Shared Responsibility Model

Failing to understand the shared responsibility model can be a major pitfall when you're diving into the world of cloud services. Imagine this: you're about to host a big cookout in your backyard and decide to hire a caterer to handle the food. You assume the caterer will bring everything needed, including the grill. But when they show up, they've got everything but the grill, because they assumed you'd provide it. Now you have a yard full of hungry guests and a big problem on your hands because of a misunderstanding about who was in charge of a single piece of equipment.

Just like in this cookout catastrophe, using cloud services involves a give-and-take relationship between you and your cloud service provider. Having a clear understanding of who's responsible for what is extremely important, because if there's a task you thought your provider was taking care of, but they thought it was your job, you can end up with some major security gaps.

The shared responsibility model is something you need to revisit regularly, especially when introducing new services or tools into your cloud environment. As we've said before, no one's perfect, and mistakes are bound to happen—but understanding exactly what you're responsible for and what your cloud services provider is responsible for means you're less likely to run into security issues down the line. And even if you do stumble, remember that each mistake is a chance to learn and improve your cloud security practices.

Cloud Security Best Practices

Now that we've looked at avoiding common cloud security mistakes, it's time to dig into best practices for cloud security. Think of your cloud environment like a shiny new car, sleek and loaded with high-tech features. It's a gorgeous machine, and you're proud to show it off. However, knowing how to handle it safely and remembering to lock it up is important.

In this section, we're going to talk about the "rules of the road" for cloud security. We'll discuss secure architectural patterns, explore well-architected frameworks, and run through key best practices. Then, to finish off this chapter, we'll get our hands dirty with a practical exercise.

Start with Secure Architectural Patterns

Just like in construction, we need to build our digital assets on a solid foundation. It's always a smart move to utilize established architectural patterns when designing your cloud environment. This will help you avoid common missteps, ensuring your setup is both secure and efficient.

Common patterns like three-tier architecture, microservices architecture, and event-driven architecture (EDA) have been thoroughly tested over time. They provide proven structures that are designed to work with the flow of data and the needs of modern applications. Let's look at each of these a little more closely:

Three-tier architecture

The three-tier architecture (*https://oreil.ly/D9LEU*) is a widely used software design pattern that separates an application into three logical layers, each with its own responsibilities. The *presentation layer* (or frontend) is typically the UI that users interact with. The *application layer* (middle) is where the business logic lives. This is often the core of the application. Finally, the *data layer* (backend) is where data is stored and retrieved; this might be a database, or a data service that stores objects.

The point of this architecture is that it allows software engineers to update one layer without impacting the others. This makes the application more scalable and more secure, as each layer can be segmented and secured independently.

Microservices architecture

A microservices architecture (*https://oreil.ly/xbN5F*) breaks down an application into small, loosely coupled services, each performing a specific business function. Each microservice can be developed, deployed, and scaled independently of the others. This approach increases an application's scalability and speed of development, as teams can work on different microservices in parallel. It also improves fault isolation, so if one microservice fails, the others can still function. However, when you look underneath the covers, it's common to discover that a microservice is really more of a mini-monolith reliant on a legacy application or data store.

Event-driven architecture

EDA (*https://oreil.ly/lI6mb*) is a software design pattern where the flow of the program is determined by events: user actions, sensor outputs, messages passed from other programs, and so on. It mainly consists of *event creators* (which generate the events), *event consumers* (which receive and process the events), and *event channels* (which pass the events from the creators to the consumers). An example of an EDA is a notification system. When a user posts a new message on a social media app, for example (the event), a notification is sent to their followers (the event consumers).

This pattern provides high flexibility and scalability, as components can be added or removed without affecting others. It also enables real-time processing, as actions are taken immediately after an event occurs.

EDA can be a lot to wrap your head around if you aren't a developer. Martin Fowler provides an excellent introduction in his article (*https://oreil.ly/9qF2a*) "What Do You Mean by 'Event-Driven?'"

When it comes to cloud security, these architectural patterns aren't just beneficial; they are fundamental. They provide a solid and predictable structure, which makes planning and implementing security measures an attainable goal. With established routes for data flow and component interactions, security becomes less of an add-on and more of a built-in feature of your system.

Let's take the three-tier web application as an example. In a perfect setup, the only layer that really needs to face the Wild West of the internet is the frontend. The other layers should be locked down behind network access control lists (ACLs), communicating only with the internal hosts they need to contact to do their jobs. Updates and patch management can be taken care of without giving these layers direct internet access.

What does that mean for you? Well, if a layer does suffer a security event or a full-blown compromise, the damage can be contained to just that layer, especially in cases where the attacker can't communicate due to tight egress filtering. It's like a safety net, preventing a single issue from turning into a catastrophic meltdown. In essence, these patterns not only help you construct your cloud environment but also aid in building your defense system, layer by layer.

Cloud providers also offer reference architectures that you can use as a starting point, often tailored to the unique features of each provider's platform. For example, AWS (*https://oreil.ly/qm57-*), Azure (*https://oreil.ly/mXkwG*), and GCP (*https://oreil.ly/hw_Te*) each provide a set of reference architectures that you can use as a base for your cloud environment.

Properly Manage Secrets

In the previous section related to common cloud security mistakes, we discussed how inadequate credentials and secrets management can lead to security mishaps in the cloud. You saw that being careless with secrets is a lot like hiding your house keys under the doormat—it's just inviting trouble. But fear not! It's time to move from highlighting problems to presenting solutions. In this section, we're going to tackle how to prevent such issues from happening in the first place. We'll walk through managing secrets effectively in the cloud step by step, from assessing your current state to deploying secure storage and beyond.

First things first: if you have an existing codebase, the first step in strengthening your secrets management is to figure out what secrets already exist within your code. You might be surprised at how many forgotten credentials there are. Once you've located them, it's time to clean up. To do this, you can kick things off by setting automated scanning tools loose on your code repositories. Tools like TruffleHog (*https://oreil.ly/WB-h2*), `git-secret` (*https://oreil.ly/vm_Dh*), and Horusec (*https://horusec.io*) can be your faithful hounds, sniffing out secrets scattered across your repositories. Don't rely on automation alone, however—when you first run these tools they are bound to create pages and pages of output that need to be manually vetted. Don't skip this step.

Next, you need time to find a secure home for your organization's secrets. Think of it as a high-tech safe where your encryption keys, API keys, and database passwords can rest easy. For this, cloud native tools like AWS Secrets Manager (*https://oreil.ly/upu0I*) or third-party tools like HashiCorp Vault (*https://oreil.ly/OyQhh*) are your best bet. Of course, simply standing up a vault isn't enough; you also have to run it properly and train your development team on how to use it and how to update their source code so that secrets are called from the vault rather than statically input into source code. Luckily, organizations like Amazon and HashiCorp provide extensive tutorial documentation (*https://oreil.ly/9wcS4*) on how to configure your environment appropriately.

If you've gotten this far, now is the time to take it one step further and get proactive. You need to prevent secrets from accidentally sneaking into your code repositories to begin with. The way to do this is by integrating checks into your CI/CD pipeline. This way, you're not just reacting to problems but preventing them from happening in the first place. All of the tools previously mentioned can function as CI/CD gates or be configured for precommit hooks (*https://oreil.ly/x9EhE*) to prevent deploying or committing code with secrets.

Lastly, you should consider creating a detection playbook that will alert you when a secret is found within your source code and lay out the steps to take in this event. Think of this like an incident response playbook. First, you need a tool that will detect the secret (this might be one of the examples we mentioned earlier, or a tool built into your source control management solution, like CodeQL (*https://codeql.github.com*)). Then, outline the process of rotating the secret, validating that it hasn't been abused, and assigning the development team the task of refactoring the code to use the secret manager.

It's important to remember that some of the largest software development teams in the world struggle with this problem. Framing this as a journey to improve DevSecOps practices tends to be more productive than simply pointing out the mistakes that were made to cause the problem.

Embrace Well-Architected Frameworks

No matter which cloud platform you're using, there's a well-architected framework that you can follow to ensure your cloud architecture is up to scratch. These frameworks offer best practices, guidelines, and checklists that can help you design and manage your cloud architecture.

The AWS Well-Architected Framework (*https://oreil.ly/Z2U2j*) is a guide that helps you understand the pros and cons of decisions you make while building systems on AWS. The framework focuses on five pillars: Operational Excellence, Security, Reliability, Performance Efficiency, and Cost Optimization and Sustainability (a relatively new addition). Under the Security pillar, AWS provides guidance on identity and access management (IAM), data protection, incident response, and infrastructure protection. If you're new to the cloud, this is foundational knowledge you'll need, so don't skip this reading.

Microsoft's version (*https://oreil.ly/bJICy*) is designed to help you build and deliver great solutions on Azure. It includes a different set of five pillars: Cost Optimization, Operational Excellence, Performance Efficiency, Reliability, and Security. The Security pillar offers guidance on aspects like managing identity and access, protecting applications and data, and ensuring your Azure environment is secure and well managed.

GCP's Cloud Architecture Framework (*https://oreil.ly/Zo_uP*) offers guidance for designing, building, and managing secure and scalable cloud applications. It also includes five pillars: Operational Excellence; Security, Privacy, and Compliance; Reliability; Cost Optimization; and Performance Optimization. Its Security pillar focuses on areas like IAM, data security, and network security and strongly encourages DevOps practitioners to shift Security left (which is to say, utilize security features in the platform earlier to prevent major issues later).

Continue Following Security Best Practices

Finally, don't forget to keep following security best practices. Make sure you:

- Understand the shared responsibility model.
- Secure your perimeter with firewalls, VPNs, and encryption.
- Monitor for misconfigurations.
- Securely use IAM.
- Enable visibility of your security posture.
- Implement cloud security policies.

- Encrypt data.
- Upskill your team as the cloud security landscape continues to change.
- Maintain logs and monitor for threats and vulnerabilities.

Exercise: Gaining Security Visibility into an AWS Environment

In the following exercise, we aim to guide you in establishing a basic level of visibility into the security status of your AWS infrastructure. Our focus is to make this as accessible as possible, catering even to those who may not be well versed with AWS. To achieve this, we'll demonstrate how to configure GuardDuty (*https://oreil.ly/ hO7w2*) to send email alerts when it detects a security event.

This exercise, like the others, is designed to equip new practitioners with an understanding of how these services operate and how they can be put to use to provide insightful visibility into the cloud. In a typical setup, you'd direct GuardDuty alerts to your SIEM system rather than an email inbox. We offer this exercise primarily as a learning and testing tool, and not as a recommendation for your production environment. However, if you currently have no security alerts configured, this could serve as a beneficial initial step.

Configure an SNS Email Notification

Follow these steps to configure an Amazon Simple Notification Service (SNS) email notification:

1. Sign in to the Amazon SNS console (*https://console.aws.amazon.com/sns/v3/home*).
2. Select Topics from the navigation pane, then select "Create topic."
3. On the "Create topic" screen (Figure 14-1), select Standard. Enter a topic name; for example, *Guard_Duty_Notification*. Keep the defaults for everything else.

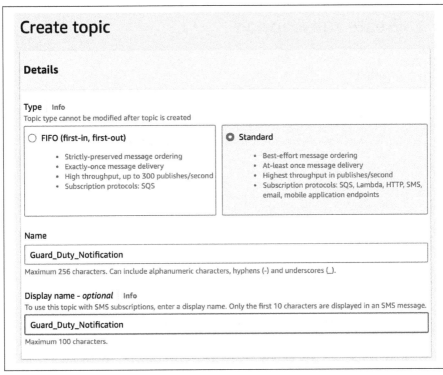

Create topic

Details

Type   Info
Topic type cannot be modified after topic is created

○ FIFO (first-in, first-out)
- Strictly-preserved message ordering
- Exactly-once message delivery
- High throughput, up to 300 publishes/second
- Subscription protocols: SQS

● Standard
- Best-effort message ordering
- At-least once message delivery
- Highest throughput in publishes/second
- Subscription protocols: SQS, Lambda, HTTP, SMS, email, mobile application endpoints

Name

Guard_Duty_Notification

Maximum 256 characters. Can include alphanumeric characters, hyphens (-) and underscores (_).

Display name - *optional*   Info
To use this topic with SMS subscriptions, enter a display name. Only the first 10 characters are displayed in an SMS message.

Guard_Duty_Notification

Maximum 100 characters.

Figure 14-1. Creating an SNS topic

4. Choose "Create topic."

5. Select Subscriptions from the navigation pane, then select "Create subscription."

6. On the "Create subscription" screen (Figure 14-2), from the Protocol menu, select Email. In the Endpoint field, add the email address that you want to receive GuardDuty alerts.

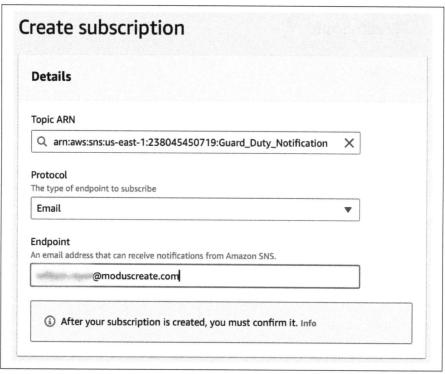

Figure 14-2. Creating an SNS email subscription

7. Choose "Create subscription."
8. Check your email and confirm the SNS subscription.

Enable GuardDuty

Now, enable GuardDuty:

1. Navigate to the AWS Management Console (*https://aws.amazon.com/console*).
2. In the Services drop-down, select GuardDuty.
3. Click the Get Started button if GuardDuty is not yet enabled. You'll see a page explaining the permissions required for GuardDuty to operate. Click Enable GuardDuty to proceed.
4. Go into Settings and scroll to "Findings export options." Change the update frequency to 15 minutes.

Set Up EventBridge to Route Alerts to Email

Now, set up EventBridge to route alerts to email:

1. Open the Amazon EventBridge console (*https://console.aws.amazon.com/events/home*).

2. In the left-hand navigation pane, under Buses, select Rules.

3. Click "Create rule." On the "Rule detail" screen (Figure 14-3), leave all options on the defaults, give your rule a name (e.g., *Guard_Duty_Finding*), and then click Next.

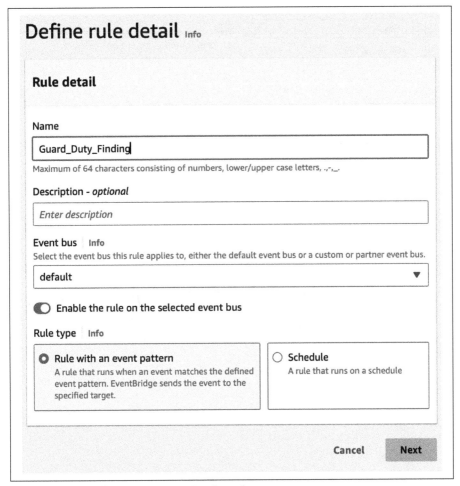

Figure 14-3. Configuring an EventBridge rule

4. On the "Build event pattern" screen, scroll to the bottom section, labeled "Event pattern" (see Figure 14-4). In this section:

- Set the event source to AWS Services.

- Set the AWS service to GuardDuty.

- Set the event type to GuardDuty Finding.

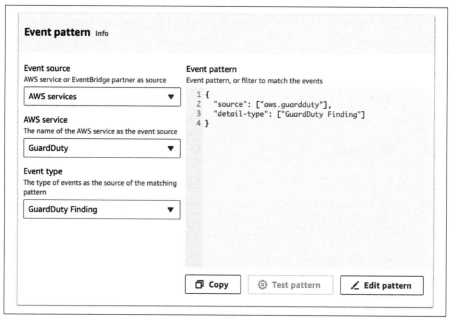

Figure 14-4. Configuring the event pattern

5. Click Next to proceed to the "Target selection" screen and add a target.

6. Select "AWS service" as the target type. Under "Select a target," select "SNS topic," and for the topic select "Guard_Duty_Notification" (see Figure 14-5).

Figure 14-5. EventBridge target configuration

7. Click Next, and you'll be presented with a summary of the EventBridge rule. Click "Create rule" at the bottom of the screen.

Testing

Now, to test and validate that you've successfully configured email notification, navigate back to the GuardDuty configuration in the console:

1. Navigate to Settings.
2. Under "Sample findings," click "Generate sample findings" (see Figure 14-6).

Figure 14-6. Generating sample findings in GuardDuty

3. Check your email. If all went well, you should have a few hundred new messages (see Figure 14-7).

Findings JSON   ×

> ⓘ **Read-only**
> This is an AWS generated finding

```
 1   [
 2     {
 3       "AccountId": "238045450719",
 4       "Arn": "arn:aws:guardduty:us-east-
       1:238045450719:detector/82be6dea9309c7a3d8ae7f050aa3a258/finding/02072bd35aea458cb1d
       015d6f5443a8b",
 5       "CreatedAt": "2024-05-07T22:01:36.006Z",
 6       "Description": "A container has mounted a host directory.",
 7       "Id": "02072bd35aea458cb1d015d6f5443a8b",
 8       "Partition": "aws",
 9       "Region": "us-east-1",
10       "Resource": {
11         "InstanceDetails": {
12           "AvailabilityZone": "GeneratedFindingInstanceAvailabilityZone",
13           "IamInstanceProfile": {
14             "Arn": "GeneratedFindingInstanceProfileArn",
15             "Id": "GeneratedFindingInstanceProfileId"
16           },
17           "ImageDescription": "GeneratedFindingInstanceImageDescription",
18           "ImageId": "ami-99999999",
19           "InstanceId": "i-99999999",
20           "InstanceState": "running",
21           "InstanceType": "m3.xlarge",
22           "OutpostArn": "arn:aws:outposts:us-west-2:123456789000:outpost/op-
       12345678890abcdef",
23           "LaunchTime": "2016-08-02T02:05:06.000Z",
24           "NetworkInterfaces": [
25             {
26               "Ipv6Addresses": [],
27               "NetworkInterfaceId": "eni-abcdef12",
28               "PrivateDnsName": "GeneratedFindingPrivateDnsName",
29               "PrivateIpAddress": "10.0.0.1",
30               "PrivateIpAddresses": [
31                 {
32                   "PrivateDnsName": "GeneratedFindingPrivateName",
33                   "PrivateIpAddress": "10.0.0.1"
34                 }
35               ],
36               "PublicDnsName": "GeneratedFindingPublicDNSName",
37               "PublicIp": "198.51.100.0",
38               "SecurityGroups": [
39                 {
40                   "GroupId": "GeneratedFindingSecurityId",
41                   "GroupName": "GeneratedFindingSecurityGroupName"
42                 }
43               ],
44               "SubnetId": "GeneratedFindingSubnetId",
```

Figure 14-7. Sample GuardDuty finding

4. Next, navigate back to GuardDuty Findings by clicking Findings on the upper-left pane of the GuardDuty service within the AWS Console and examine the generated sample findings (see Figure 14-8).

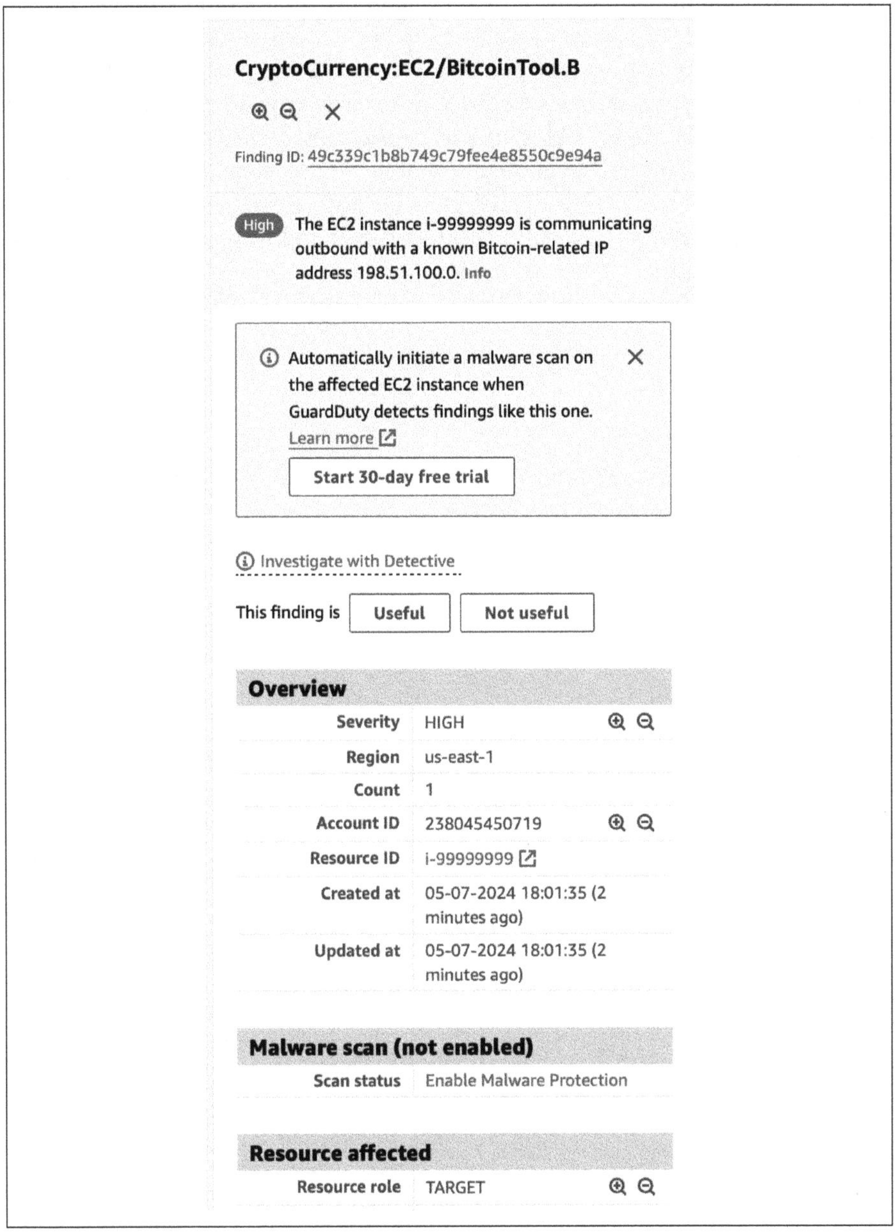

Figure 14-8. GuardDuty Console findings

Conclusion

While checkbox and compliance-driven security has a place in your toolbox and can be useful to establish a baseline and a foundation, this should be the beginning, not the end, of your cloud security journey. The best security outcomes require developing deep knowledge of how each cloud service works and interacts with your applications. Then, use your security knowledge to ensure your architecture has strong security controls in place, baking in and considering security from the start at each layer. This requires a mindset and culture of being proactive, ensuring you're following core principles such as least privilege while also considering everything you need for proactive monitoring and automation to detect and respond to threats in as close to real time as possible.

CHAPTER 15

Authentication

Authentication is a cornerstone of information security and one of the few subjects that will impact almost everyone. From protecting access to email to state secrets and now even being able to start and drive cars, authentication is ingrained in almost everything we do. In this chapter, we'll look at some high-level concepts around access and authentication and dig into how some of them work.

Identity and Access Management

Identity and access management (IAM) is a term that collectively describes the processes, policies, and products used to manage access for user identities/entities in an environment. The rest of this chapter is divided into three main sections, covering passwords, authentication protocols, and MFA; however, you can think of both passwords and MFA as subcategories of the broader IAM category. We'll also cover encryption, hashing, and salting, as those usually come up in relation to protecting passwords.

There are a handful of common best practices when it comes to IAM. While the individual cloud providers all provide their own specific technical guidance, the following concepts are universal regardless of whether you're operating systems on premises, in the cloud, or as SaaS:

Least privilege
> We've talked about the principle of least privilege a few times already. As a reminder, this is the concept of granting users and endpoints (collectively called an identity or entity) access to only the applications, endpoints, files, etc., to which they need access, and nothing more.

Centralization

Centralization is pivotal for efficient access tracking and management. There are some cases in which segmented authentication may be a good idea. However, with respect to tracking access and accounts, this is not the case, because there needs to be a single source of truth. One of the biggest worries for companies when someone with a high level of access leaves is whether all of their access has been removed. If everything is tied to a central authentication platform, there is much less hunting to do for accounts to disable.

Centralization may also encompass the implementation of single sign-on (SSO) authentication. SSO enables users to authenticate across various systems using a single access token. This approach minimizes the need for multiple passwords, simplifies user login processes, and enhances security measures like automated onboarding and offboarding using SCIM (*https://scim.cloud*).

Removal of unwanted/unneeded assets

Eliminating superfluous assets is a critical (and in many cases regulatorily mandated) practice for maintaining a secure environment. Throughout this book, we've touched on this in several different contexts. In Chapter 2 we discussed asset management, emphasizing the importance of decommissioning no longer active accounts. Taking the proactive approach of revoking access for former employees and vendors, updating or phasing out outdated software and hardware, and ensuring your infrastructure is tidy and well managed is a strategic move in any security program. The fewer unneeded items that you have to worry about defending and securing, the more you can reduce the risk of one of them being used for nefarious purposes.

Effective password management and MFA implementation

Password management is a critical element of IAM that we'll consider in depth in this chapter. MFA is a security control that adds an extra layer of security by requiring users to provide two forms of verification before being granted access. We've found in practice that mandatory MFA is an effective way to prevent phishing-related account takeovers (although there are ways around this, so don't assume MFA alone will prevent all such attempts—as with all security controls, you should never put all of your security eggs in one basket!).

Let's start with the most obvious aspect of IAM: passwords.

Passwords

Passwords have been used in computers since the early 1960s, when the first shared environments were born. MIT's Compatible Time-Sharing System (CTSS) was the first multiuser operating system. At this early stage, there was no password security, as previously only physical security had been used to limit access. The CTSS passwords (stored in plain text) were in theory only accessible by the administrators, but an admin error in the late '60s caused the widespread display of all users' passwords during login after the message-of-the-day file was swapped with the password file. Oops!

Passwords have come a long way since then, but some security professionals today view them as outdated and think they shouldn't be used anymore. While we agree that some password implementations can be incredibly insecure, there are many ways to ensure that the transmission and storage of passwords are securely implemented. In this case, they can still add another valuable layer of security.

Password Basics

Simple password hashes can be cracked in less than a second with some trivial knowledge and the right tools. Password cracking software like Cain and Abel and John the Ripper supports the cracking of hundreds of types of hashes using brute force or rainbow tables. Brute-force attacks often use dictionary files, which are large text files containing thousands upon thousands of plain-text passwords that are commonly used and have been stripped from data breaches and other sources. Both the tools and the dictionaries are readily available on the internet.

The 2023 Verizon Data Breach Incident Report (*https://oreil.ly/becO1*) stated that 86% of web application attacks and 76% of social engineering attacks involved compromised user credentials. According to the 2024 report (*https://oreil.ly/LK4LJ*), credentials remain the most sought-after data type, with half of social engineering attacks and over 70% of web app attacks involving compromised credentials. Looking at some numbers from the Identity Theft Resource Center's 2023 Data Breach Report (*https://oreil.ly/qut7v*), the numbers of victims affected are staggering (see Table 15-1).

Table 15-1. Data breaches and victims

Industry	# of breaches	# of victims
Healthcare	809	~56M
Financial services	744	~61M
Manufacturing	259	~5M
Educational	173	~4M
Government	100	~15M
Hospitality	45	~6M

Good password security will allow you to minimize the impact of consistent breaches on personal accounts and make it less likely that the enterprise will have a breach. Let's begin with some basic math surrounding the length and complexity of passwords. The times listed here (based on Random-ize's "How Long to Hack My Password" (*https://oreil.ly/J06_j*) tool) are approximate and don't take into consideration if a service doesn't allow certain characters or how fast and amazing your password-cracking GPU cluster may or may not be:

- Using 8 characters in only lowercase equals 26^8 possible combinations. Extremely easy, will crack in <2 minutes.

- Using 8 characters in upper- and lowercase equals 52^8 possible combinations. Still not the best, will crack in <6 hours.

- Using 8 characters in uppercase, lowercase, and numbers equals 62^8 possible combinations. A little better, will crack in <24 hours.

- Using 10 characters with uppercase, lowercase, numbers, and symbols equals 94^{10} possible combinations. Much better, will take approximately 600 years to crack.

A rainbow table is a database of precomputed hash values for a wide range of plaintext passwords. Rainbow table attacks utilize these tables to quickly find the original password corresponding to a provided hash value, which negates the need for real-time computation of a hash value for cracking passwords. While rainbow tables were once powerful tools for cracking password hashes, their effectiveness has been greatly reduced by modern cryptographic security measures such as salts (*https://oreil.ly/ arzYm*) and key derivation functions (*https://oreil.ly/Wf5gz*) that are intentionally slow and cryptographically demanding.

While long and complex passwords won't matter if the backend encryption is weak or there has been a breach involving them, it will protect against brute-force attacks. So, teaching users and requiring administrators to create complex passwords is an overall win for everyone. Users who make use of password management software (discussed in "Password Management" on page 180) no longer have to remember their passwords or try to come up with them on their own. However, if you can't or prefer not to use such software, there are a few ways of coming up with them on your own. One way of making secure passwords easier to remember is using phrases from books, songs, favorite expressions, etc., and substituting characters. They then become passphrases instead and are inherently more secure. For example:

Amanda and Bill really love their password security = A&BillR<3TPS

Another method is using Diceware passphrases, as outlined in the now famous *XKCD* comic (*https://xkcd.com/936*). The gist of this method is that you roll a six-sided die multiple times in succession, recording the number from each roll to get a random five-digit sequence. You then use this sequence to look up a corresponding word in a pre-established Diceware wordlist, repeating this process four or more times until you have a random sequence of words that you combine to form a strong, memorable passphrase. The benefit here is that the password is random, has high randomness and unpredictability, and is long, making it difficult to crack.

Here's an example, using three words for simplicity's sake:

1. The first roll sequence is 15624, corresponding to *Galaxy*.

2. The second roll is 46315, corresponding to *Dolphin*.

3. The third roll is 52431, corresponding to *Sunset*.

Combining these words, Amanda and Bill's new Diceware passphrase might become *Galaxy!Dolphin!Sunset*. This approach is preferable to the previous one because each word is selected randomly, the password is longer, it's memorable, and no personal info is used (e.g., the name Bill in the previous example; also, <3 is a predictable combination that password crackers will check for).

Another important point to make, which may represent a learning opportunity for end users (and possibly even an enterprise-wide shift in process), is not to trust others with your passwords. Help desk staff should not be asking for passwords, ever, period. Users should be educated that no one in the organization will ask for their password, and they should do the right thing and report anyone who does, as they may be asking for malicious purposes. If it's the person next to you, that just presents a great collaboration and learning opportunity—maybe you can read this chapter together!

This idea of keeping passwords to yourself doesn't only apply to humans. Web browsers store passwords encoded in a way that is publicly known and thus easy to decode. Password recovery tools, which are easily available online, enable anyone to see all the passwords stored in the browser and open user profiles.

Encryption, Hashing, and Salting

There is a common misunderstanding of these three terms. It will be extremely helpful to understand what encryption, hashing, and salting mean and the difference between them in general. All three can be involved with password implementations, and it's best to know a little about them and how they work.

Encryption

Encryption has evolved significantly from its ancient origins with the Egyptians and Romans. Today, it underpins the security of data in transit (moving over a network) and at rest (stored). Encryption works by applying an algorithm to make data unreadable without the correct decryption key.

Modern encryption methods include the Advanced Encryption Standard (AES) and Rivest–Shamir–Adleman (RSA) algorithms and elliptic curve cryptography (ECC), among many others. AES, for instance, is widely recognized for its strength and efficiency, making it a preferred choice for securing data.

However, quantum computing is presenting new challenges to these established methods. Quantum computers use qubits, which can exist in multiple states at the same time; this allows them to potentially crack passwords much faster than the classic computers we use today. For example, a sufficiently powerful quantum computer utilizing Shor's algorithm (*https://oreil.ly/ePxYR*) could factor out the prime numbers that underpin algorithms like RSA and break many modern encryption algorithms. Similarly, Grover's algorithm (*https://oreil.ly/4-XF6*) could be applied to speed up breaking protocols like AES by accelerating random searches.

This new risk to encryption has necessitated the need for *quantum-hardened* or (*post-quantum*) encryption protocols and methods. At the time of writing, NIST (*https://oreil.ly/G4Lef*) is in the process of evaluating and standardizing these new hardened algorithms, which are expected to be secure against both classic and quantum-enabled attacks.

Hashing

Hashing is a fundamental method for transforming data into a fixed-size string of characters. Unlike encryption, which is designed to be reversible with the correct key, hashing is a one-way process. This means that once data has been hashed, it can't be directly reversed or decoded back to its original plain text. For example, applying SHA256 to the phrase "Amanda and Bill are awesome" yields a hash of:

```
e6a5214c6f2b21244bbcd9fb53911f92980fdbcb0cc10af50d1ed0617e9d9cb8
```

And for the longer phrase "Amanda and Bill are awesome at creating examples," it results in:

```
9e2327099eb270a1cf6899ad245ae97be08bcfc4581fd8c0a163e5071bcb93d0
```

Notice that the results are both the same length, demonstrating the algorithm's fixed output size. This ensures that no matter the length of the input, the hash will occupy a consistent amount of storage space. However, it also implies the possibility of collisions, where different inputs produce the same output hash. While collisions are mathematically rare with strong and well-tested algorithms like SHA256, they are possible due to the finite size of the output space.

Hashing is particularly useful for password storage. Rather than storing passwords in plain text, systems can store passwords as hashes. Then, when someone types in their password, the same hashing algorithm is applied to the clear text, and the resulting cipher text is compared with what is located in the database, looking for a match. Even the slightest change in the clear-text data results in significantly different cipher-text output. This means hash functions can also test whether information, programs, or other data has been tampered with and provide the basis for nonrepudiation (i.e., signatures) in a cryptographic context.

Because hashing algorithms only work one way, the only way to derive the original value is to use brute force, trying multiple values to see if they produce the same cipher text. However, the simplicity and predictability of the passwords users pick can make them vulnerable to brute force attacks, especially if the attacker has knowledge of how the user may have picked the password. To mitigate brute forcing, salting is applied; we'll look at that next.

Salting

Salting works by adding an extra secret value to the input, extending the length of the original password. Suppose the password is *Defensive* and the salt value is *Security.Handbook*. The hash value would be derived from the combination of the two: *DefensiveSecurity.Handbook*. This provides some protection for those people who use common words as their passwords. However, this protection is limited: if someone learns the salt value that is used, they can just add it to the end (or start) of each dictionary word they try in their attack. To make brute-force attacks more difficult, random salts can be used, one for each password (bcrypt (*https://oreil.ly/_dNC8*) is an example of a hashing algorithm that uses a random salt for each hash by default). Salts can also be created from multiple parts, such as the current date/time, the user's ID or username, a secret phrase, a random value, or a combination of these.

Encryption and hashing recommendations

There are many insecure encryption and hashing algorithms currently in use that should be upgraded to stronger methods. NIST recommends the following upgrades:

- Upgrade MD5 to SHA512 (or above)
- Upgrade SHA1 to SHA512
- Upgrade DES/3DES to AES3

Depreciated encryption/hashing algorithms include:

- SHA1
- 1,024-bit RSA or DSA
- 160-bit ECDSA (elliptic curve DSA)
- 80/112-bit 2TDEA (2-key triple DES)
- MD5 (this was never an acceptable algorithm)

For password hashing specifically, NIST SP 800-132 (*https://oreil.ly/DLxG4*) recommends using key derivation functions like PBKDF2 (Password-Based Key Derivation Function 2). PBKDF2 should be used with a salt of at least 32 bits and an iteration count as high as possible (typically >10,000) in combination with hardened memory functions (in the case of application architectures storing passwords).

Password Management

In this day and age, we have passwords for everything. Some of us have systems that make remembering passwords easier, but for the majority of users it isn't feasible to expect them to remember a different password for each piece of software or website they use. At the same time, it's vital not to make the mistake of reusing passwords. Whenever a website with stored password hashes gets hacked, attackers inevitably start trying to crack the passwords (particularly those associated with an email address). If they succeed, they will probably attempt to reuse those credentials on other sites. This type of attack can be thwarted by never reusing passwords (or similar permutations of passwords). Whether it's a personal account or an enterprise account, passwords should not be reused. Unique, complex passwords should always be used for sites and services with confidential information or powerful access.

Password management software

Password reuse is a common problem that can be solved by using a password manager. There are many different options available, both free and paid. Password management implementations vary from the rudimentary password-storing features in most browsers to specialized products that synchronize the saved passwords across different devices and automatically fill login forms as needed. You should do some careful research to identify the best fit for your organization.

Before deciding on a password manager, read reviews of various products in order to understand how they work and what they are capable of doing. Some reviews include both strengths and weaknesses. Also, read the background information on vendors' websites. Some questions to ask when evaluating password management software are:

- Are there certain passwords that need to be shared among admins, such as for a root or *sa* account?

- Will you be using MFA to log in to the password manager? (Hint: you should.)

- Do you want to start with a free solution that has fewer features or with a paid option that offers more room to grow and better ease of use? You may want to start with a free tool and decide later if it makes sense to move to something more robust. Take note, however, that many free versions of software are for personal use only.

- Is there a one-time cost or a recurring fee?

- Should the system have a built-in password generator and strength meter?

- Is there a need for it to auto-fill application or website fields?

- Does the password manager use strong encryption?

- Does it have a lockout feature?

- Does it include protection from malicious activity, such as keystroke logging? If so, which kinds of activity?

- What kind of logging does the solution have? You may need to log for auditing purposes or want to create detections around improper use or attempts at malicious activity.

In all cases, the master password should be well protected; it's best to memorize it rather than write it down, although writing it down and keeping it in a secure location is also an option. (It's never a bad idea to have a physical copy of major user account names and passwords written down or printed out and stored in a vault, in case of emergency—yay, disaster planning!)

When you've chosen a password manager, get it directly from the vendor and verify that the installer is not installing a maliciously modified version by checking the MD5 hash. If a hash is not available, request one from the vendor; if the vendor cannot provide a verification method, be skeptical.

Although moving to a password manager may take a little effort, in the long run it is a safe and convenient method of keeping track of your organization's passwords and guarding specific online information.

Password resets

Password reset questions when not using MFA (or when it's poorly implemented) can be a surefire way for an attacker to get into an account and cut the user off from accessing it. Answers to the questions like "What is your mother's maiden name?"; "What city were you born in?"; or "Where did you graduate high school?" are often added onto an account for "security" purposes. The majority of answers to these questions can easily be found on the internet, guessed, or even socially engineered out of the user.

When designing a system that allows password resets, try to not use standard everyday questions that are easily guessed. One method for users to ensure the security questions are not brute forced is to supply false information. For example, the answer to the question "What is the name of your elementary school?" could be "Never gonna give you up" or "Never gonna let you down." The answers should then be stored away in a password manager, as it will likely be difficult to remember them.

Password storage locations and methods

Many password storage locations and methods are insecure by default. For example, in 2015, a high-profile Linux vulnerability in the Grand Unified Bootloader (GRUB2) allowed physical password bypass by pressing the backspace button 28 times in a row. GRUB2, used by most Linux systems to boot the operating system when the PC starts, would then display a rescue shell, allowing unauthenticated access to the computer and the ability to load another environment.

The following are some recommendations to protect Microsoft Windows clients from interception attacks:

- Ensure Server Message Block (SMB) signing and encryption are forced:
  - Configure the "Microsoft network client: Digitally sign communications (always)" Group Policy setting to enable SMB signing.
  - Set the "Microsoft network server: Digitally sign communications (always)" policy to require signing on the server side as well.
  - Enable SMB encryption by setting "Encrypt data access" to "Enabled" in the SMB server configuration.
  - To allow for mandatory SMB encryption, all clients must support SMB 3.0 or later.
- Disable weak SMBv1 and require newer SMB dialects:
  - Set the `MinSMB2Dialect` registry value to `0x000000311` to require SMB 3.1.1 or higher. SMB 3.1.1 introduced pre-authentication integrity, which protects the initial connection negotiation against tampering.
  - Set `MaxSMB2Dialect` to the same value to prevent downgrades to older, less secure dialects.
- Disable guest authentication and fallback. You can do this using the following PowerShell command:

```
Set-SmbClientConfiguration -EnableInsecureGuestLogons $false -Confirm:$false
```

For additional guidance on hardening SMB in Windows networks, see the Microsoft article on protecting SMB traffic from interception (*https://oreil.ly/63qYj*).

In June 2023, the Cybersecurity and Infrastructure Security Agency (CISA), together with the National Security Agency (NSA), released direct guidance (*https://oreil.ly/Mb3F2*) on hardening baseboard management controllers (BMCs), also known as Integrated Lights-Out (iLO) cards, which are a type of embedded computer used to provide out-of-band monitoring for desktops and servers. They are used for remote access to servers, enabling control of the hardware settings and status without physical access to the devices themselves. The card allows system administrators to connect through a web browser as long as the unit has power running to it; they can power up the device, change settings, and remotely connect to the OS. A major security risk here is that often the default passwords on the cards are not changed.

The protocol that BMCs/iLOs use is also extremely insecure. Intelligent Platform Management Interface (IPMI) v1 has cipher suite zero enabled by default, which permits logon as an administrator without requiring a password. So, in addition to taking care to change the default passwords, you should take steps to protect against this critical vulnerability by upgrading the iLOs to v2 or greater. There are specific modules in Metasploit (*https://www.metasploit.com*) that will allow scanning a network for iLO cards with vulnerabilities (the Metasploit scanner in this case is *auxiliary/scanner/ipmi/*).

As covered earlier in this chapter and discussed further in Chapter 16, using centralized authentication when possible—such as a cloud provider, Active Directory, Terminal Access Controller Access-Control System Plus (TACACS+), or Remote Authentication Dial In User Service (RADIUS)—will allow you to have fewer overall instances of password storage to keep track of.

It's also recommended that you segment the management of your servers (especially as it relates to BMCs/iLOs/IPMI) to a control network using a virtual LAN; we'll talk more about this in Chapter 17.

Additional Password Security

In addition to what we've discussed so far, there are many other solutions and configurations that offer amazing features, tools, and visibility with regard to IAM and passwords. Let's look at a few examples to round out this section.

Fine-grained password policies (FGPPs)

In Windows Server 2008, Microsoft introduced the capability to implement fine-grained password policies (FGPPs) (*https://oreil.ly/PysE5*). Using FGPPs can be extremely beneficial in cases where certain users or groups require different password restrictions and options. However, they can be difficult to set up and manage, so it's important that a long-term plan is created for deploying them.

To use FGPPs in a domain, all of the domain controllers must be running Windows Server 2008 or later. Also, FGPPs can only be applied to user objects and global security groups (not computers).

Cloud IAM

With the introduction of cloud-hosted authentication and other complete services focused on IAM, it's now possible to add controls to new and existing infrastructure that we never could before. In addition, cloud IAM has benefits beyond password management, such as increased scalability, reduced infrastructure costs, and remote access management.

For example, for many years it was nearly impossible to prevent Active Directory users from setting their passwords to something like *MyCompanyName1* or *summer2005* without custom-creating a *.dll*. Even that was only supported on some operating system versions, and it isn't exactly an enterprise solution. Now, with Azure AD, you have the ability to add custom banned passwords in the Azure portal, along with conditional access policies and a variety of other controls around access.

You can find more information on cloud features in Chapter 14. As with any type of infrastructure decision, however, don't automatically jump to a cloud solution because you think it will fix all of your problems with access. The important thing is to find a solution that fits well with your environment.

Common Authentication Protocols

An authentication protocol enables a receiving entity (such as a server) to verify the identity of another device or user. User authentication protocols secure communication between computer networks. Establishing the right authentication protocol for your business is one way to achieve better security, but the process can be overwhelming.

NTLM

Windows NT LAN Manager (NTLM) is a suite of protocols used to authenticate a client to a resource in an Active Directory domain. It includes the NTLMv1, NTLMv2, and NTLM2 Session protocols.

NTLM was the primary method of authentication prior to Windows 2000. It is vulnerable to many types of attacks, including pass-the-hash and brute-force attacks. However, it is still widely deployed to maintain compatibility with older systems that cannot use newer cryptography.

As illustrated in Figure 15-1, NTLM uses a challenge/response method of authentication where the domain controller or target computer checks the hash the client provides against its stored hash to ensure it is a match. If it is, the client is allowed access to the resource. The hashes are stored either in the Security Account Manager (SAM) database in the registry (when local authentication is happening) or on the domain controller, in the *ntds.dit* file.

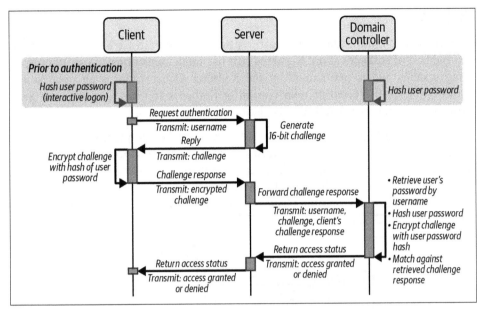

Figure 15-1. NTLM

To summarize, here's how it works:

1. The client makes an authentication request.

2. The resource being accessed challenges authentication with a 16-bit random number.

3. The client encrypts the challenge with its stored hash of the user's password and sends it back.

4. The resource being accessed forwards that response (along with the challenge and the username) to the domain controller.

5. The domain controller encrypts the challenge itself using its stored hash of the user's password in *ntds.dit*, compares it to the forwarded response, and returns the access status, allowing access to the resource if it matches and otherwise denying it.

Kerberos

Starting with Windows 2000, Microsoft replaced NTLM with Kerberos as the preferred method of authentication. Kerberos also has implementations across other operating systems and is maintained by the Kerberos Consortium as an open source project. Microsoft created its own version of Kerberos and has used it as the go-to protocol for authentication across its platforms ever since.

As illustrated in Figure 15-2, Kerberos adds in secret-key cryptography as well as a third-party ticket authorization to make it a more secure method of authentication. The protocol derived its name from Greek mythology's guardian of the underworld— Cerberus, the three-headed dog. The three "heads" in Kerberos are the client, the server, and the Key Distribution Center (KDC). The KDC acts as both Authentication Server (AS) and Ticket Granting Server (TGS).

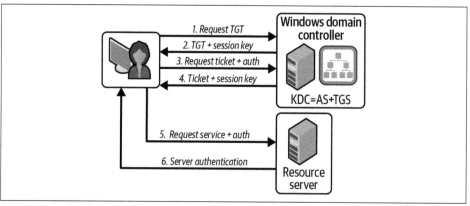

Figure 15-2. Kerberos

Here's a summary of how it works:

1. The client requests an authentication ticket (Ticket Granting Ticket, or TGT).

2. The KDC verifies that the client has sent the correct credentials and, if so, returns an encrypted TGT and a session key. The client stores that TGT until it expires, at which point it will need to ask for another one.

3. The client sends the current TGT to the TGS with the Service Principal Name (SPN) of the resource the client wants to access.

4. The TGS sends a valid session key for the resource to the client.

5. The client uses that session key for access.

LDAP

The Lightweight Directory Access Protocol (LDAP) is a protocol that makes it possible for applications to query user information rapidly. LDAP has been in use since the early 1990s and has been a significant part of many networks over the past decades.

LDAP not only is used for authentication but can also be used to find files and devices on a network or modify entries in a database. In fact, most environments do not rely on LDAP for authentication, as it is not as secure by default as other options and is easy to misconfigure. For example, if LDAP is not configured with the use of SSL/TLS, it sends authentication in plain text over the network. Obviously, we strongly recommend against this!

Figure 15-3 illustrates the basic authentication process with LDAP. First, the client sends a bind request to the LDAP server, including its distinguished name and credentials (e.g., a password) to prove its identity. If the credentials match the client's directory entry on the server, the bind is successful and the server establishes an authenticated session that authorizes the client for subsequent directory operations.

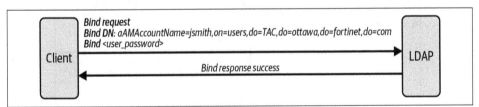

Figure 15-3. Simple bind authentication with LDAP

RADIUS

Remote Authentication Dial In User Service (RADIUS) is a client/server network protocol that was originally designed to authenticate remote users to a dial-in access server, with low-bandwidth conditions in mind. Figure 15-4 shows how it works.

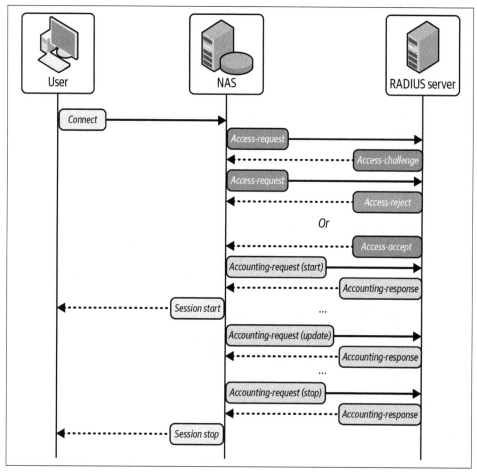

Figure 15-4. RADIUS

RADIUS authentication begins when the client attempts to access a network resource, such as a WiFi network or a VPN connection. Here are the steps:

1. The user's device sends an Access-Request message to a RADIUS server through a Remote Access Server (RAS) or Network Access Server (NAS), along with the user's credentials, such as a username and password.

2. The RAS/NAS passes along the authentication request to the RADIUS server, which checks the information against a locally stored database file or other external source (such as Active Directory). To verify that the information is correct, it uses an authentication scheme such as the Password Authentication Protocol (PAP), Challenge Handshake Authentication Protocol (CHAP), MS-CHAP (Microsoft's version of CHAP), or Extensible Authentication Protocol (EAP).

3. If the credentials are valid, the RADIUS server sends an Access-Accept message back to the user's device. Alternatively, if the credentials are invalid, the RADIUS server sends an Access-Reject message back to the user's device.

4. Once the user is authenticated, the RADIUS server can also authorize the user to access specific network resources, such as certain servers or applications. This is done through an Access-Accept message that includes the user's authorization information.

5. The RADIUS server keeps track of the user's activity on the network through accounting messages, which can include information such as the duration of the user's session, the amount of data transferred, and the user's IP address.

Differences Between Protocols

Table 15-2 outlines the differences between the protocols discussed here, as well as a few others.

Table 15-2. Comparison of authentication protocols

Protocol	Authentication	Encryption	Common attacks
NTLMv1	Challenge/response	DES	• Authentication downgrade LDAP relay • Pass-the-hash
NTLMv2	Challenge/response	HMAC-MD5	• Pass-the-hash • Link-Local Multicast Name Resolution (LLMNR) / NetBIOS Name Service (NBT-NS) poisoning • SMB relay
Kerberos	Third-party ticket	• DES_CBC_CRC • DES_CBC_MD5 • RC4_HMAC_MD5 • AES128_HMAC_SHA1 • AES256_HMAC_SHA1	• Pass-the-ticket • Golden ticket • Silver ticket • Credential stuffing/brute force • Encryption downgrade • DCShadow • As-rep roasting • Kerberoasting
LDAP	Simple bind	None	• Account discovery • Brute force • Domain enumeration
RADIUS	Challenge/response	Many, but most common are: • EAP-TLS • PEAP-MSCHAPv2 • EAP-TTLS/PAP	• Response authenticator • User-password attribute cipher design • Shared secret attack • User password–based password attack • Request authenticator

Protocol	Authentication	Encryption	Common attacks
OIDC	Token-based using OAuth 2.0 flows	TLS for transport security operational ID token encryption	• Token interception • Client impersonation • Cross-site request forgery (CSRF) • Open redirect
SAML	XML-based assertions	TLS for transport security, XMLEnc for assertion (optional)	• Replay attacks • Signature wrapping • Man in the middle • XML injection • Assertion theft

Protocol Security

To determine what authentication protocol is being used, you can check the network configuration settings on the device or service that you are using to authenticate.

Here are some steps you can follow:

- Validate the authentication settings on the device or service (you may do this via a configuration file, management interface, or GUI). Look for settings related to authentication and security.
- Depending on the device or service, you may see specific protocol names such as Kerberos, NTML, PAP, CHAP, MS-CHAP, or EAP.
- Many authentication services log authentication attempts and results. Check the logs for any mention of the authentication protocol used.
- Network analyzers like Wireshark can capture and analyze network traffic. By capturing authentication traffic, you can identify the protocol used.
- The documentation for the device or service may provide information on what authentication protocols are supported and how to configure them.

 Protocols such as Telnet, FTP, SNMPv2, HTTP, and older versions of SMB transmit login credentials in plain text, making them susceptible to interception and unauthorized access. Unless you have no other choice, disable and avoid using these protocols.

Choosing the Best Protocol for Your Organization

Identifying the best choice of authentication protocol depends on several factors related to your organization's infrastructure and application requirements. Authentication mechanisms have strengths and weaknesses, and (like Indiana Jones in *The Last Crusade*) it's important that we choose wisely, because doing otherwise can mean our systems get compromised and we go out of business.

To guide your decision, consider the following questions:

- What does the application limit us to?
- Do we need this system to scale?
- Will technical debt prevent adequate management and control?
- What are the security requirements of this system?
- What are the performance constraints?
- Do we need to support interoperability?

As system designers, these are among the questions we ask ourselves to frame out and threat model (*https://oreil.ly/nzqUw*) our systems before we release them to production. This can help us identify the security requirements and design more secure systems.

Multi-Factor Authentication

Managing multiple accounts or access systems using the same or separate authentication can be challenging. With the sheer volume and sensitive nature of the data that's in cyberspace and today's computing power, with extensive botnets and entire server farms dedicated to password cracking, you can no longer safely rely only on a password for protection. Why compromise regarding the security of your data, access to your systems, or the possibility of giving an attacker a foothold into your corporate infrastructure? In addition to doing your best to increase password complexity, MFA is an essential part of a complete defense strategy—not just a box to check on a compliance list.

While the number of services and websites that provide MFA is increasing, it's rarely implemented as completely as it should be in enterprise environments. A surprising number of companies and services decide to implement MFA only after a large-scale or high-visibility breach. For example, Figure 15-5 shows the false tweet from the hacked AP Twitter account (*https://oreil.ly/_Ylto*) that caused the stock market to plunge (Figure 15-6) in April 2013. Twitter started offering MFA in August of that same year, less than four months later. While it could be argued that this specific hack, being the result of a phishing attack, might have occurred regardless, it is still likely that MFA could have lent a hand in preventing it.

Figure 15-5. False tweet from the hacked @AP Twitter account

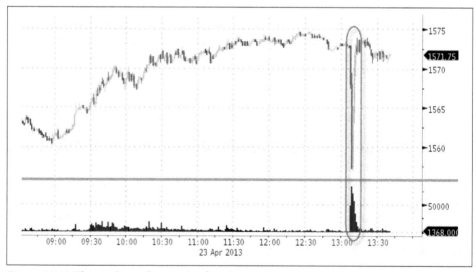

Figure 15-6. The stock market crash after the tweet

MFA Weaknesses

Of course, there are various ways that MFA may fail to be the necessary security blanket, especially when it comes to poor implementation. To give an example of how important it is to be rigorous about applying MFA (going back to that "as completely as it should be" comment), consider the case of the 2014 JPMorgan Chase attack (*https://oreil.ly/NaX65*), where the names, addresses, phone numbers, and email addresses of 83 million account holders were exposed in one of the biggest data security breaches in history—the attackers managed to gain a foothold on a server that had accidentally been overlooked when MFA was enabled across the organization.

As another example, suppose Company A decides to implement MFA by using the push notification or phone call method. A criminal or pentester comes along and attempts to break in by either phishing, using passwords harvested from a recent breach, or using a password brute-forcing technique. Somehow, they end up with a legitimate username/password combo—they should be stopped from authenticating because of MFA, right? But in this case, the user gets the usual phone call or application alert that they've gotten so many times before (and which doesn't tell the user what it is that they're supposedly logging in to) and, as a force of habit and without paying much attention, they acknowledge the alert or answer the phone call and press the # key. Boom, the threat actor or pentester is in. There have also been case studies where attackers have used password reset options to bypass MFA. The level of security boils down to how the implementation has been designed, how the users have been trained, and what options are configurable.

The scenario described here is technically using the "something you have" MFA factor (in addition to "something you know," the harvested credentials), allowing Company A to be compliant, but it's not really leveraging the security potential of this authentication approach. Requiring the user to enter a code into the application or service they're trying to connect to rather than simply acknowledging the authentication attempt with a click or the push of a button would be a more secure implementation.

There are many other ways of getting around MFA that we won't get into here (for example, SIM jacking, social engineering, and intercepting emails). In the words of Bruce Schneier (*https://oreil.ly/SPhlQ*):

> Two-factor authentication isn't our savior. It won't defend against phishing. It's not going to prevent identity theft. It's not going to secure online accounts from fraudulent transactions. It solves the security problems we had ten years ago, not the security problems we have today.

Still, the bottom line is that passwords alone are weak, and adding MFA strengthens that authentication method and makes it more secure.

Where It Should Be Implemented

MFA is here to stay, and it can significantly increase network security. We recommend that it be implemented wherever possible. If there is any type of remote access in your organization, such as via VPNs, portals, or email, MFA should be required—and not just for administrators, but for vendors, employees, consultants, and everyone else. Your data is worth protecting. Implementing an effective MFA solution in an organization enables remote and local access to firewalls, servers, applications, and critical infrastructure to be secured. We also suggest that you use it personally for your home accounts, such as email, social media, banking, and other services, where offered.

Conclusion

Our goal in this chapter was to provide a basic introduction to IAM, passwords, and MFA. However, we recognize that what we've omitted could fill several volumes in itself, and we strongly suggest that you do some further reading to continue to grow your understanding of this area.

The following books are good starting points:

- *Privileged Attack Vectors: Building Effective Cyber-Defense Strategies to Protect Organizations*, 2nd ed., by Morey J. Haber (Apress). This book focuses on defending against attacks that exploit privileged accounts, detailing the risks associated with poor privilege management, possible avenues of attack, and proper defensive measures.

- *Identity and Access Management: Business Performance Through Connected Intelligence* by Ertem Osmanoglu (Syngress). Even though it's a decade old, this is still one of the best guides for understanding the fundamentals, strategies, and best practices.

- *Access Control and Identity Management (Information Systems Security & Assurance)*, 3rd ed., by Mike Chapple (Jones & Bartlett). This book focuses on the components of access control; it provides a business framework for implementation and discusses legal requirements that impact access control programs.

We also recommend that you consult the relevant vendor guides, such as:

- Microsoft
    - Identity and Access documentation (*https://oreil.ly/pXlFV*)
    - What is identity and access management (IAM)? (*https://oreil.ly/F5hgH*)
    - Identity and access management overview (*https://oreil.ly/Sfk0e*)

- Amazon
  - AWS Identity and Access Management Best Practices (*https://oreil.ly/hGUW1*)
  - Policies and permissions in IAM (*https://oreil.ly/e_MGt*)
  - Identity and access management (*https://oreil.ly/nwGYD*)
- Google
  - Identity and Access Management documentation (*https://oreil.ly/EtQcO*)
  - Google Cloud security best practices center (*https://oreil.ly/sBpOv*)
  - Google Cloud Architecture Framework (*https://oreil.ly/frunB*)

Finally, there are many excellent online courses available. The following are just a few examples:

- Coursera | Azure: Identity and Access Management (*https://oreil.ly/ymh1z*)
- Simplilearn | Introduction to AWS Identity and Access Management (IAM) (*https://oreil.ly/yi4KD*)

CHAPTER 16

Secure Network Infrastructure

When we talk about securing network infrastructure, we're referring to the hardware and software that enables network connectivity, communication, operations, and management of business networks. This includes routers, switches, wireless access points (WAPs), cables, firewalls, network security devices, and management software often used for network orchestration.

When we think about securing our IT environments, it's easy to focus our attention on application and operating system security while overlooking fundamental building blocks of an environment, such as the network infrastructure.

However, attacks against network infrastructure can have a very real business impact. The threats include denial of service (DoS) attacks, which cause unexpected outages, and man-in-the-middle attacks, where the attacker reroutes traffic on a network to a system they control, allowing them to intercept, inspect, and possibly modify it.

A solidly built network with proper segmentation, access controls, monitoring, and hardening will significantly hamper an attacker's efforts to move laterally within a network or to exfiltrate data and help to keep them contained within a particular area of the network in the event that a breach should occur.

There are many books specializing in network security, of all shapes and sizes. In this brief chapter, we won't dive deeply into every single aspect of how to secure a network; we'll focus on the general concepts you should be aware of and introduce the fundamentals of network management practices that you can employ within your environment to harden your network infrastructure against a range of attacks.

Device Hardening

Hardening network devices is an effective way to drastically reduce the risk of compromise or abuse of a network device and, by extension, your environment. It requires that you do significantly more than just bring devices online in their default state and forget about them. Hardening is about securely configuring your routers, switches, and WAPs by disabling unnecessary services, optimizing device settings from their default state (creating secure configuration benchmarks), employing encryption, restricting access, and keeping devices patched and updated.

Firmware/Software Patching

Network devices run software or firmware that requires regular patching to address vulnerabilities. It's a common misconception that firmware-based devices are somehow more secure and less susceptible to security flaws than devices like desktops, servers, or mobile phones. This is not the case—network infrastructure needs to be maintained and updated like any other device you're responsible for securing.

Unlike operating system patches, patches for network devices are often delivered as a single firmware image that updates the entire system rather than incrementally updating individual components such as drivers or applications. This means upgrading typically involves replacing the existing software with a completely new version, preserving only the device configuration. This isn't the case for all devices, though; for example, enterprise firewalls from vendors like Cisco, Palo Alto, Fortinet, and Checkpoint support incremental patching rather than requiring a full firmware install, so it's best to consult the device's documentation before you begin.

Automated and scheduled updates for network infrastructure are unusual, so a more manual approach to vetting and installing patches is typically required. Manually managing core infrastructure patching isn't a bad thing, though, as a failed update means you just caused an outage that likely has a business impact that can be measured in dollars. Patching requires care and diligence to ensure you don't cause an outage, but it's important to keep on top of it so that you can mitigate risk and remediate security issues as they're discovered and patched. Typically, vendors will include release notes with updates that contain details of the changes and the bugs, including security vulnerabilities, that have been fixed.

Patching and updating deployment methods will vary from vendor to vendor, as will the requirements for backing up configuration beforehand and the amount of time required for an update. We recommend getting to know your vendor documentation before you initiate an upgrade process so that you fully understand the requirements and the backout/recovery process in case the upgrade fails.

On consumer-grade equipment, the process is generally as simple as downloading a binary package from a website, verifying the signature, and installing it via a web interface by uploading it to the relevant form. With enterprise-grade equipment upgrades, it can be a bit more complicated, and it's important to prepare adequately. Again, you should consult the specific vendor's documentation when upgrading software or firmware, but in our experience a typical upgrade/patch process will flow something like this:

1. Notify stakeholders and schedule the change/patch using your existing change control process (this is especially important if the patching process will create a temporary outage).

2. Download the right update or firmware image from the vendor.

3. Make sure your device supports the patch (depending on the device type, you may need to meet hardware requirements for the patch to work).

4. Trust but verify the patch. Hash the version you download and match it up with the vendor's documentation to make sure you have the right image and not something backdoored.

5. Back up the configuration of the existing device (and be familiar with how to restore the device from scratch).

6. Once you're in the change window for the upgrade, upload the new update or firmware to the device.

7. Execute the upgrade process, following the vendor's instructions (which may call for the device to be restarted).

8. Perform functional testing to validate that the device is working as expected. If you're using network management software (such as PRTG, Nagios, OpManager, etc.), this can be automated as you observe alarms automatically clearing.

9. Communicate the result of the upgrade. (You just worked all night to get this thing patched, so let people know about it!)

Services

In the past, hardening network devices was a largely manual process: you'd run a port scan, manually review the results, and turn off unneeded services, all by hand. Modern approaches to network management, however, utilize IaC and DevOps to automate as much of this process as possible.

By treating device configurations as code and managing them in version control (e.g., GitHub), you can use the same deployment methodology used in CI/CD pipelines to configure servers and deploy applications to your network infrastructure. The configuration files essentially become the "source code" that defines the desired state you want the network device to be in.

If you're working in an enterprise, both Red Hat (*https://oreil.ly/uDVnq*) and Ansible (*https://oreil.ly/oBZq7*) have published case studies that provide in-depth examples of how CI/CD can be adapted to network management, and it's worth noting that many DevOps engineers today already are managing cloud infrastructure this way.

 Legacy network configuration files are full of secrets. Before you move toward CI/CD, be sure you have a solid understanding of how to use CI/CD with a secret management platform (HashiCorp Vault, GitHub Secrets, etc.).

If moving toward DevOps is too big of a change to manage minimally, you should be completing a manual security review before deploying to production. This is ideally done by executing an authenticated vulnerability scan against the device, which can parse the device's running configuration for any problems. If you're working in a security program that hasn't been funded yet, you can lean on open source tools like Nmap. Even though this isn't the most efficient method, it's still a valid one, and one that as a practitioner you should be familiar with. With Nmap, you can determine which TCP and UDP (Transmission Control Protocol and User Datagram Protocol) ports are listening on equipment and make educated inferences to determine which services may be running.

To scan all TCP ports, use the command:

```
nmap -sT -p1-65535 10.0.10.1/32
```

where:

`-sT`

Sets the scan type to TCP connect. Nmap has many scanning options, many of which are used to circumvent poor firewalling or ACLs. However, if you're on the same network as the equipment being scanned and it's not using any counter-measures, you can connect using a true TCP handshake and obtain more accurate results.

`-p1-65535`

Tells Nmap to scan ports from 1 to 65535—i.e., all of them. This can be time-consuming, but it will give you a more complete view, especially if the vendor has taken the not-unusual approach of running additional management interfaces on higher ports.

`10.0.10.1/32`

Indicates the target to scan: in this case, the host 10.0.10.1. The /32 is CIDR notation for a single host. Entire networks can be scanned by using the correct CIDR notation for a wider range.

This will produce something like the following output:

```
$ nmap -sT -p1-65535 10.0.10.1/32
Starting Nmap 7.12 ( https://nmap.org ) at 2016-01-01 00:00 UTC
Nmap scan report for targethost (10.0.10.1)
Host is up (0.00043s latency).
Not shown: 1021 closed ports
PORT    STATE SERVICE
23/tcp  open  telnet
80/tcp  open  http
443/tcp open  https
```

In this case, ports 23, 80, and 443 are open. Typically, these ports are assigned to Telnet, HTTP, and HTTPS. This is not an entirely unusual set of results; Telnet is most likely used for command-line remote administration, while HTTP and HTTPS are used to present the same web-based management interface with and without encrypted transport.

In this example, we will consider how the host should be administered. If the command line is to be used exclusively, disabling the HTTP and HTTPS interfaces is likely to be worthwhile, as this will remove the opportunity to pass data to the code that runs the internal web server, thus reducing the attack surface available to an attacker. In this case, it would also be advisable to determine if the device can use an encrypted protocol, such as SSH, as opposed to the clear-text Telnet. If SSH is available, enabling that protocol and disabling Telnet is a must.

This process can be repeated, substituting the -sT with -sU to scan all the UDP ports. UDP ports are likely to highlight SNMP and time synchronization services.

SNMP

The Simple Network Management Protocol (SNMP) is a widely used protocol for monitoring and managing network devices. It allows administrators to collect performance metrics, configure devices, and receive alerts. However, SNMP has had a history of security vulnerabilities, particularly in its earlier versions:

- SNMPv1, the original and least secure version, uses plain-text community strings for authentication, which can be intercepted easily.
- SNMPv2c adds some security enhancements but still uses the weak community string authentication model.
- SNMPv3 (the most recent version at the time of writing) includes authentication, encryption, and access control.

SNMPv1 and v2c should be considered insecure and deprecated protocols and should not be allowed on your network. They lack encryption, can be intercepted, and increase the network's attack surface.

Access to SNMP is granted via *community strings* (essentially, passwords). By default, these are set to "public" for read-only access and "private" for read/write access.

The number one configuration change to make with regard to SNMP is changing the community strings to something other than the defaults. There are three main reasons for this:

- Data that can be obtained even via the public community string is often very sensitive and, at the very least, will leak information about your organization's network architecture. This sort of information can be very useful for attackers in determining other targets within your network and avoiding your defenses. The available data ranges from IP addressing information to, in some cases, user credentials stored in the configuration.

- The private community string allows an attacker to reconfigure devices. If an attacker can control your organization's network infrastructure, then your defenses are no longer effective, and you may not even know about it.

- SNMP produces vastly disproportionate output compared to its input. This means an open SNMP service (i.e., one using the default credentials) can easily be used by others as an amplifier for DoS attacks.

Encrypted Protocols

Historically, network devices have often lagged behind servers and operating systems in their support for secure, encrypted management protocols. While modern servers almost universally support SSH for command-line access and HTTPS for web-based management, network gear has been slower to adopt these best practices.

It's not uncommon to find network devices, especially older models, with insecure protocols like Telnet and HTTP enabled by default. In the earlier port scanning example, we saw a device with both HTTP and HTTPS configured for the web interface, but only Telnet was available for CLI access. This is a risky configuration that exposes management traffic to potential eavesdropping and credential theft.

However, the situation is improving as network vendors increasingly prioritize security in their products. Most current-generation network operating systems support secure protocols like SSHv2 for the CLI and HTTPS/TLS for the web GUI. The challenge, especially when working in environments with high amounts of legacy (unsupported) infrastructure, is ensuring that these capabilities are consistently enabled and insecure legacy protocols are disabled.

If your vulnerability management program has identified unencrypted protocols in your core network services, and you have no mechanism to force secure remote management mechanisms, you essentially have three options:

1. Schedule the device for replacement.

2. Disable all remote administrative functionality and manage the device locally using a serial cable. (Obviously, this is an option of last resort as you can now only manage the device in person.)

3. Accept the risk.

Management Network

Networking equipment typically allows configuration that restricts access to configuration and management functions to a single physical network interface. It's a best practice to build a dedicated management network and configure all devices to restrict access to their management consoles to network interfaces that are connected only to that network.

Access to the management network can be exclusively through a bastion host or VPN, meaning that no management consoles are placed on either public or internal networks other than for those with credentials to access the bastion host VPN. Restricting access to these interfaces means that an attacker will have to compromise the management network before attempting to compromise a targeted device's management interface.

 Even with a bastion host or VPN, it's important to apply the principle of least privilege and grant access only to the specific devices and functions that are needed. Role-based access control and privilege account management solutions (like HashiCorp Boundary (*https://www.boundaryproject.io*), Apache Guacamole (*https://guacamole.apache.org*), and Teleport (*https://goteleport.com*)) can help you achieve this and provide a secure path to IaC management, but you should test and understand how they work before actually using these services in production.

In a more advanced network, the management network might employ the software-defined perimeter (SDP) or zero trust network access (ZTNA) principle. With these approaches, there's no permanent network access at all; each administrative session is dynamically authenticated and authorized based on multiple factors like user identity, device health, and behavioral context. For more on zero trust architectures, consider reviewing NIST special publication 800-207 (*https://oreil.ly/dHlX9*).

Hardware Devices

The security of network hardware devices can sometimes be overlooked. However, they form the backbone of our communications. Devices such as bastion hosts, routers, and switches each play specialized roles in protecting sensitive data and maintaining robust network security.

Bastion Hosts

Bastion hosts (or jump boxes) play a critical role in securing access to sensitive infrastructure and management interfaces. These specifically hardened servers act as the single entry point to a protected network and provide a controlled and auditable gateway for administrative access. They run only the software and services that are required, which keeps the attack surface low.

Routers

While the general device hardening principles (like patching, disabling unnecessary services, and using encrypted management protocols) apply to routers as well, there are some additional router-specific security measures to consider. Access control lists (ACLs) are sets of rules that allow or deny traffic based on IP address, protocol, or port. They're stateless, meaning that (unlike a stateful firewall) they do not keep track of the TCP connection state.

A typical Cisco router ACL looks like this:

```
access-list 100 permit tcp 10.10.10.0 0.0.0.255 any eq 80
access-list 100 permit tcp 10.10.10.0 0.0.0.255 any eq 443
access-list 100 permit tcp host 10.10.20.5 any eq 22
access-list 100 permit udp 10.10.30.0 0.0.0.255 host 10.10.40.10 eq 161
access-list 100 deny ip any any
!
interface GigabitEthernet0/0
ip access-group 100 in
!
```

which:

1. Permits HTTP (TCP/80) traffic from the 10.10.10.0/24 subnet to any destination
2. Permits HTTPS (TCP/443) traffic from the 10.10.10.0/24 subnet to any destination
3. Permits SSH (TCP/22) traffic from host 10.10.20.5 to any destination
4. Permits SNMP (UDP/161) traffic from subnet 10.10.30.0/24 to host 10.10.40.10
5. Denies all other traffic

And the last lines (6–9) apply the ACL (100) to the interface (ethernet port) 0/0.

Routers may, depending on the vendor and default configuration, ship with dynamic routing protocols such as the Interior Gateway Protocol (IGP), Routing Information Protocol version 2 (RIPv2), Enhanced Interior Gateway Routing Protocol (EIGRP), or Open Shortest Path First (OSPF). These protocols, if used properly, can dynamically determine the fastest routing path between two hosts and route around failed devices, links, and network segments. However, if they're improperly configured, an attacker can leverage such protocols to route traffic via a malicious device that they control for the purposes of eavesdropping or launching a man-in-the-middle attack.

As a best practice, you should review the appropriate CIS Benchmark (*https://oreil.ly/ GhiXr*) for the device you are responsible for to understand its intricacies, as each routing protocol and device has specific areas of concern you should be aware of.

Switches

As with routers, while the general device hardening principles discussed earlier apply to switches too, there are some additional switch-specific security features worth exploring in more depth. For example, modern managed layer 2 switches support VLANs, which provide logical segmentation of the network. VLANs allow you to group devices together and isolate them from other parts of the network, restricting the scope of broadcast traffic and applying ACLs to control traffic between segments. However, VLANs are not as secure as physical air-gapping and are still susceptible to attacks like VLAN hopping if switches are misconfigured.

Another important switch security feature is port security. This allows you to lock down switch ports to allow only specific MAC addresses to connect (either statically configured or dynamically learned). Port security helps prevent unauthorized devices from being plugged into the network and protects against MAC spoofing attacks. It should be enabled on all access ports where end user devices connect.

In addition to using VLANs and enabling port security, other switch-hardening best practices include disabling unused ports, limiting the number of MAC addresses per port, enabling DHCP snooping and dynamic ARP inspection, using private VLANs, and securing the spanning tree protocol. The specific configuration varies by vendor, so consult your vendor's product documentation and security baseline guides.

Again, it is highly recommended that you download and review the appropriate CIS Benchmarks for the switches you use, as each brand has its own unique challenges you will need to be aware of.

Wireless Devices

With the rise in popularity of Internet of Things (IoT) devices, we have a lot more to worry about when it comes to wireless equipment today than just WAPs. Almost anything can have a MAC address, from toasters to gaming devices, lightbulbs to medical implants. While we won't go into the specifics of how to secure your wireless toaster, we will cover the basic wireless protocols and security protocols to be aware of. If you need help with the toaster, just make sure to keep up-to-date on patches, firmware upgrades, and burnt toast.

Communication protocols

There are a handful of different wireless protocols to be aware of. Many of these protocols are commonly forgotten about in a security context but can be used as a way of attacking larger infrastructure or making social engineering attempts more successful. The Flipper Zero, for example, with its many uses, has the capability of compromising or cloning devices using each of the following protocols in some way or another:

Bluetooth
Bluetooth uses a short-range wireless signal to communicate between devices up to 10–100 meters away. The easy pairing makes Bluetooth convenient for consumers to connect personal gadgets without wires. However, Bluetooth security depends on device-specific PINs that often use guessable or default codes which are vulnerable to threats like Bluesnarfing (data theft) or Bluebugging (device control). Each new Bluetooth version attempts to improve security, but eavesdropping and data theft are still possible.

4G/5G cellular networks
4G LTE and the emerging 5G standard provide wireless connectivity across the mobile phone network. They offer much wider coverage and higher speeds than WiFi and are more secure, thanks to standardized encryption across the infrastructure. However, weaknesses have been found in older 2G and 3G networks.

Zigbee
Zigbee is a low-power, low-data-rate wireless protocol common in IoT devices like home security systems, home automation/controls, and sensors that transmit small amounts of noncritical data. Security relies on established encryption standards, but risks remain if devices have poor access controls or vulnerable web interfaces.

Near-Field Communication (NFC)
NFC powers tap-to-pay transactions and quick connections between smartphones and payment terminals up to 1–2 inches apart. This very short range limits its eavesdropping threats, and encryption is required by payment standards, but account theft is still possible in crowded spaces.

Security protocols

Wireless security protocols prevent unauthorized access to the wireless packets floating through the air. There are several protocols in use, all with their own strengths and weaknesses:

Wired Equivalent Privacy (WEP)

In 1997, when the original 802.11 WiFi standard was released, it included WEP, which supposedly offered the same level of confidentiality that users today now expect from wired networks. That was not true. Not only did it have poor "password" standards, but it also relied on a weak encryption algorithm (RC4) and was designed in a way that all traffic was encrypted by the same preshared key (PSK). This allowed anyone on the same network to sniff data in clear text.

Wi-Fi Protected Access (WPA)

WPA, released in 2003, was designed to replace WEP. It used a new protocol (the Temporal Key Integrity Protocol, or TKIP) to dynamically generate unique keys for each packet; however, it was still riddled with vulnerabilities such as brute-force and replay attacks.

WPA2

Arriving in 2004, WPA2 offered further wireless security advances using the more powerful AES encryption and CCMP (*https://oreil.ly/nnt09*) data protection. WPA2 is still widely used today due to its good blend of proper encryption and compatibility with preexisting hardware. However, weaknesses in underlying protocols like Wi-Fi Protected Setup (WPS) combined with crackable PSKs mean determined attackers can still compromise WPA2 security.

WPA3

Launched in 2018, WPA3 represents the current WiFi security standard, with upgraded defenses including improved cryptographic handshakes, individualized data encryption, and stronger password requirements. WPA3 is designed to mitigate previous exploits, but adoption has been gradual as many devices still don't fully support it.

Design

While we'll talk more about network infrastructure design in the following chapter, there are a few areas of this topic that we'd like to address here.

Egress Filtering

Egress filtering refers to filtering outbound traffic—traffic originating from your internal network and destined for another network, such as the internet. But why would you want to filter network traffic exiting your network? Aren't all the bad people and viruses trying to get in from the outside? (Hint: no.)

Even if we discount the issues surrounding insider threat, egress filtering is a very useful, cheap, underused technique. Not only could internal traffic heading outbound be worthy of blocking, but it could be a useful indicator that there is an active breach that you should address. For example:

- Malware command and control traffic typically originates from infected desktops "calling home" to C&C infrastructure. By restricting outbound traffic to only protocols and IP addresses that are expected as part of normal use, you can make C&C infrastructure running on other ports and IP addresses unavailable to the malware. In addition, by reviewing logs of dropped traffic it is possible to determine which internal hosts may be infected with malware and are worthy of further scrutiny.

- Data exfiltration attempts by someone trying to steal data from a compromised host often take the form of outbound connections from the internal network. Remember the example from Chapter 13? Data theft attempts commonly involve using network resources rather than copying data to removable media. By blocking access to all but the expected resources, you can make data exfiltration much harder to achieve. And again, by reviewing logs of dropped traffic, it may be possible to spot failed attempts at data exfiltration.

IPv6: A Cautionary Note

IPv6, the successor to IPv4, has been in existence for quite some time, but it has not yet managed to overtake its predecessor (IPv4 is still used to route nearly two-thirds (*https://oreil.ly/LeXLb*) of internet traffic). The two versions are not directly compatible; consequently, the major operating systems all ship with both IPv4 and IPv6 stacks, and they have for some time. This means that most networks are (possibly unbeknownst to the network administrators) running a dual IPv4 and IPv6 stack.

Furthermore, many security devices are not yet fully IPv6 aware. Without configuration, IPv6-enabled hosts will configure themselves onto the `fe80::/10` prefix and can communicate on, at least, the local LAN using native IPv6. If devices are prebuilt to use a tunneling protocol such as Teredo, 6in4, 6to4, or 6rd, then they may well have not only internet access using IPv6, but also internet access that is effectively unfirewalled and unmonitored. Why is this? Your network equipment will most likely only see IPv4 traffic and not inspect inside the tunnel to see the true IPv6 destination, and thus access controls and monitoring facilities will be ineffective. This, if it is not clear, is bad.

 Teredo, 6in4, 6to4, and 6rd are the four flavors of tunneling protocol allowing the use of IPv6 addresses transported over IPv4 to a tunnel broker. This allows the use of IPv6 when connected to an ISP that only supports IPv4.

While it is common guidance to simply recommend blocking IPv6 at the borders of your network, we have found that in practice this creates unintended complications and compatibility issues; so, rather than sweeping the issue under the rug, the best solution is to properly secure and monitor IPv6 traffic and not ignore it. This means auditing your network to understand where IPv6 is in use and crafting appropriate firewall rules to control and log traffic.

The last thing you want to do is build a network that assumes IPv6 isn't in use only to find out that an attacker has been moving laterally across your network using it, knowing that they're invisible to your security controls. To avoid this, the ideal solution is to take control of the situation and run an IPv6 network yourself. However, this is not a minor undertaking and requires a book in its own right.

Egress filtering may take care of the tunneling portion of the problem, but the issue remains that many network security devices may not be capable of properly detecting or preventing IPv6-based attacks. There is no panacea, as many devices are still catching up; self-education and vigilance are required until such time as IPv6 becomes the de facto standard in networking protocols.

TACACS+

Whenever you hear TACACS mentioned, it most likely means TACACS+, which has replaced the earlier TACACS and XTACACS. TACACS+, or the Terminal Access Controller Access-Control System Plus, provides AAA architecture for networking equipment, covering authentication, authorization, and accounting.

By setting up a TACACS+ server, you enable networking equipment to make use of centralized authentication, which (as with server and desktop operating systems) brings with it all the benefits of having a single point for provisioning and deprovisioning of users. Additionally, the accounting features provide centralized storage of accounting data in a central logging repository.

Both centralized authentication and central logging are discussed elsewhere in this book, but it is still worth mentioning that you should have a separation of duties when it comes to the administrative accounts that are permitted to access vital networking devices and software.

Networking Attacks

Just like with any other piece of architecture, there are a multitude of different attacks that may be carried out on networking infrastructure. They do seem to have become less prominent with the rise of malware and ransomware but are still frequently coupled with other attacks to bring down certain architecture or to gain access to aid in other malicious actions. In this section, we'll consider some of the most common attack vectors.

ARP Cache Poisoning and MAC Spoofing

ARP cache poisoning and MAC spoofing attacks are both used to capture or modify data flows between hosts. With ARP cache poisoning, attackers send malicious ARP messages to corrupt ARP cache tables and re-route traffic through their own machines. With MAC spoofing, they just change their own MAC address manually to attempt to bypass access controls or impersonate a trusted device.

To mitigate layer 2 attacks such as these, we recommend reviewing the CIS Benchmark for the device you're managing, looking for security features such as port security, sticky ports, DHCP snooping, and dynamic ARP inspection, which can shut down a switch port when attack traffic is observed.

DDoS Amplification

DDoS amplification is a technique whereby an attacker who wishes to attack a host X will find an amplifier host Y (a host whose output is larger than the input) and, by spoofing (faking) network packets so that they appear to have been sent from host X to host Y, cause host Y to send disproportionately larger responses back to host X, which it thinks it is the originator of the requests. The result is that host X is flooded with much more traffic than the attacker produced originally, thus "amplifying" the attack.

To prevent such attacks, there are two areas for consideration:

Avoid being an amplifier.
> As a network administrator or security professional, you have a responsibility to make sure that your infrastructure can't be used to unwittingly attack others. This means that you need to think about how you have network protocols configured and available on the public internet, especially for services like DNS (see the Cloudflare whitepaper "DNS and the Threat of DDoS" (*https://oreil.ly/xNfAS*) for more information on this).

Avoid being the victim.
> Where at all possible, public-facing services should be deployed behind a content delivery network (CDN) that protects against DDoS attacks. At the time of writing, services like Cloudflare (*https://oreil.ly/wlflf*) that can be used for reverse proxying still provide reliable free plans that offer good protection against DDoS attacks. However, it's important to remember that once you configure your public-facing services to use such a service, you need to go back and restrict access to those public services so that only that service can connect.

VPN Attacks

Flaws in widely used SSL-VPN and IPSec-VPN enterprise solutions have offered increased opportunities to breach company networks with stolen credentials or unpatched bugs. Don't forget to check regularly with your hardware manufacturer for patches and disclosed vulnerabilities!

Wireless

Wireless technologies have become ubiquitous. From smartphones to connected home appliances, we love the convenience. Wireless protocols allow a large array of different devices with different security capabilities to communicate. This convenience comes with security risks that we as security professionals (and boy is that weird to write) need to be aware of. So, let's quickly outline the big ones you should be aware of.

WiFi abuse

As we mentioned earlier, 802.11 (WiFi) has for the past 20 years or so been something of a security cat-and-mouse game. From 1999 to 2003 we had to deal with WEP cracking, which involved collecting RC4 initialization vector (IV) packets using tools like AirSnort and Aircrack to recover a wireless preshared key. WPA-TKIP then replaced WEP as the de facto standard, but it was vulnerable to having the PSK captured during the four-way handshake and cracked (along with other attacks, like MIC key recovery (*https://oreil.ly/G4JVu*)). WPA2/3 overcame many of the vulnerabilities that were present in WEP and WPA-TKIP; however, cracking weak PSKs is still possible, and in 2017 a key reinitialization attack (*https://www.krackattacks.com*) vulnerability was found in WPA2 (and later patched by vendors) that allowed attackers to read information that was previously assumed to be safely encrypted.

Rogue access points and evil twin attacks

The 802.11 protocol allows sending management frames that disconnect other clients without authentication. This means that attackers can flood the airspace with a disconnection management frame while, at the same time, advertising a duplicate (but malicious) access point. This can have serious implications when combined with social engineering, where a user is tricked into connecting to a rogue access point and presented with a fake login portal that looks like their company portal to log in to.

This can be detected by monitoring for malicious rogue access points. Some access points also contain the capability to automatically deauthenticate clients from rogue access points.

Jamming

Causing purposeful interference to a wireless network, while illegal, is unfortunately trivial to accomplish and difficult to detect. For instance, mdk3 (*https://oreil.ly/ bySzF*), included in Kali Linux, can be set up to send nonstop deauthentication packets, disconnecting all nearby clients. Sweep jammers, which are available for purchase on many international marketplace websites (like AliExpress), are an even lower-tech method of preventing clients from connecting: the sweep jammer simply fills the radio spectrum with noise, preventing the connection attempts from clients and access points from being received.

It's often difficult to hunt down jammers, and specialized equipment can be required to even detect them. This is important to consider when you're configuring how your devices connect to the network. Imagine for a moment you're planning to install video surveillance monitoring (cameras) for a bank. Installing wireless cameras might be the least expensive option, but anyone walking in off the street could potentially knock all the cameras offline using a pocket jammer if they were looking to rob the bank.

Conclusion

Network infrastructure is often considered "just plumbing," as it typically does not directly serve requests to applications. However, the underlying integrity of the network is core to the security of other components.

By following good practices such as patching, hardening, enabling encryption, and filtering connections, you can vastly reduce the risk this equipment poses to the rest of your environment.

CHAPTER 17

Segmentation

Segmentation is the process of compartmentalizing a network into smaller zones. This can take many forms, both physical and logical. Segmentation has many benefits, especially with regard to security. Unfortunately, however, flat networks with little to no segmentation are still common in many organizations. In this chapter, we will walk through various segmentation practices and designs that can help boost the security of your environment.

Network Segmentation

There are two main approaches to network segmentation: physical and logical. Physical segmentation involves using hardware to divide the network into segments. It requires either the use of equipment already in the environment or additional capital for purchasing new devices (or both). Logical segmentation involves segregating different parts of the network on the same hardware. It requires sufficient knowledge of your specific network, routing, and design. The two approaches are often combined, and both must take many design elements into consideration.

Physical

Network segmentation should start, when possible, with physical devices such as firewalls, switches, and routers. Effectively, this divides the network into more manageable zones, which (when designed properly) can add a layer of protection against network intrusion, insider threats, and the propagation of malicious software or activities. Placing firewalls at all network ingress/egress points will offer control over and visibility into the flowing traffic. However, you can't just install a firewall and assume that the default configuration will enhance the security of your network; you'll need to configure an appropriate ruleset that takes into account the design of the network and the specific needs of your organization.

This basic first step gives you several advantages, including:

- The ability to monitor traffic easily with packet capture software or a network flow analysis tool
- Improved troubleshooting capabilities for network-related issues
- Less broadcast traffic over the network

As well as adding physical devices at the ingress/egress points of the network, strategically placing additional devices inside the environment can greatly increase the success of segmentation. Other areas where you may want to implement segmentation include between the main production network and any of the following:

A development or test network
There may be untested or nonstandard devices or code that will be connected to this network. Segmenting new devices from the production network should not only be a requirement stated in policy but also be managed with technical controls. A physical device between such a large amount of unknown variables creates a much needed barrier.

Networks containing sensitive data (especially PII)
Segmentation is required in the majority of regulatory standards, for good reason.

The demilitarized zone (DMZ)
The DMZ is a subnetwork that sits between the production network and the internet or another larger untrusted network. The servers and devices in this zone will likely be at greater risk of compromise, as they are accessible from the external network. An example of a device in this zone would be the public web server, but not the database backend that it connects to.

A guest network
If customers or guests are permitted to bring and connect their own equipment to an open or complementary network, you'll want to install a firewall between this and your production network in order to protect your corporate assets from the unknown assets of others. Networks such as this can be air-gapped as well, meaning that no equipment or intranet/internet connection is shared.

Logical

Logical network segmentation can be successfully accomplished with VLANs, access control lists, network access control, and a variety of other technologies. When designing and implementing such controls, you should adhere to best practices in all of the following areas:

Access control

The principle of least privilege should be included in the design at every layer as a top priority (yes, this is a recurring theme!), and it fits well with the idea of segmentation. If a third-party vendor needs access to your network, ensure that their access is restricted to only the devices that are required.

Layering

We've already talked about physical segmentation, but data can be segmented at the data, application, and other layers as well. A web proxy is a good example of application layer segmentation.

Organization

The firewalls, switches, proxies, and other devices in your network, as well as the rules and configurations within those devices, should be well organized with common naming conventions. This will make it easier to troubleshoot and add/remove devices and configurations as needed.

Default deny / allow listing

The default policy for any type of firewall (application, network, etc.) should be to deny everything, followed by a set of rules and configurations specifically allowing what is known to be legitimate activity and traffic. The more specific the rules are, the more likely it is that only acceptable communications will be permitted. When implementing a firewall in a live production environment, however, it may be best to begin with a default allow policy, carefully monitor all traffic, and specifically allow certain traffic on a granular basis until the final "deny all" can be safely achieved at the end.

Endpoint-to-endpoint communication

While it's convenient for machines to talk directly to each other, the less they are able to do, the better. Using host-based firewalls gives you the opportunity to lock down the specific destinations and ports that endpoints are permitted to communicate over.

Egress traffic

All devices do not need access to the internet—especially servers! Software can be installed from a local repository, and updates can be applied from a local source. Blocking internet access when it is not required will save you a lot of headaches.

Adherence to regulatory standards

Specific regulatory standards (such as PCI DSS and HIPAA) mention segmentation in several sections and should be kept in mind during the design process. Regulatory compliance is covered more in depth in Chapter 8.

Protecting sensitive data

Every network is different, and the design of yours should take that into consideration. Be sure to identify where different types of sensitive information are stored and take that into account: define different zones and customize your design based on where the sensitive data resides.

With that in mind, let's look at some of the options for logical network segmentation. You might use one or more of these approaches, together with physical segmentation.

VLANs

A VLAN allows geographically distributed network-connected devices to appear to be on the same LAN, using encrypted tunneling protocols.

The main security justification for using VLANs is the inherent security they add to the network by ensuring that when broadcasts are sent, the frames are delivered only within the target VLAN. This makes it much harder to sniff the traffic across the switch, as it will require an attacker to target a specific port, as opposed to capturing them all. Furthermore, when utilizing VLANs it is possible to make the division according to a security policy or ACL and provide access to sensitive data only to users on a given VLAN, without exposing the information to the entire network.

Other positive attributes of VLAN implementation include the following:

Flexibility

Networks are independent from the physical location of the devices.

Performance

Specific traffic such as VoIP in a VLAN and transmission into this VLAN can be prioritized. There will also be a decrease in broadcast traffic across the network as a whole.

Cost

VLANs reduce the need for additional hardware (routers, cabling, etc.), which can decrease overall expenditures.

Ease of management

VLAN configuration changes only need to be made in one location as opposed to on each device.

VLAN segmentation should not be solely relied on for network security, as it has been proven that it is possible to traverse multiple VLANs (*https://oreil.ly/MBfQh*) by crafting specially crafted frames in a default Cisco configuration.

There are a few different methodologies that can be followed when customizing your approach to VLAN planning. One common approach is to separate endpoints into risk categories based on the data that traverses them. For example, the lower-risk category would include desktops, laptops, and printers; the medium-risk category would include print and file servers; and the high-risk category would include domain controllers and PII servers. Alternatively, VLAN design can be based on endpoint roles, with separate VLANs created for desktops, laptops, printers, database servers, file servers, access points, and so on. In a larger environment, this method tends to make more sense and can result in a less complicated network design.

> Remember, just because you have all of these VLANs present and configured doesn't mean they need to show up at every site. VLAN pruning can be configured to allow only certain ones to cross physical devices.

ACLs

A network access control list (ACL) is a filter that can be applied to restrict traffic between subnets or IP addresses. ACLs are often applied by equipment other than firewalls (typically network routers).

Expensive firewalls cannot always be installed between segments, and for the most part this isn't necessary. All data entering and leaving a segment of a network should be controlled, however. ACLs can be applied to the network to limit as much traffic as possible. Increased granularity increases security and also makes it easier to troubleshoot any malicious behavior. Creating rules specifying exact matches of source and destination host, network addresses, and ports rather than using the generic keyword "any" in ACLs will ensure that it is known exactly what traffic is traversing the device. Be sure to include an explicit deny statement at the end of the policy to ensure the logging of all dropped packets.

NAC

Per Techopedia (*https://oreil.ly/oXzb0*), network access control (NAC) is "an approach to network management and security that enforces security policy, compliance and management of access control to a network." NAC uses the 802.1X protocol, which is part of the IEEE 802.1 group of protocol specifications. One of the key benefits of 802.1X is that it provides authentication at the port level, so devices are not connected to the network until authenticated. This differs from more traditional approaches, such as domain logon, where a host is on the network with an IP address and is capable of making connections before the authentication process begins.

NAC can be amazingly effective when implemented correctly, with solid processes surrounding its use. It makes us particularly happy, as it combines asset management with network security. The captive portals that pop up after you've connected to the wireless network at a hotel or airport are usually run by a NAC appliance. They can separate unknown and known devices onto their own VLANs or networks depending on a variety of categories.

NAC is implemented for a variety of reasons. Here is a list of some common uses and examples:

Guest captive portal

A visitor walks into your lobby and needs to use your guest connection. After agreeing to your end-user license agreement, they are switched from the unroutable internal network to a guest access VLAN that only has access to the internet on port 80 or 443 and is using DNS filtering. This enables them to access needed resources without the ability to easily perform any malicious activity.

Initial equipment connection

Installing new equipment from a third-party vendor has inherent risks. For example, suppose a representative from your third-party vendor Moon Ent is required to plug in a PC as part of a new equipment purchase and installation. This device happens to be running a very old version of Java and has malware that the vendor isn't aware of. NAC enables you to give this PC access to a sectioned-off portion of the network so that full vulnerability and antivirus scanning can be conducted prior to adding the equipment to a production network.

Boardroom/conference room

While you do want to turn off all unused ports by default, doing so in a conference room can be difficult due to the variety of devices that may require connection. For example, suppose your IT team, legal, and HR show up for a meeting with a vendor for a presentation. NAC offers the ability for the vendor to be on a separate network with access to a test environment, but only after a full antivirus scan and check for outdated, vulnerable software. Most NAC solutions allow for automated detection and restriction of noncompliant devices, based on a configured policy set.

BYOD policies

Now that we are in an age where most people commonly carry one or more devices capable of wireless access around with them, a BYOD policy is something that many organizations struggle to implement securely. NAC can be used in conjunction with the data stored within an asset management tool to explicitly deny devices that are foreign to the network.

VPNs

A virtual private network (VPN) is a secure channel specifically created to send data over a public or less secure network, utilizing some method of encryption. VPNs can be used to segment sensitive data from an untrusted network (usually the internet).

 This section will assume the reader has a general understanding of how VPNs work and focus more on baseline security practices surrounding them.

Many devices will allow an insecure VPN configuration. Following these guidelines will ensure a secure setup:

- Use the strongest possible authentication method.
- Use the strongest possible encryption method.
- Limit VPN access to those with a valid business reason, and only when necessary.
- Provide access to selected files through intranets or extranets rather than VPNs.

Two main types of VPN configuration are used in enterprise environments: IPsec and SSL/TLS. Each has its advantages and security implications to take into consideration.

Here are the advantages of an IPsec VPN:

- IPsec is an established and field-tested technology in widespread use.
- IPsec VPN is a client-based VPN technology that can be configured to connect to only sites and devices that can prove their integrity. This gives administrators the assurance that the devices connecting to the network can be trusted.
- IPsec supports multiple methods of authentication and allows for the flexibility to configure the appropriate authentication mechanism, making it difficult for intruders to perform man-in-the-middle and similar attacks.

Security considerations with IPSec VPNs include:

- They can be configured to give full access to all intranet resources to remote users. While this has the benefit of making users feel as if they are at the office, a misconfigured connection can also open the door to a large amount of risk. Steps should be taken to ensure that users only have access to what they need.
- Depending on the configuration of the remote network (if traveling to customers, clients, etc.), it may be impossible to use an IPSec VPN due to firewall restrictions at the site you are connected to.

SSL/TLS VPNs have the following advantages:

- They allow for host integrity checking (the process of assessing connecting devices against a preset security policy, such as checking the latest OS version or OS patch status, whether the antivirus definitions are up-to-date, etc.) and remediation. This addresses the first security consideration in the following list; however, it has to be enabled to effectively assess endpoints.
- They can provide granular NAC for each user or group of users, to limit remote user access to certain designated resources or applications in the corporate network.
- They support multiple methods of user authentication and integration with centralized authentication mechanisms like RADIUS/LDAP, Active Directory, etc.
- They allow the configuration of secure customized web portals for vendors or other restricted users, to provide access to certain applications only.
- They have exhaustive auditing capabilities, which is crucial for regulatory compliance.

Security considerations with SSL/TLS VPNs include:

- They're browser-based, which allows corporate resources to be accessed by users from any computer with internet access after proper authentication. This opens up the potential for attack or transmission of a virus or malware from a public device to the corporate network.
- They open up the possibility of data theft. They are browser-based, which means information can be left in the browser's cache, cookies, history, or saved password settings. There is also a higher possibility of keyloggers being present on noncorporate devices.
- There have been known man-in-the-middle attacks against the SSL protocol.
- Split tunneling, or the ability to access both corporate and local networks simultaneously, creates another entry point for security vulnerabilities. If the proper security measures are not in place, it may be possible for a threat actor to compromise a device from the internet and gain access to the internal network through the VPN tunnel. Many organizations do not allow split tunneling for this reason.

Physical and Logical Network Example

Figure 17-1 shows an example network in which the majority of the designs discussed previously have been implemented. Although we wouldn't recommend using this exact setup for a live working environment, the basics have been covered. (Live environments should be inherently more complex, with hundreds or sometimes thousands of firewall rules.)

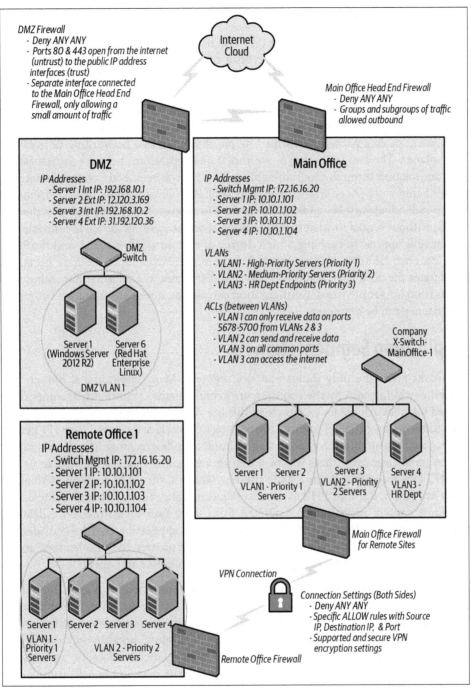

Figure 17-1. Physical and logical network example

Software-Defined Networking

While software-defined networking (SDN) is neither a cheap nor an easy solution for segmentation, we still feel that it deserves a short explanation. As technology advances and we start to drift away from needing a hardware solution for everything, the concept of "microsegmentation," where traffic between any two endpoints can be analyzed and filtered based on a set policy, is becoming a reality. SDN uses software-based controllers or APIs to direct network traffic (the control plane), with the actual movement of data packets performed by physical or virtual networking devices (the data plane). The key technologies are functional separation, network virtualization, and automation through programmability. In a software-defined network, a network administrator can shape traffic from a centralized control console without having to touch individual switches and deliver services to wherever they are needed in the network, without regard to what specific devices a server or other device is connected to. It's an agile approach, enabling a high degree of customizability, speed, and flexibility at a low cost. However, this approach does have some drawbacks. Notably, because it eliminates the need for traditional routers and switches, the security that comes with them is no longer provided. Configuration can also be time-consuming and complex, and latency can be a concern.

Application Segmentation

Networks aren't the only things you can segment. Many applications, though perceived as a single unit by the end user, are actually made up of multiple components linked together. An obvious example of this is a simple web application, which is consumed by the user in the form of a browser-based interface delivered over HTTPS. In reality, such an application is not a single chunk of code executing in isolation; rather, in the most basic form there will be a web server such as nginx or Apache to handle the HTTPS requests and serve static content, which in turn uses a scripting language such as Python, Ruby, or PHP to process requests that generate dynamic content. The dynamic content may well be generated from some user data stored in a database such as MySQL or PostgreSQL. Of course, a larger application may be considerably more complex than this, with load balancers, reverse proxies, SSL accelerators, and so on. The point is that even a simple setup will have multiple components.

The temptation, particularly from a cost perspective, may be to run something like a LAMP (Linux, Apache, MySQL, and PHP) stack on a single host. The perceived complexity is low because everything is self-contained, the components can communicate on localhost with no obstruction, and the cost is minimal because only one host is needed. Putting aside discussions about the performance, scalability, and ease of maintenance of this type of solution, however, security does not benefit from such a setup.

To illustrate, suppose you have an application that uses the LAMP stack, and that application allows your customers to log in and update their postal addresses for the purpose of shipping products to them. If there is a flaw in one of the PHP scripts that, for example, allows an attacker to gain control of the web server, then it is quite possible that the entire application will be compromised. On the same disk, the attacker will have access to the raw files that contain the database, the certificate files used to create the HTTPS connections, and all the PHP code and configuration.

Compromising the web server would, of course, still yield some value for an attacker if the application components were separated onto different hosts, but this approach would have a few key benefits. For example:

- There would be no access to raw database files. To obtain data from the database, even from a fully compromised host, they would need to execute queries over the network as opposed to just copying the database files. Databases can be configured to return only a set maximum number of responses, and the attacker would be restricted to only records that the PHP credentials could access. Raw access to the files, on the other hand, could also have provided access to all sorts of data stored in the database.

- SSL keys would not be accessible to the attacker, as they would most likely be stored on a load balancer, SSL acceleration device, or reverse proxy sitting between the web server and the internet.

These are some significant gains in the event of a compromise, even in the case of a very simple application. Now consider some of the applications that you access—perhaps some that hold sensitive data such as financial information or medical records— and the regulatory requirements surrounding the storage and transmission of such data. You should see that segregating application components is a necessary aspect of application security.

Segmentation of Roles and Responsibilities

Segmenting roles and responsibilities can and should be done at many levels, in many different ways, with regard to users and devices. You should design this segmentation in whatever way works best for you and your environment; however, no individual should have excessive system access that enables them to execute actions across an entire environment without checks and balances.

Many regulations demand segregation of duties. Developers shouldn't have direct access to the production systems housing corporate financial data, and users who can approve a transaction shouldn't be given access to the accounts payable application. A sound approach to this problem is to frequently review and refine your RBAC role assignments. For example, you might want to assign permissions such that the sales executive role can approve transactions but never access the accounts payable application; no one can access the developer environment except developers and their direct managers; and only application managers can touch production systems.

Whenever possible, development and production systems should be fully segregated. At times, a code review group or board can be of use to determine if development code is production ready. Depending on the footprint of the organization, the same developers working on code in the development environment may also be the ones implementing it in production. In this case, ensure the proper technical controls are in place to separate the environments without hindering the ability to achieve the desired end result. The developers shouldn't have to rewrite every bit of code each time it's pushed to production, but it shouldn't be an all-access pass either.

Make sure that environment backups, backup locations, and the ability to create backups are not overlooked. A physical copy of backup media can prove to be an extremely valuable cache of information in the hands of someone malicious. Approved backup operators should be identified in writing with the appropriate procedures.

While the security or technology departments may be involved in creating structured access groups, they are not always the ones who should be making the decisions—at least, not alone. This should be a group effort between information stakeholders and management.

Not only should system access be of concern, but permission levels locally and domain-wide should also be taken into account. Much of this was covered in Chapters 10 and 11, in regard to Windows and Unix user security. Additional points include:

- Generic administrative accounts should be disabled and alerted on if they are used.

- Database administrators are often the hardest accounts to control. Database administrators should only have database administrator authority, not root or administrator access.

- Administrators and database administrators should have two accounts for separate use: one with elevated rights and one with normal user rights. The normal account should be used to perform everyday functions such as checking email, while the account with elevated rights should be used only for administrator-type activity. Even going as far as having a separate endpoint for administrative activities would be a fantastic idea, as the endpoint itself could then be monitored closely as well as the user accounts.

It's also in your best interest to separate server roles. As mentioned previously, having a SQL database on the same server as an application increases the danger posed by a successful attack. Some smaller applications can share servers, when the risk associated has been determined to be acceptable. Conversely, there are some server roles that should always remain isolated, such as Active Directory domain controllers, mail servers, and PII servers.

Conclusion

Segmentation can span almost every aspect of an information security program, from physical to logical infrastructure and administration to documentation. With each design decision, sit back and look at the details. Can and should the design be more segmented? What benefits or hurdles would the segmentation create for users or attackers? There is always going to be a balance between a certain level of security and usability.

CHAPTER 18

Vulnerability Management

Contrary to what some vendors' marketing materials would have us believe, a huge proportion of successful breaches do not occur because of complex zero-day vulnerabilities lovingly handcrafted by artisanal exploit writers. Although such attacks do happen, a lack of patching, failure to follow good practices for configuration, or neglect to change default passwords is to blame for a far larger number of successful attacks against corporate environments. Even those capable of deploying tailor-made exploits against your infrastructure will typically prefer to make use of these types of vulnerabilities.

Vulnerability management is the term used to describe the overall program of activities that oversees everything from vulnerability scanning and detection right through to remediation. An effective vulnerability management program raises the security of your network by identifying, assessing, and addressing potential flaws.

Vulnerability assessment is a different discipline from penetration testing, typically carried out by different people; however, the two terms are often used interchangeably by those who are not aware of the differences. Unlike penetration testing, vulnerability assessment is automated or semiautomated, continuous, and less focused on bespoke systems and applications. Vulnerability assessment tools generally search for flaws such as missing patches, outdated software, common configuration errors, and default passwords. Vulnerability scans ideally operate on an ongoing basis, rather than taking the form of a one-time or annual assessment.

Issues discovered through vulnerability assessment tend to be known issues found in widely distributed software. Vulnerability scanners are less likely to discover vulnerabilities in your own code—that is the role of penetration testing and code analysis. Also, these tools do not attempt to adapt to the environment; rather, they attempt to enumerate an environment, discovering which software is installed, which versions of the software are in use, what some of the configuration options are, and whether any default accounts are still using the default passwords.

In this chapter, we will discuss vulnerability scanning at a technology level and how this can form part of a larger program designed to better manage vulnerabilities across your environment—and ultimately improve the overall security of your systems.

Authenticated Versus Unauthenticated Scans

Of course, the exact techniques used by a vulnerability scanner will vary from tool to tool, especially in an industry like information security, where techniques fall into and out of favor fairly quickly. However, in its simplest form, a vulnerability scanning tool will attempt to determine the information that it requires by probing the target and trying to solicit a response that will allow it to determine some detail about the software running on the host and its configuration. How this is achieved will vary depending on the type of scan you're performing.

Vulnerability scans can be either *authenticated* or *unauthenticated*; that is, operated using a set of known credentials for the target system or not. Authenticated scans typically produce more accurate results with both fewer false positives and false negatives. An authenticated scanner can simply log in to the target host and carry out actions such as querying internal databases for lists of installed software and patches, opening configuration files to read configuration details, and enumerating the list of local users. Once it has retrieved this information, it can look up the discovered software, for example, and correlate this against its internal database of known vulnerabilities. This lookup will yield a fairly high-quality list of potential defects, which may or may not be further verified before producing a report (depending on the software in use and its configuration).

An unauthenticated scanner, however, will most likely not have access to a helpful repository of data that details what is installed on a host and how it is configured. Therefore, it will attempt to discover the information that it requires through other means. It may perform a test such as connecting to a listening TCP socket for a daemon and determining the version of the software based on the banner that several servers display. This technique can be easily demonstrated against an SMTP server using Telnet, for example:

```
$ telnet my.example.com 25
Trying 192.168.1.25...
Connected to my.example.com.
Escape character is '^]'.
220 my.example.com ESMTP Exim 4.82 Ubuntu Tue, 01 Jan 2016 00:00:00 +0100
```

In this example, an unauthenticated scanner would typically assume that the SMTP server is running Exim version 4.82 on Ubuntu. The scanner would then compare this server to an internal database of vulnerable SMTP servers and output a report based on whether or not this version was listed as being susceptible to any vulnerabilities.

However, there is nothing to say that the administrator of the server isn't really running a much older or more vulnerable version of Exim, or any other mail server for that matter, and is just displaying a false banner via a configuration option in order to hamper this sort of profiling. This could be achieved in Exim with this simple configuration option:

```
smtp_banner = "${primary_hostname} ESMTP Exim 4.82 Ubuntu $tod_full"
```

Ideally, the tool would use the version in the banner as a best current guess but conduct other tests to determine if that is the true version. For example, different mail servers and different versions of the same mail server may act differently with regard to supported features, the ordering of header information, or other nuances that can be used to fingerprint a system. This, however, is not always the case; it depends on the toolset. In lieu of tools that automatically complete these tasks, it often falls to the person reviewing the results to verify them, or at least make decisions with the knowledge that there is a chance of incorrect results being gathered this way.

Authenticated scans not only remove the ambiguity from results of this nature—as described earlier, an authenticated scanner will log in to the host and execute commands to determine the correct version of the software installed, not just make assumptions based on the banner—but can also often highlight issues that are not discoverable from an unauthenticated scan. For example, a local privilege escalation vulnerability via an installed command-line tool would most likely not be visible by probing services that are listening for network connections via an unauthenticated scan. These sorts of vulnerabilities are still important to discover and remedy, as when combined with another exploit such as a remote code execution vulnerability they can create a remote root vulnerability. That is, vulnerability #1 may be used to remotely execute a command as an unprivileged user, and that command may execute an exploit against vulnerability #2 to escalate that user's privileges (perhaps taking on the role of a privileged user such as root in Unix or Administrator in Windows).

Given the benefits of authenticated scans, which as we mentioned earlier can reduce both false positives and false negatives, why is there even an option for unauthenticated scans? There are a couple of reasons.

While it is true that authenticated scans are more accurate, there is one risk that should be highlighted before running headlong into using them. Namely, they are authenticated, which means that the scanner by definition will have access to some sort of authentication credential, be that a username and password combination, SSH keys, or something else. These credentials need to be managed as carefully as any other credentials would be. It is therefore sensible to set up dedicated credentials just for the scanning server to use. If possible, schedule these credentials to be active only during preauthorized scanning windows; that is, they should be disabled during times when scanning is not scheduled to take place, to minimize the chances of abuse. If this is not possible, ensure that an audit log of login times and IP addresses is produced and that this audit log is reviewed to ensure that those times and locations align with the expected scanning times and locations.

Also, the results of unauthenticated scans are what attackers would see, assuming that they do not already have credentials for your systems; so, even if they're not a completely true representation of the systems' vulnerabilities, unauthenticated scans can provide valuable insight into what is available from an attacker's perspective.

There have been cases of legacy applications and network equipment encountering performance issues and in some instances crashing during a simple port scan, never mind a full vulnerability assessment. For this reason, scans should take place during a prearranged engineering window, and under change control. After a couple of successful scans, it will become easier to make the case for regular scans to take place on a predetermined schedule.

Using some trial runs to place people at ease, we have managed to take organizations from being unwilling to run scans at all to having a fully automated scanning program that tests a different area of the network each day, recurring every week. Such an organization is never more than a week out of date with regard to vulnerability data for any host.

Vulnerability Assessment Tools

As with most other security disciplines, there are many tools available for vulnerability assessment, both free and commercial. The value that each tool brings is entirely dependent on your particular environment and the staff that will be operating it. When selecting a tool or tools to use, the key areas to consider are:

Coverage for your particular technology stack
Many vulnerability assessment tools will have gaps in coverage, especially for more esoteric systems. For example, we once discovered that one of the leading commercial solutions that had thorough coverage for Windows and Linux systems had a gaping hole when it came to AIX systems. (A guess as to which system we were running in our environment is left as an exercise for the reader.) Some tools are aimed at very specific areas, such as web applications. While quite useful in those specific areas due to their narrow focus, such tools tend not to give much visibility into operating system issues and should be used in tandem with other tools to provide the appropriate coverage.

Automation

Some tools are heavily automated, run on a schedule, self-update, and can effectively be left to run with only minimal maintenance on a day-to-day basis, producing reports as scheduled. Others are almost like guided penetration testing tools that require specific technical knowledge to obtain reasonable results. Picking the right tool based on the experience, technical knowledge, and available time of the person who will be using it is essential. Most organizations tend to lean toward a general-use tool for vulnerability assessments and favor regular penetration tests, code review, and code analysis to find weaknesses in these areas.

Scope

Vulnerability scanners come with a wide range of features, and it is worth determining what the scope of your vulnerability assessments will be when assessing possible tools. For example, some will focus on missing operating system patches, while others will have more options with regard to web application scanning. Some will use autodiscovery, while others will need to be told which IP addresses to include in the vulnerability assessment. Understanding each tool's scope will allow you to make more informed decisions regarding which tool is most appropriate for you.

 More in-depth results can be gained by using the guided penetration test–type tools, if used by an experienced operator. A better use of time, however, is probably to use automated tools to capture low-hanging fruit such as missing operating system patches and older versions of software and have an external company undertake a full penetration test to uncover issues in bespoke applications.

Open Source Tools

As with any type of security tool, there is a large list of vendors who will be more than happy to sell you a commercial offering. That's often a good solution, but when you're operating on a tight budget or bootstrapping a vulnerability management program, open source tooling is a cost-effective and speedy way to get started. Here are a few suggestions:

FlanScan

FlanScan (*https://oreil.ly/xns7d*) is a wrapper around the popular Nmap tool (*https://nmap.org*) that can be used to perform an unauthenticated scan across a network, either internally or externally. It is available as a Docker image and can be deployed very easily, requiring only a list of IP addresses to target to get started.

osquery + CVE/National Vulnerability Database (NVD) data

osquery (*https://oreil.ly/K1sMy*) is an open source tool for gathering telemetry from individual endpoints. Often this is used by IT administrators to check various characteristics of hosts, which can be queried in a SQL-like fashion. One of the characteristics that can be scanned is the installed software on a host, including which version of the software is currently installed. With a little scripting (or a lot of manual effort), the results can be compared against the NVD (*https://nvd.nist.gov*) and CVE (*https://www.cve.org*) vulnerability databases for a fairly thorough exploration of vulnerable software installed on endpoints.

Vulnerability Management Program

The vulnerability management program is not only a matter of technology; it comprises all the policies, processes, and procedures that are used to discover vulnerabilities and see them through to remediation. After all, what's the point in discovering flaws in your system if you're not going to fix them?

Working on the assumption that if you are reading this, you probably do not have a vulnerability management program in place at this point, we're going to need to catch you up before we move on to business as usual.

Program Initialization

If you have existing infrastructure but no vulnerability management program in place, it is incredibly likely that when you run your first scan you are going to end up reading a very long report. This can be a daunting experience filled with red lines on graphs. Fret not—with some pragmatic planning and prioritization, this is a manageable task.

Let's assume that the results of your first scan have highlighted vulnerabilities across a wide range of hosts, with a wide range of criticality ratings, and that you probably have a mixture of different operating systems in the mix. If you can skip directly to the business-as-usual process outlined in the following section, you should, as it permits the use of better prioritization techniques. However, the normal methods of prioritization may not be practical in your situation.

The first step is to break down the vulnerabilities in the report by the operations teams that will most likely have the required access to the systems in question and the appropriate job responsibilities to deploy fixes. Typically this is done either by technology type (Linux team, Windows team, network team, etc.) or by function (finance servers, IT servers, human resources servers, etc.). Now you have a separate list of fixes for each team to implement.

Next, try to create batches of multiple fixes or instances of fixes that can be deployed during a single change or engineering window, to maximize the number of fixes that can be deployed at any one time. The easiest two approaches are:

- Look for vulnerabilities that occur frequently throughout your environment. By patching the same vulnerability or making the same configuration change over and over across the entire environment, you enable certain tasks (such as preimplementation testing) to be performed only once, reducing the amount of time needed to roll out the fix. The remediation steps are likely to be repeated identically on each host that it is deployed to, leading to a predictable outcome on each host and less friction for those who are making the changes.

- Pick a particular host or group of hosts and attempt to address all, or at least many, patches on that host or group. Although the range of patches in this case will likely be more varied than with the previous option, the advantage is that there is only one host or group of hosts to raise change requests for, manage outages for, and monitor throughout the process. This will result in fewer reboots because, hopefully, a single reboot can be used to roll in multiple patches, and you may only have one team that needs to work to deploy all the patches.

Once the patches are grouped using whichever system works best for your particular organization, you should prioritize the batches of remediation work (see "Remediation Prioritization" on page 234) to ensure that the most important changes are implemented as quickly as possible.

By using one of these approaches, it is possible to deploy large numbers of patches during an engineering window. By repeating this process regularly, it should be possible to catch up to a point whereby you can move to the business-as-usual phase.

Business as Usual

Unlike the program initiation phase, which is often predominantly composed of "catching up" remediation activities in bulk patching, config change, or upgrade cycles, operating vulnerability management as a business-as-usual process relies upon a more systematic approach to handling vulnerabilities. The process should look something like this:

1. Discover vulnerabilities within your environment. This is typically done via a combination of scheduled automated scans, vendor announcements, and scheduled releases.

2. Prioritize remediation activities in order to determine the priority order and timeline to remedy each vulnerability.

3. Assign remediation activities as appropriate. In many organizations, there may be separate teams to manage different systems.

4. Track and monitor remediation activities. This will often be done by checking change control tickets and ensuring that items are not present during the next scheduled vulnerability scan, indicating that they have been fixed successfully.

Remediation Prioritization

It's all very well having a long list of vulnerabilities that require remediation, but the reality is that for most people the ability to remediate everything quickly is purely aspirational. Not only is there the problem of having sufficient time and resources to carry out the work, but you'll also have to deal with issues like obtaining a maintenance window, raising change control tickets, patch testing, and all manner of other potential bugbears. For us mere mortals, there is a need to prioritize the work in order to ensure that the more important vulnerabilities are addressed in the most timely manner, while less important issues can wait a little longer. This brings us to the important factor in prioritization: what *is* "important"?

Typically, this is the point in a book like this where you will find a 3 × 3 or 5 × 5 matrix with differing levels of panic along each axis to tell you how to deal with your vulnerabilities (like the one in Figure 1-1 back in Chapter 1). Ultimately, what these diagrams come down to is having a repeatable process to determine how quickly a vulnerability should be remediated that works for your organization.

Nearly every system of vulnerability prioritization, matrix-based or otherwise, will use the *severity rating* of the vulnerability as one of the metrics. The severity rating is often derived from a combination of the estimated impact of successful exploitation *without any specific context about your environment*, and the "likelihood" of exploitation. The likelihood estimate is typically based on factors such as complexity, necessary preconditions, whether user interaction is required, and other items that could influence the chances of a successful attack.

There are multiple systems used to calculate severity ratings. The most common is probably the Common Vulnerability Scoring System (CVSS (*https://oreil.ly/J2LHE*)). However, some vendors, such as Microsoft, produce their own severity ratings (*https://oreil.ly/9TEAA*). These vendor-specific systems are often higher fidelity, as they're based on more specific information and context.

Unless you are someone who is well versed in risk and risk language, or you have a particular interest in the field, it's probably advisable to accept the vendor-supplied rating and continue. The severity rating doesn't always need to be completely accurate; for the purposes of this exercise, it serves to provide an approximate categorization.

As we alluded to earlier, the missing element from the universal and vendor-supplied severity ratings is context. A vulnerability present on a standalone PC with no sensitive data and no network connection is going to have a very different potential impact from the same vulnerability discovered on an internet-facing web server—context makes all the difference. If your infrastructure is suitably small, you may be able to prioritize based on vendor rating alone, but context can provide further granularity to help you prioritize more effectively. This context typically forms, in one way or another, the other axis of the aforementioned matrix.

There are multiple ways that you can add context, and their relevance will depend on your organization. Some examples are:

Sensitivity
The more sensitive the data held on the device, the higher the priority. This is mostly driven by concerns about breach-type scenarios, where loss of personal or financial data is a worst-case scenario both from a regulatory and a PR point of view.

Volume of hosts
If all hosts are equal, then this approach can work well, as a vulnerability affecting 300 hosts will be more important than one that affects only 5 hosts. In reality, however, most hosts are not created equal.

Exposure
Another important consideration is how likely it is that a host will be exposed to an attacker. For example, an internet-facing host will probably have a higher exposure than one on an internal network.

Having determined how you are going to rate each vulnerability, the final step is to set timelines for remediation to ensure a consistent approach. For example, an internet-facing, critical vulnerability should be remediated within 1 day, while one with a low criticality rating affecting only desktops could perhaps wait 30 days. Mapping out your strategy with timelines brings consistency, which in turn makes it easier to set expectations and to track the progress of remediation activities. Meeting the timelines could be part of internal SLAs or key performance indicators (KPIs) for teams and is a relatively easy metric to track. Table 18-1 shows an example, which should of course be modified to suit your own needs.

Table 18-1. Vulnerability remediation timetable

	Isolated LAN	Internal LAN	Partner-facing	Internet-facing
Critical	7 days	2 days	1 day	1 day
High	7 days	5 days	3 days	3 days
Medium	14 days	7 days	5 days	5 days
Low	21 days	7 days	14 days	14 days

Risk Acceptance

In the event that a vulnerability cannot be mitigated, either within the agreed timeline or at all, you may need to engage in a process known as *risk acceptance*. This is just what it sounds like: the process of a member of staff of predetermined seniority documenting acceptance of a risk. That is, they agree that for whatever reason, the risk is permitted to remain within the environment and that they accept responsibility for this decision. Typically this is for reasons such as software interdependence, where remediating a vulnerability will cause some other sort of issue, or because an upgrade would require the procurement of a license, for example.

Security professionals wince, quite rightly, at the mention of risk acceptance. Although this may seem entirely obvious, experience has shown that this warning bears repeating, quite possibly twice.

When a risk is "accepted" via a process, it does not, in reality, disappear. The software is still vulnerable, the risk is still present on the system, and an attacker can still make use of it. All that has happened is that a suitably senior member of staff has acknowledged the existence of the vulnerability and accepted responsibility for the decision to permit its continued existence in the environment.

This is only a "fix" on paper.

(Read this just one more time.)

Risk acceptance should be used as a last possible measure, and all acceptances should have an expiry placed on them and not remain in perpetuity. This helps to ensure that risks are reviewed, revisited, and hopefully remediated instead of living on forever in an accepted and perpetually renewed acceptance state. Even a vulnerability that is expected to remain for a long period of time should only have a short acceptance period, with the acceptance decision reviewed and reissued upon expiry if needed. This ensures that its continued existence is a cognizant decision, with a named individual responsible for that decision.

Conclusion

A vulnerability management program allows you to assess, log, and remediate vulnerabilities within your environment using a largely automated set of processes and tools. By following even a simple such program, you can drastically reduce the issues responsible for a large number of breaches, unpatched systems, and simple configuration errors.

CHAPTER 19

Development

As we have discussed in previous chapters, any code that is executed on a system can contain errors, and if these errors can be leveraged by an attacker, this becomes a vulnerability in the system. This is, of course, something that you do not want.

The aim of securely developing code is, somewhat obviously, to reduce the chances of this occurring, as well as to reduce the impact if it does.

Secure coding insofar as particulars within any one language is a large and complex field, far too expansive to cover in its entirety within this book. However, in this chapter we'll go over the high-level concepts so that you can understand enough of the topic to be able to identify specific areas that it will be useful for you to go and research separately.

Language Selection

Anyone who's done any coding is probably aware that a variety of programming languages are available. They are probably also aware that the choice of programming language can have an effect on a number of areas, including ease of development, speed of execution, availability of libraries, resources required, operating system compatibility, and a wide array of other factors that contribute to the decision. One of the less-considered factors is the impact on security.

Of course, the choice cannot be entirely about security. Failure to meet other business objectives for the sake of security alone tends to lead to organizations going out of business (unless the purpose of the business is security). But security should be a factor, especially when other requirements leave several options open.

In the interests of keeping this section from spilling over into an insane number of pages and trying to characterize every language, we have selected some common examples to illustrate the main themes and characteristics. If you are running a development department, you should conduct your own research into your language options; however, these examples can serve as a guide to the types of features to consider.

Assembly

Assembly is about as close to the hardware as you can get, and with that power comes enormous room for error. In comparison to other languages, writing directly in assembly provides very few checks that the instructions you are asking the processor to execute make any sense or will work. The scope of the potential issues this can create is far beyond that of a simple off-by-one error in other languages. In addition, assembly is made further complicated by having no abstraction from the processor, which means that (unlike most other languages) it needs to be written with specific knowledge of the type of processor being used.

Thankfully, outside of a few key disciplines, assembly is a very unlikely choice of language. It's still useful for security practitioners, but not really for software development. For example, assembly can be incredibly valuable for someone who works in fields such as reverse engineering or malware analysis, as it provides a route for examining an executable binary via a disassembler, without access to the source code. Assembly is also useful for exploit development for classes of bugs such as buffer, heap, stack, and other memory management vulnerabilities.

C and C++

C and (to a lesser degree) C++ are the next best thing after assembly for being close to the hardware, but without the burden of needing to deal with nitty-gritty details like processor registers. C and C++ are written as ASCII text files that are compiled into binary executables. They offer familiar statements such as if and else for flow control. A lot of code at the operating system layer is written in C, C++, or a combination of the two; prime examples of this are the Linux and BSD kernels.

At compile time, a modern compiler will perform some basic checks against the code. However, the very features that provide the power to C and C++ are also their downfall. For example, both languages allow the use of *pointers*, which are variables that point to another location in memory that holds a variable (or another pointer) as opposed to holding a value themselves. This feature leaves lots of scope for unchecked buffers, use after free, double free, and other memory-related conditions, as pointers that are not managed properly can easily end up pointing to the wrong location in memory. These conditions in turn lead to entire classes of bugs that are much more difficult to introduce when using other languages.

Go

Go, also referred to as Golang, is also a compiled language, but it's much more modern than C/C++ and has more of the protections traditionally offered in scripting (rather than compiled) languages. One of these is that it's garbage collected, meaning that, unlike C, C++, or assembly, Go is designed to manage memory (mostly) automatically rather than leaving it in the hands of the developer. This avoids many of the bugs that can be introduced in languages that run closer to the bare metal.

Pointers still exist in Go, but pointer arithmetic does not. Additionally, accessing out-of-bounds memory locations results in a panic, reducing the impact of their presence as the code will simply stop rather than exhibiting unknown, potentially dangerous behaviors. This makes accidentally introducing an exploitable buffer overflow very difficult. Most unsafe methods are contained within the `unsafe` package, so if a developer does decide to use them, it is abundantly clear that this is a bad idea.

Go is also strongly typed—that is, the type of every object is known at compile time. Variables cannot be cast to another type; rather, they need to be type switched, which is a safer operation from the perspective of introducing vulnerabilities to the system.

Go has a large community and tools to scan Go code for vulnerabilities and vulnerable dependencies are getting more and more common, meaning that the ecosystem lends itself well to secure development.

Rust

Rust is another modern language that, like Go, aims to produce code that is more likely to fail to compile (or simply crash) rather than be exploitable via a memory corruption or similar bug. Rust uses a different system for managing memory, however, involving an ownership system for variables along with protections for race conditions.

Rust produces high-performance compiled binaries, but it's considered by many to be more difficult to learn than Go.

Python/Ruby/Perl

Scripting languages such as Python, Ruby, and Perl are written in human-readable files that are parsed by an interpreter at runtime, rather than being compiled into executable binaries. The interpreter translates each statement into a series of precompiled routines and executes those. There is typically very little in the way of memory management required of the developer, with variable sizes automatically adjusting, garbage collection being automated, and so on. This removes many of the risks associated with memory-related vulnerabilities, but it does not, of course, remove all bugs.

Interpreted languages offer greater flexibility and ease of development than compiled languages, but they can fall foul of other vulnerabilities. For instance, the ease with which data can be consumed often leads to failures to correctly parse input, and automated memory management can lead to issues caused by lazy management of data. Unexpected function behaviors are also a common flaw in interpreted scripts. And of course, if there is a flaw in the interpreter itself, then problems will manifest across all scripts (although likewise, patching the interpreter will fix the issue everywhere).

PHP

Strictly speaking, PHP should fall into the same category as Python, Ruby, and Perl, as it too is interpreted and has many of the same advantages and disadvantages. However, PHP deserves a special mention because it is often called out as having a high incidence of security flaws.

Much of the negative press PHP gets is not because the interpreter itself contains vulnerabilities but because developers often abuse features of the language, like remote file inclusion, that make it incredibly easy to write insecure code without realizing it. This has, in turn, led to many issues in a wide range of popular PHP-based applications. For instance, a programmer might decide to dynamically generate the filename for a server-side include based on some user input, without realizing that the function to include files also permits remote includes as an argument. A prime example of this is having the name of a theme stored in a cookie, which dynamically loads a locally included file to present that theme to the user. However, in PHP, if a URL is provided as the `include` argument, it will perform a remote include. This means an attacker can craft a cookie to provide a theme name that is a URL to a script that they control, which causes a remote include of that script and subsequently runs the code.

Secure Coding Guidelines

When you're working on a project alone or in a small group, it can seem pointless to have secure coding guidelines. However, if you are part of a larger development team, outsource components of development, or have frequent rotations in staffing, the necessity becomes clear. These guidelines not only educate less experienced staff with regard to expectations surrounding the level of code quality in areas such as input validation and memory management but also provide a level of consistency across the entire codebase.

Secure coding guidelines are in many ways like the policies, standards, and procedures discussed in Chapters 3 and 4, with respect to code. For example, with regard to validation of user input, the following statements could be applicable, depending on the environment:

User-supplied input is defined as data that is received over a network, from a file, from the command line, from interactions with the GUI, or from a peripheral device.

User input must never be processed without prior validation.

Validation includes:

- Data is of the expected type (e.g., numeric, alphanumeric, binary blob).
- Data is of the length expected.
- Data is within the range expected.
- Data is received in conjunction with other data that passes validation.

Data that fails to correctly validate will be discarded, along with any other data, valid or not, received in the same transaction.

Additionally, coding guidelines may stipulate that specific libraries or code snippets should be used for commonly occurring tasks to ensure further consistency across the codebase.

Similar guidelines should be included for a wide range of areas, such as the use of cryptography, database access, memory management, network communication, error handling, authentication, audit trails, and access management. There may be further guidelines for specific types of applications as well; for example, a web application will almost certainly require guidelines with regard to session management and differences between requirements for client-side and server-side components.

Testing

Once code has been written, it should be tested before being released into production. This is a fairly well-understood process from the perspective of quality assurance, performance, and meeting functional requirements. However, many forget that security testing should also be performed in order to prevent detectable bugs from making their way into a production environment.

There are many types of tests (some with subtle variants), and which one is most appropriate and will yield the most useful results will vary depending on the environment. For example, the average lifespan of a release can vary from minutes in a continuous deployment environment to years in some more traditional configurations. The amount of time it takes to run tests could be a significant factor if rapid turnaround to production is a necessity.

Automated Static Testing

Static testing is a type of analysis where the code is not executed as part of the testing process, but rather source code is analyzed by specialist tools that search for a number of programming flaws that can often lead to the introduction of a vulnerability. In the context of modern software development practices, "automated" static testing often implies integration into CI pipelines that are triggered at commit time. This approach enables teams to systematically evaluate new and modified code for potential flaws every time changes are pushed to a repository.

This kind of testing is quick and fairly easy to set up, but it is prone to false positives and can often require the involvement of someone who understands secure development practices. This understanding gives them the ability to explain to the development team why the issues highlighted are a problem and to determine which of the findings are false positives.

The types of issues that are easily highlighted are often of the ilk of memory bugs, such as buffer overflows, and the use of unsafe functions. Static testing does not normally fare well with the identification of design-type issues such as incorrect use of cryptography, flaws in authentication mechanisms, and replay attacks, as these flaws are due to implementation choices, not code that is operating in an unexpected manner. It can also be useful for secrets detection, alongside traditional static scanning and linting techniques. Secrets detection involves scanning the source code for unintentional inclusion of confidential information, such as passwords, tokens, API keys, and private cryptographic keys.

Automated Dynamic Testing

Dynamic testing is performed by executing the application in real time and analyzing how the running code operates under various conditions. Rather than trying to formulaically "understand" the operation of the application based on the content of the source code, dynamic testing will apply various inputs. These inputs in turn create outputs and internal state changes, which are used to identify potential flaws in the executing code.

This type of testing is more complex and time-consuming to set up than static testing. It may also lack complete coverage, as some areas of the application may not be tested due to a lack of visibility to the test tool. That said, dynamic testing can uncover entire classes of vulnerabilities that are much more difficult to test for using static testing techniques, such as temporal issues, certain types of injection, and reflection techniques.

Peer Review

Peer review, or code review, is a manual process whereby another developer will conduct a systematic review of either the entire application or, more commonly, the area that has most recently been updated. The intention is to assess the code for mistakes of all types using an experienced eye.

This is not an automated process, so the number of false positives is often lower. The reviewer will typically validate their findings, naturally filtering out false positives in the process. Of course, this is a human process, and as with the initial creation of the code, it is subject to human error. Additionally, the level of coverage will probably depend on the experience of the person conducting the testing. Someone who is not well versed in a particular type of issue or the specific nuances of the language being used could well miss certain classes of vulnerabilities.

Software Development Lifecycle

As we have touched on in other chapters, having consistent processes is a good way to ensure that you are in control of your environment and able to spot when things are not working quite as they should. It is of note that in many system or software development lifecycle (SDLC) models, security is not mentioned formally. If possible, being able to inject security directly into the SDLC could be very beneficial. Otherwise, security may be treated as an afterthought or optional extra, rather than a core component, which leads to it being viewed as of lower priority than other criteria.

The SDLC is the normal way that processes around development are defined. There are a few variations, but most align to approximately the same structure, with a few changes in nomenclature. The typical stages are described here, from a security-oriented perspective:

Stage 1: Training
> This is the building block upon which all other work is founded. Staff should not only be trained in the art of software development but also should receive training in secure software development, threat modeling, security testing, and privacy principles. This will equip developers with the knowledge to both write better code in the first place and understand the results and take appropriate action during testing and review.

Stage 2: Requirements
> It is a common tendency to define functional requirements and security requirements as two separate lists. We recommend that security requirements be included as functional requirements. This avoids ambiguity as to whether or not security requirements are mandatory. It also simplifies documentation and keeps security at front of mind, as opposed to it being an afterthought addressed after the all-important functional requirements.

Stage 3: Architecture and design
> Determining the architectural model for a system prior to coding should lead to a more secure system overall. This is because the process of architecture and design should set high-level expectations such as where encryption will be used, where access controls will be enforced, and where sensitive data will be located.

Additionally, part of the architecture and design process should include threat modeling exercises to focus on high-level methods of attacking proposed solution designs. This will facilitate redesigns to reduce the attack surface to an acceptable level and ensure that the appropriate controls are implemented in the right places.

Stage 4: Code and build

Coding takes place based on a combination of the architecture and design specifications, which in turn should meet the requirements laid out previously. Code should be written using a predetermined language, conform to any coding guidelines that have been set out by the organization, and align with any other agreed-upon best practices.

Stage 5: Test and review

The code should be tested, not just functionally, but using security testing methodologies—multiple, if applicable—to identify any security defects. Defects should be assessed and the code sent back to developers for the appropriate fix.

Stage 6: Release

Release the code as per the internal release process. This includes a final security review, ensuring that the system has been operationalized in terms of documentation, processes, and procedures such as incident response and business continuity, as well as handing over to operational support teams.

If you would like to learn more about the SDLC, we suggest reading the work that Microsoft (*https://oreil.ly/UcclY*) has done in this field.

Conclusion

If your organization produces code, either as a product or for internal use, there is always a risk of that code containing errors. Errors are what lead to vulnerabilities. By establishing clear coding guidelines, testing your code, and incorporating a security focus into your software development lifecycle, you can greatly reduce these risks.

CHAPTER 20

OSINT and Purple Teaming

Have you ever watched a sports team practice? You've got your main team, and then there's this "scrimmage" team playing against them. It's not about winning or losing but rather about honing skills, finding weaknesses, and preparing for real games. Now, imagine something similar, but in the cybersecurity world. That's where *purple teaming* comes into play.

Picture your company's security operations staff as the main team, dressed in blue (the blue team). Now, in place of a scrimmage team, you've got a red team pretending to be cyber bad guys trying to find cracks in your cyber defenses. This is often an ongoing exercise, so it differs a little from a penetration test, which is usually held in a defined time period with a defined scope of systems to attack.

Purple teaming—where red meets blue—is like a friendly match between the red team (simulated attackers) and the blue team (the defenders). Only we're not playing football or basketball; the field is your organization's security. It's a constant learning process, with the defenders trying to get the hang of the attackers' strategies and the attackers trying to figure out what they're up against. It's like a never-ending dress rehearsal for a potential cyberattack. Sounds intense, right?

So what's the big deal, and why engage in this exercise? Purple teaming brings a bunch of benefits to the table. It helps your security team anticipate threats, discover vulnerabilities, and improve their defensive tactics. And the best part? You're learning from your own simulated attacks, which means you're prepping for realistic threats, not theoretical ones. Each practice run allows the blue team to defend your assets under realistic conditions. And because the red team is using actual attack techniques, they get to see firsthand how cyber crooks might target your systems and what they might be after.

In this chapter, we'll take a look at some of the tools that are used and walk through a real-world example of purple teaming in action. Let's start by exploring the different types of assets you should be thinking about protecting, and how attackers might gather information about those assets.

Open Source Intelligence

Open source intelligence, or OSINT, is a strategic process where you collect, process, and analyze relevant information that's in the public domain. This information can then be used to respond to certain intelligence needs. Attackers or security teams often harness the power of OSINT to learn more about your business or key players in your team, sifting through publicly available information and digging deep to uncover details about your company and employees. This knowledge can then be used to craft a detailed, personalized attack strategy.

The world of OSINT is fascinating, but it also underlines why we need to be vigilant about the information we make publicly available.

Types of Information and Access

OSINT can uncover details about everything from your company's physical assets to the technologies you use and your personnel. Trying it yourself can give you a snapshot of the range of information about your company that's freely available online. The results will probably surprise you.

Taking the initiative to discover what OSINT can reveal about your own company isn't just an academic exercise; it's a practical one. Emulating an attacker and seeing what details you and your team can hunt down about your organization gives you a real-world, hands-on understanding of what information potential threat actors may be able to make use of for their exploits.

This activity can provide a valuable reality check, offering insights that can help you strategically tweak your processes, policies, and defenses. But remember this important caveat before you get started: just like with a pentest, *it's essential to secure written approval from your management chain.* Verbal acknowledgments aren't enough; make sure you have it in black and white. This isn't just a matter of posterior protection, but also that of making sure everyone's on the same page and understands the purpose behind this activity.

Once you have that approval (and are clear on expectations regarding respecting privacy and upholding ethical practices), dive in. Welcome to the intriguing world of OSINT!

Physical assets

Physical assets—all the things in your work environment that you can touch, from your laptop to your servers to the stack of papers on your desk—are brimming with information such as account numbers, names and addresses, what services you're using, and even some real top-secret stuff. And it's not just physical access you need to worry about. Attackers are savvy; they can find out about your organization's physical footprint and then take a virtual stroll through your spaces using all sorts of online tools. Guard your information carefully, both digital and physical, and keep a clean and secure environment to raise the level of difficulty for any would-be attacker.

These are some of the kinds of attacks you'll need to guard against:

Dumpster diving

While dumpster diving might lack appeal, don't underestimate its effectiveness. Your discarded materials could inadvertently reveal a lot of sensitive information, and it's crucial not to provide potential attackers with this opportunity. Establish robust processes that safeguard against improper disposal of sensitive information. If you have papers that need to be shredded, secure them under lock and key or use a readily accessible, locked shred bin, especially in areas where sensitive information is commonplace (think departments like accounting, IT, HR, etc.).

Remember, every bit of trash or recyclable material leaving your business premises is a potential risk. Invoices, scrap papers, personnel records, USB keys, old hard drives, and other seemingly mundane items might contain valuable or sensitive business or personal information. Be vigilant with disposal processes and controls. Your physical assets hold an array of data, and safeguarding them effectively is a crucial step in information security.

Shoulder surfing

Shoulder surfing is another technique attackers may employ to gather sensitive information. It's as simple as it sounds: by peering over a person's shoulder as they use a computer or smartphone, an attacker may be able to gather valuable information about the software, services, deployed operating systems, and controls in use—or even specific sensitive data.

Defending against this seemingly straightforward activity necessitates some thoughtful measures. Using a privacy screen protector or filter is one effective approach; it helps limit the viewable angle of your screen so that only someone directly in front of the device can see it clearly.

Consider the physical setup of your workspace, too. Position computers and devices in areas where they aren't easily visible to casual passersby. Lastly, don't underestimate the power of awareness. Train users to be conscious of their surroundings, particularly when accessing sensitive information. Prevention of shoulder surfing begins with acknowledging its potential occurrence and taking proactive steps to mitigate it.

Email addresses and outsourcing considerations

Email addresses are like digital footprints, easily found scattered around the internet. We'll delve into the automated harvesting of these nuggets of information later in this chapter, but it's important to be aware that these lists of addresses aren't just sitting there; they're potential targets for large-scale phishing campaigns.

You might be wondering, "So how do I keep these addresses private?" Speaking frankly, that's not possible. However, you can turn this situation on its head: by creating decoy email accounts, often called canary addresses or honey accounts, you can track and get alerts on suspicious activities.

The trick is to make these email addresses blend in seamlessly with your organization's real ones. How? Add them to your organization's main website, where an email harvesting tool might find them, or better yet, build an entire fake online persona. To prevent a genuine customer from reaching out to the fake email address, consider hiding it in plain sight, for example, by using white text on a white background.

Another aspect to consider in safeguarding your company assets involves third-party services. Outsourcing can be a cost-saving move, freeing your business to focus on its specialty rather than spending time on peripheral duties. Roles like housekeeping, food services, safety inspectors, and other professional services are often outsourced.

However, outsourcing also opens doors—doors that a savvy social engineer might walk through to gain physical access to your buildings. To counter this risk, physical security training (discussed in Chapter 9) and maintaining current information on vendor access is paramount. In short, while outsourcing can be beneficial, it's important to stay alert to potential risks and educate your team accordingly.

Technology assets and metadata

Automated scanning tools, browser plug-ins, and scripts can provide attackers with a wealth of information about your external-facing servers, such as which operating systems and software versions are in use. By analyzing the data from other public-facing devices and systems, an attacker can add more information to their profile. This data can reveal vulnerable applications or devices to anyone with access, amplifying the risk.

Take, for instance, BuiltWith (*https://builtwith.com*), an online tool for web infrastructure profiling. You can use this tool to determine what technologies are powering a website, including analytics tools, advertising platforms, hosting providers, content management system (CMS) versions and types, and more. For instance, if you plug *https://www.sans.org* into the lookup box, you'll discover that the SANS website employs tools and services like Google Analytics, WordPress, Cloudflare, and AWS, among others. This information can offer insights into the underlying structure, capabilities, and potential weaknesses of a website, providing a useful complement to tools like Shodan or Maltego (which we'll dive into later in this chapter).

It's also important to consider metadata, or data about data. Metadata can spill a ton of information about its source, be it a person or a company. A common metadata type you'll come across is Exchangeable Image File Format (EXIF). EXIF properties are attached to documents, images, and sound files and can include details like the creator's username, custom comments, creation date, geographic location information, sharing permissions, and more. These may seem like minor details, but in the hands of a knowledgeable attacker they can be used to piece together a comprehensive profile that could pose a threat to your organization.

 Analyzing document metadata is a useful skill beyond OSINT and purple teaming and is routinely included in incident response activities and forensic investigations. FotoForensics (*https://fotofor ensics.com*) is a good online tool for extracting metadata from photo files, while ExifTool (*https://exiftool.org*) is a great tool that covers most office document types, including Microsoft Office and PDF files.

Web pages and documents

While it's essential to share information within your organization (otherwise, how would we get work done?), you've got to be careful about what gets out in the public that everyone can see. Tactics like Google dorking (*https://oreil.ly/ra9cs*) (aka Google hacking), a favorite among information seekers, can help unearth sensitive information contained in documents never meant for public viewing. The Exploit Database (*https://oreil.ly/xFBa7*), for example, keeps an up-to-date catalog of Google dorking searches specifically designed to uncover hidden data.

Here's a quick example: suppose you search Google for *inurl:wp-config -intext:wp-config "'DB_PASSWORD'"*. The *wp-config.php* file is a crucial setup file for WordPress sites. It's packed with database information and other settings and is typically placed in the site's root directory. Public access to this file? That's a big no-no. So how did your Google dork find the file? Let's break down this search query:

inurl:wp-config
> This is like saying to Google, "Hey, show me URLs with 'wp-config' in them." You'll see URLs like *example.com/wp-config.php* or *example.com/wp-config.bak*.

- intext:wp-config
> This part is like saying, "Ignore URLs with 'wp-config' in the page text." This helps weed out pages that only mention "wp-config" but don't include the file-name in the URL.

"'DB_PASSWORD'"

This tells Google to look for URLs containing the exact phrase "DB_PASS-WORD." You'll hit the jackpot with URLs exposing the *wp-config.php* file and the database password.

While this is an overly broad example intended to be used to demonstrate how to identify misconfigurations of WordPress, you can easily tune down the scope of Google dorking and narrow it to your company or organization by simply appending the *site:<yourdomain.com>* argument. You might even consider creating Google Alerts (*https://www.google.com/alerts*) focused on the technologies you know your organization uses (WordPress, for example); this way, as soon as a misconfiguration makes its way to Google you'll receive an email notification, and you can take appropriate action right away.

Personal assets and data breaches

Many individuals fail to grasp how telling their social media activities can be. Every casual check-in at a local café, every enthusiastic post about the new software introduced at work, and every other snippet of personal information that's disclosed all serve as valuable resources for a potential attacker planning a targeted offensive. These discrete pieces of information may seem insignificant individually, but collectively, they can paint a detailed portrait of an individual's habits, preferences, and even the technologies employed at their workplace.

Consequently, mastering privacy settings and being circumspect about the content we share online is really important. It's not merely about protecting our personal information; it's also about defending the integrity of the organizations we are affiliated with. From an organizational perspective, implementing an all-encompassing security awareness program that extends from workplace to home can significantly lessen this threat.

Online forums, regardless of their public or private status, can also potentially unleash a myriad of security vulnerabilities. In their sincere attempt to troubleshoot a technical issue or assist others, employees may (and historically have) unintentionally leak sensitive information, such as software build numbers, log files, and error messages. These seemingly harmless exchanges are a treasure trove for cyber adversaries.

Large corporations are all too familiar with data breaches. From CVS to the IRS, many high-profile organizations have suffered substantial breaches over the years, making the records of millions of customers freely available to anyone with an internet connection. These breaches often yield a vast repository of data that's ideal for mining, and they supply invaluable information for those orchestrating an OSINT campaign. The disconcerting practice of password reuse across various platforms can further enable attackers to breach multiple sites, which is why many credential stuffing attacks are so successful (see more at Have I Been Pwned? (*https://haveibeenpwned.com*)).

Let's delve into a fictitious scenario involving Zephyr University to illustrate how OSINT gathering can be weaponized to facilitate attacks and fraud.

Zephyr University, an imaginary academic institution, recently transitioned from using Banner to Workday as its enterprise resource planning (ERP) system, to enhance operations and increase productivity. However, this transition didn't go unnoticed. Cybercriminals spotted LinkedIn posts announcing the university's initiative and decided to capitalize on it. With the knowledge that a major shift was underway at Zephyr University, they harnessed the power of OSINT to collect more data. The attackers closely monitored the university's official website and social media outlets, hunting for clues about the transition timeline. A post from a member of the IT department enthusiastically discussing the impending change and the planned training sessions stood out.

Next, the perpetrators scoured the university's website and located a faculty and staff directory, which conveniently provided email contact information for the entire university body. Seizing upon this opportunity, the cybercriminals orchestrated the next phase of their scheme. They craftily assembled phishing emails that convincingly mimicked official communications from Zephyr University's IT department. The emails appeared to invite employees to a "mandatory" Workday training session and included a link for employees to "sign in" and "confirm their attendance." However, this link was a ruse, redirecting users to a bogus login page designed to harvest their login credentials.

Eager to adapt to the new system, many unsuspecting faculty and staff members who received these emails clicked on the provided link and attempted to log in. In doing so, they unwittingly handed over their credentials to the attackers. Armed with these details, the attackers infiltrated the authentic Workday platform and manipulated the direct deposit information, stealthily diverting employees' paychecks into their accounts.

The scam went undetected until a staff member, perplexed by their absent paycheck, reported the anomaly to the finance department. The ensuing internal investigation laid bare the full extent of the phishing attack, serving as a stark reminder to Zephyr University of the critical role online security and OSINT play in cyber defense.

This hypothetical incident highlights the need for maintaining rigorous online privacy, especially during significant transitions that may pique attackers' interest. It also emphasizes the importance of providing comprehensive security awareness training to all members of an organization. An informed staff is less prone to falling for such tricks, leading to a safer organizational environment.

It's worth noting that this particular attack scenario isn't merely a product of our imaginations. Between 2016 and 2018, several universities fell prey to similar attacks, underscoring the relevance and realism of this example.

Modern OSINT Tools

Many professional tools and websites are utilized for basic and advanced OSINT gathering, some free and open source and others hosted and subscription-based. In this section, we'll briefly cover some of the most popular options out there today and how to use a handful of their features.

The OSINT Framework

The OSINT Framework (*https://osintframework.com*) is more than just a website; it's a comprehensive resource hub designed to facilitate OSINT gathering. What makes it unique and effective is its structure, which is inherently intuitive and user-friendly, designed to cater to both the seasoned investigator and the curious enthusiast.

The framework is built around a visual interface resembling a mind map (see Figure 20-1). Each node in this map represents a specific category of information encompassing various types of data (domain names, IP addresses, email addresses, social networks, business records, and many more). The nodes branch out into subcategories, providing a streamlined way of accessing tools or resources related to that specific area of information. When a user hovers over or clicks a node, a series of tools and resources specifically tailored to that category appear. These could include online databases, search engines, digital forensic tools, or data visualization platforms, among other resources. Each tool or resource is linked directly, enabling the user to quickly navigate to it and streamlining the process of data collection and analysis.

It's important to note that while the OSINT Framework provides access to a myriad of tools and resources, it doesn't replace the need for proper training (like that provided by Antisyphon Training (*https://www.antisyphontraining.com*)) and understanding of how to ethically and effectively use OSINT techniques. It serves as a guide and toolbox, but the art of OSINT gathering (and it really is an art that requires continuous practice) still depends on the skill and judgment of the individual practitioner.

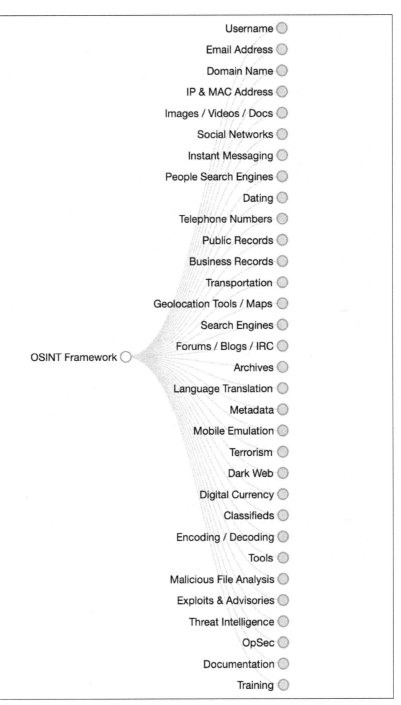

Figure 20-1. The OSINT Framework

In essence, the OSINT Framework serves as a comprehensive roadmap to the vastness of OSINT gathering. It's an invaluable resource for anyone interested in exploring, understanding, and leveraging the power of OSINT for various applications, from cybersecurity and threat intelligence to market research and investigative journalism, and we strongly encourage using it as a starting point.

Maltego

Maltego is a highly sophisticated reconnaissance tool that harnesses the power of OSINT. It can aggregate a wealth of information from various sources across the internet, from router configurations to geolocation data on high-profile individuals. Maltego's effectiveness lies in its capacity to not only locate and aggregate this data but also visualize it in an easily understandable way. Additionally, Maltego Machines (*https://oreil.ly/rnB6-*) (macros) can help you streamline and automate typical OSINT workflows that can otherwise be very time-consuming to complete (think due diligence for mergers and acquisitions).

Many professional organizations utilize Maltego for its ability to build and visualize comprehensive profiles. The software's user-friendly graphical interface allows for seamless drag-and-drop operations and enables the execution of complex queries with just a few clicks. Its value to an organization may depend on the frequency of data change and the importance of presenting data in a visually engaging format.

Maltego is available in a community version, which can be found on Kali Linux and the official website (*https://oreil.ly/YMfvm*), and multiple tiers of paid versions offering additional features (*https://oreil.ly/x3nfR*). For the purposes of our discussion, we'll be using the community edition of the software to guide you through setting up a single domain on Kali Linux.

First, walk through the basic setup guide (*https://oreil.ly/-HcfE*) to get Maltego installed and register for transforms. When you're finished, simply open up a blank canvas to follow along. To add a domain, drag and drop the Domain object from the Infrastructure tab in the Palette menu on the left onto the canvas (see Figure 20-2). Then double-click the Domain object on your new graph to update the domain to the domain you'd like to enumerate.

Figure 20-2. Maltego

Next, right-click anywhere on the graph and select All Transforms (Figure 20-3). This action will populate all identifiable information related to your domain and the transforms to which you have access (paid account tier accounts tend to have access to better data).

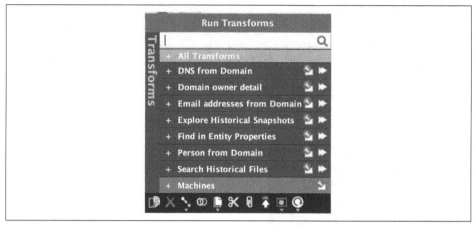

Figure 20-3. Running all transforms

While the Maltego graph is helpful, it's often necessary to pivot into different data views, such as List View (Figure 20-4), to be able to make sense of all of the information. The different layout options are available in the sidebar.

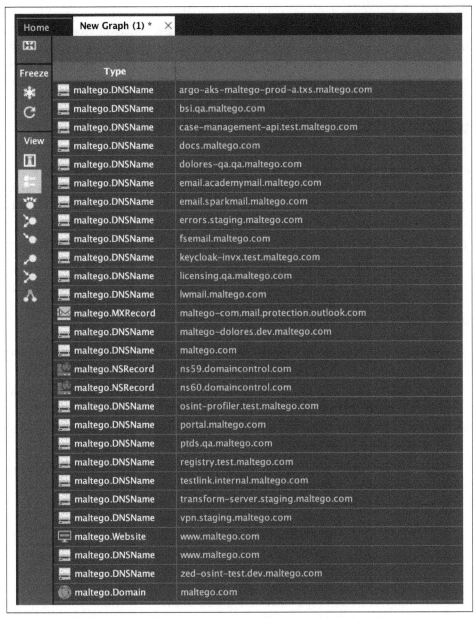

	Type	
🖥	maltego.DNSName	argo-aks-maltego-prod-a.txs.maltego.com
🖥	maltego.DNSName	bsi.qa.maltego.com
🖥	maltego.DNSName	case-management-api.test.maltego.com
🖥	maltego.DNSName	docs.maltego.com
🖥	maltego.DNSName	dolores-qa.qa.maltego.com
🖥	maltego.DNSName	email.academymail.maltego.com
🖥	maltego.DNSName	email.sparkmail.maltego.com
🖥	maltego.DNSName	errors.staging.maltego.com
🖥	maltego.DNSName	fsemail.maltego.com
🖥	maltego.DNSName	keycloak-invx.test.maltego.com
🖥	maltego.DNSName	licensing.qa.maltego.com
🖥	maltego.DNSName	lwmail.maltego.com
📧	maltego.MXRecord	maltego-com.mail.protection.outlook.com
🖥	maltego.DNSName	maltego-dolores.dev.maltego.com
🖥	maltego.DNSName	maltego.com
🖥	maltego.NSRecord	ns59.domaincontrol.com
🖥	maltego.NSRecord	ns60.domaincontrol.com
🖥	maltego.DNSName	osint-profiler.test.maltego.com
🖥	maltego.DNSName	portal.maltego.com
🖥	maltego.DNSName	ptds.qa.maltego.com
🖥	maltego.DNSName	registry.test.maltego.com
🖥	maltego.DNSName	testlink.internal.maltego.com
🖥	maltego.DNSName	transform-server.staging.maltego.com
🖥	maltego.DNSName	vpn.staging.maltego.com
🖥	maltego.Website	www.maltego.com
🖥	maltego.DNSName	www.maltego.com
🖥	maltego.DNSName	zed-osint-test.dev.maltego.com
🌐	maltego.Domain	maltego.com

Figure 20-4. Maltego's List View

Following this, you can run a series of individual transforms such as resolving to IP address, discovering which websites are hosted on the servers, and determining their GeoIP location.

The domain transform (as pictured earlier) can also uncover interesting files and email addresses. This feature scours the domain using a variety of Google dorks to identify different types of Microsoft Office files. It can be insightful to see the results of a comprehensive scan, but be aware that running All Transforms can be overwhelming due to the amount of data it produces. It can take a considerable amount of time to fill the graph with a large volume of data that may not be particularly useful.

Shodan

Shodan (*https://www.shodan.io*), often referred to as "the search engine for everything else," is another powerful tool for OSINT investigations. Unlike conventional search engines like Google or Bing that index web pages, Shodan indexes information about specific devices connected to the internet. This includes servers, routers, webcams, and smart devices, among others.

There are a number of features that make Shodan especially powerful, including API access, its search language, and its graph interface.

To get started, you'll want to review the fundamentals of how to search Shodan (*https://oreil.ly/gfiXe*). But the best part of Shodan lies in the ability to quickly pivot, so let's walk through an example:

1. We start by looking at the CISA Known Exploited Vulnerabilities (KEV) catalog (*https://oreil.ly/LeBfB*) to identify which services are currently most exploited.

2. From this we identify a vulnerability within Ivanti Endpoint Manager Mobile (*https://oreil.ly/mxbCA*).

3. We know Endpoint Manager uses many ports, with a full list (*https://oreil.ly/YpSEb*) published by Ivanti.

4. Next, we can see if we can find a pattern simply by searching for the word "Ivanti." Figure 20-5 shows some example results.

```
X-Frame-Options: SAMEORIGIN
X-Powered-By: Ivanti Service Manager
X-Content-Type-Options: nosniff
X-UA-Compatible: IE=9, IE=edge
X-XSS-Protection: 1; mode=block
X-Frame-Options: SAMEORIGIN...
```

Figure 20-5. Shodan search results for "Ivanti"

5. Great—we just found a header we can key on: X-Powered-By: Ivanti. Now we can drill in further, digging into the port information that's returned along with this result (Figure 20-6) to align with what we've discovered about this service from CISA KEV and Ivanti's own documentation.

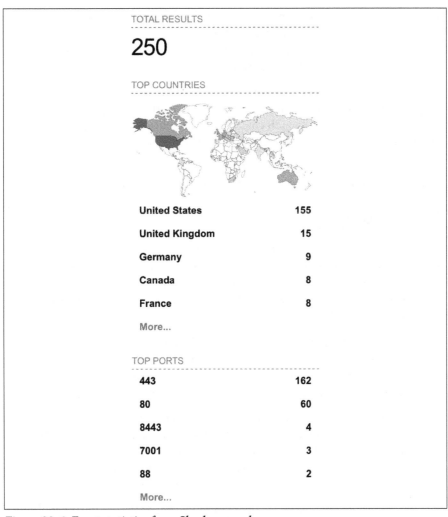

TOTAL RESULTS

250

TOP COUNTRIES

United States	155
United Kingdom	15
Germany	9
Canada	8
France	8
More...	

TOP PORTS

443	162
80	60
8443	4
7001	3
88	2
More...	

Figure 20-6. Facet statistics from Shodan search

6. At this point, we can refine, filter, and export our lists of targets, potentially zeroing in on a specific organization (like the one we want to protect).

It's essential to highlight that when it comes to safeguarding your organization, a good starting point often involves keeping tabs on pertinent information related to it. This information could include the organization's name, DNS entries, SSL common names, autonomous system numbers (ASNs), or subnets. Instead of conducting a facet analysis–style investigation (searching by drilling into results by facets such as port, location, or other metadata), you might find it more useful to monitor changes in your organization's external attack surface continuously.

If this approach seems relevant and beneficial to your organization, you may want to consider using a tool like Shodan Monitor to automate this process. Shodan Monitor provides a proactive solution for tracking your digital footprint, making it easier to identify potential risks and vulnerabilities.

To get started with Shodan Monitor, simply open the Monitor tab within Shodan and add the IP range that you wish to monitor. You can then set up a notification mechanism, such as a webhook (which could be integrated with Slack, for example), or provide an email address where you'd like to receive updates.

By employing these strategies, you can transform passive data into proactive security measures, creating a more secure digital environment for your organization.

Purple Teaming

Once an organization has established a strong security posture, it becomes vital to put those defenses to the test regularly. This is where the practice of red teaming, also known as offensive security, comes into play. In essence, red teaming involves the use of offensive measures to test and challenge the existing defensive controls, providing a real-world gauge of their efficacy.

Many organizations (particularly small to midsized companies) opt to outsource this offensive testing to specialized penetration testers and consultants rather than having a dedicated in-house team. This approach is not only cost-effective but also brings the advantage of an external, impartial perspective to the security assessment.

Red teaming extends beyond just OSINT, incorporating a range of offensive drills and skills. Popular penetration testing distributions like Kali Linux and Pentoo come preloaded with many of the tools necessary to execute these tests and exploits. These tools equip red teams with the means to simulate a diverse array of threat scenarios, further enhancing the comprehensive nature of the security assessment.

In the context of purple teaming, where offensive red team tactics are combined with defensive blue team strategies, these penetration tests play a crucial role. Challenging the defenses with simulated attacks enables the blue team to gain valuable insights into potential vulnerabilities and areas for improvement.

Conducting disaster drills is an integral part of this process. These drills simulate severe security incidents to evaluate how effectively the organization can respond and recover. In doing so, they contribute to the continuous refinement and fortification of the organization's security infrastructure.

A Purple Teaming Example

In this final section, we're going to talk a lot about Responder (*https://oreil.ly/2Dv0J*), which was written in 2012 by Laurent Gaffié. After more than a decade of conference talks, highlights, and easy pentest wins, you might think that this common pentester shortcut is no longer relevant—but you'd be wrong. In this section, we'll walk through how to use the tool from a beginner's perspective and then highlight some examples of using Responder in more state-of-the-art coerced authentication attacks.

Responder is a multithreaded application designed to spoof responses to IPv4 Link-Local Multicast Name Resolution (LLMNR) and NetBIOS Name Service (NBT-NS) queries. These queries are typically broadcast by Windows workstations on a network. In default settings, when a Windows workstation initiates a name lookup, it conducts three separate queries: checking the local hosts file, contacting configured DNS servers, and making NetBIOS broadcasts. If the first two approaches fail, the machine sends out a network-wide NBT-NS request to which any network device can respond. In addition, if a DNS query fails, an LLMNR query is made to check if the desired device is on the local network.

Responder's capabilities lie in answering these requests, potentially granting access to usernames and password hashes. This tool exploits the Windows workstation's network behavior to extract valuable information.

Here are some of the options you can use with Responder:

- `-I` is used to specify the network interface to which traffic is being redirected.
- `-w` launches the Web Proxy Auto-Discovery Protocol (WPAD) proxy server.
- `-r` allows the device to respond to NetBIOS `wredir` queries. This should be used with caution, as it can cause complications in a production environment.
- `-f` fingerprints the host, determining the operating system it is running.

Using `./Responder.py -I eth0 -wrf`, for instance, will start Responder listening on interface `eth0` and start the WPAD, fingerprinting, SMB, and HTTP modules so that, as a simulated attacker, we capture our target's hashes.

`./Responder.py` will display a comprehensive list of available options.

While Responder on its own, with its built-in NetBIOS, WPAD, and LLMNR response functionality, is undeniably helpful for red team operations to capture sensitive authentication information, contemporary penetration testers, red teams, and capture the flag competition participants frequently pair it with other attack methodologies (such as advanced coerced authentication attacks) to simplify execution.

Let's dig in a bit deeper with a more complex example that you can reproduce in your own lab. We'll detail the steps required to perform a coerced authentication attack using Responder, crackmapexec (*https://oreil.ly/d3DCU*), and Coercer (*https://oreil.ly/ arn7p*). This type of attack involves exploiting Windows services with malicious network traffic to coerce a remote server into authenticating against a system controlled by the attacker, potentially revealing sensitive information such as hashed credentials.

Ensure that each tool is installed and configured correctly on your system. You will require at least three terminal windows (shells) to perform this attack simultaneously; this example also assumes Active Directory–joined Windows hosts are on the same network. With the setup complete, follow these steps:

1. *Start Responder in listen mode (shell 1).*
   Open your first terminal window and start Responder to listen for incoming authentication requests:

   ```
   responder -I eth0
   ```

2. *Enumerate SMB targets (shell 2).*
   Open a second terminal window to enumerate available SMB targets within the network. Here we're assuming the local subnet is 172.16.2.0/24:

   ```
   crackmapexec smb 172.16.2.0/24
   ```

   This command scans the specified subnet for machines that utilize the SMB protocol, listing potential targets for the coerced authentication attack.

3. *Execute the coerced authentication attack (shell 3).*
   Based on the identified SMB hosts from step 2, use Coercer in a third terminal window to initiate a coerced authentication attack. Specify a listener IP (e.g., 172.16.2.254, where we have Responder running), a target IP running SMB that you've identified (e.g., 172.16.2.95), and valid user credentials:

   ```
   Coercer coerce -l 172.16.2.254 -t 172.16.2.95 -u <known_user>
   -p <known_password> -d <known_domain.org>
   ```

4. *Observations and analysis (shell 1).*
   Return to your first terminal window (shell 1), where Responder is running. Monitor the output for any signs that the machine credentials are being transmitted. This output will provide evidence of successful exploitation and the potential capture of hashed credentials.

Conclusion

As a defender, you are confronted with the paradox that while an attacker needs to succeed only once to breach your defenses, you must succeed consistently to keep them at bay.

While it might be a cliché to invoke Sun Tzu's wisdom at this point, like countless other defensive strategy resources, we cannot understate the importance of understanding your adversary's mindset to focus your security defenses. More than just regular vulnerability scans, it is necessary to weave elements of professional penetration testing and red teaming into your routine defensive measures. Incorporating proactive, offense-minded techniques into your defense strategy broadens your security perspective and strengthens your organization's overall security perspective. Every test, discovery, and rectified vulnerability contributes to building a stronger defense.

CHAPTER 21

Understanding IDSs and IPSs

Intrusion detection systems (IDSs) and intrusion prevention systems (IPSs) are important tools that offer a bird's eye view of your network activity. Unlike endpoint-focused controls like antivirus software, which operates on individual devices, an IDS or IPS monitors the entire network. By not depending on end devices, you sidestep the risk that a potentially compromised device could undermine your checks, thereby maintaining the integrity of your detection and alerting mechanisms.

Furthermore, IDSs and IPSs can highlight activities that endpoint security tools might overlook. For instance, certain legitimate file-sharing activities wouldn't raise eyebrows from an antivirus solution; however, if this activity involved your financial database server, it should certainly be flagged for investigation.

The difference between an IDS and an IPS lies in their response to potential threats. Both systems can detect, log, and alert you about suspicious traffic. However, an IPS steps it up by trying to block this suspect traffic. Think of an IDS as your vigilant security camera and an IPS as an active security guard ready to intervene.

Even if you're running a smaller operation, don't think you can't benefit from these tools. *Next-generation firewalls* (NGFWs) come with built-in IDS and IPS capabilities. They are fairly affordable and well suited to the needs of small- and medium-sized businesses. These NGFWs offer an all-in-one solution that's not just a boon for your security but also great news for your business's budget.

Why use an NGFW? Think of it as an upgrade to your standard firewall. NGFWs still filter traffic based on port, protocol, and IP address (i.e., networking 101). But they also include features like application awareness and control, integrated intrusion prevention, and threat intelligence feeds.

This means that while your firewall is doing its usual job of managing traffic, it's also looking out for any application-level anomalies, just like a dedicated IDS/IPS. It can then alert you, or even take action to block the threat, without you needing separate IDS/IPS infrastructure.

If you're considering investing in a commercial NGFW, a good starting point for research could be industry analysis providers like Gartner. However, from a practical standpoint, you might find it easier and more effective to stick with a platform you already know. If there's an option to upgrade the existing devices within your environment, it could be a preferable choice. Finally, don't overlook open source solutions. There are some incredibly mature options available that are worth your time to evaluate. We'll be digging deeper into these throughout this chapter.

Role in Information Security

The field of information security is vast and complex, and IDSs and IPSs serve essential roles in it. These tools are critical in maintaining the safety and integrity of your network infrastructure.

The first role is detection, primarily handled by an IDS. Its purpose is to monitor and analyze the system for unusual patterns or behaviors that could indicate a potential threat. However, it's important to note that an IDS is not designed to take preventative action against these threats. Its primary function is to identify and report these anomalies.

On the other hand, an IPS, while also involved in detection, takes an additional step. Once it identifies a potential intrusion or threat, it actively works to prevent it from causing harm to your systems. Therefore, an IPS not only recognizes the potential issues but also takes measures to mitigate them.

Apart from their individual roles in detection and prevention, both IDSs and IPSs play a significant part in incident response. They provide crucial data about detected threats, including their origin and nature. This information aids incident response teams in comprehending the threats and deciding on appropriate response actions.

Here's a quick story to illustrate the point.

Meet Paul. They're an incident responder at Red Passion Fruits Inc., a tech company that's pretty savvy about its security. The company has EDR software installed on all its devices, which is a great step for security. But Paul knows that you can't be too careful when it comes to cybersecurity, so they've also implemented an IDS to monitor inbound and outbound traffic from the internal LAN and the internet.

One day, Paul starts receiving alerts from the IDS (a system they built around the open source Security Onion (*https://oreil.ly/HyqmU*), which leverages Zeek and Suricata, which we'll talk about more in the next section). An internal IP address on the

LAN is generating Internet Relay Chat (IRC) traffic over port 80. For those not in the know, IRC is a communication protocol that's pretty old-school and isn't typically used for business operations. Even more suspicious is that this traffic is on a port normally used for web traffic.

Determined to understand what's happening, Paul reconfigures the IDS to cross-reference data with a threat feed. Their investigation leads them to discover that the IP address the endpoint is communicating with is associated with malicious activity. This is a red flag—something isn't right.

Paul employs a technique known as jack tracing using a shareware tool called LanTopoLog (*https://www.lantopolog.com*) to identify the network switch port associated with the suspicious endpoint. Once they've located it, they shut it down to prevent any more sketchy communication. Upon examining the endpoint, Paul finds that the EDR software has been removed and the endpoint was infected with a botnet (a network of private computers infected with malicious software and controlled as a group without the owners' knowledge).

Without the IDS, Paul wouldn't have known that one of the endpoints was infected. Because the EDR tool had been removed, it was the IDS that raised the alarm. This story underscores the critical role that IDSs play in security. They can help catch things that might slip through other defenses, giving teams like Paul's a fighting chance against cyberthreats.

Next, let's explore the different types of IDS and IPS. We'll look at how they work, where they're used, and why each type might be the right choice for different scenarios.

Exploring IDS and IPS Types

Terms like IDS, IPS, NIDS, and NGFW are commonly encountered in information security. However, to use these tools effectively it's critical to understand their distinct functionalities and roles. A network intrusion detection system (NIDS) might be overlooked or misclassified as antivirus software, or simply grouped under the generalized term IDS. Similarly, the advanced features of NGFWs can sometimes lead to misunderstandings or underutilization of these tools.

To provide clarity, it's essential to properly define what each of these terms represents. In the following sections, we'll dive into the key characteristics of each, their specific roles within the scope of information security, and how they contribute to a comprehensive security strategy.

Network-Based IDSs

With a NIDS, the traffic flowing through your network is under constant surveillance. These systems operate in *promiscuous mode* (*https://oreil.ly/g1OM5*), listening in on network traffic, analyzing it in real time, and alerting you to anything that looks suspicious or unusual. Snort, Suricata, and Zeek (formerly Bro) are three popular open source NIDS solutions that each offer different architectures, features, and capabilities. For our discussion, we'll be focusing on these open source offerings rather than commercial solutions. In fact, many commercial solutions leverage these NIDS engines under the hood.

Snort (*https://www.snort.org*) is a widely recognized IDS/IPS platform that has been around for a long time. It's mature, and its free signatures can be found all over the internet. Snort 2 used a single-threaded architecture (*https://oreil.ly/nXFoI*), meaning it relied on one process to analyze network packets. While it's equipped with signature-based detection, anomaly-based detection, and heuristic analysis, its single-core CPU utilization meant it struggled (*https://oreil.ly/MS5vw*) with high-speed networks or heavy traffic. However, Snort 3 (*https://oreil.ly/2BR-1*), released in 2021, is fully multithreaded.

Suricata (*https://suricata.io*) is similar to Snort 3; it also uses a multithreaded architecture, spreading the workload across multiple CPU cores. This means it's equipped to handle higher network speeds and heavy concurrent connections. Suricata can also flex its muscles when it comes to signature-based detection, anomaly-based detection, heuristic analysis, and protocol analysis. Some other useful features include file extraction, TLS/SSL inspection, and network security monitoring (NSM). While Suricata can support Snort signatures, it primarily relies on the Emerging Threats (ET) ruleset (*https://community.emergingthreats.net*), which hasn't always been updated as frequently. So, you might not find as many free signatures as you would with Snort, and there could be some compatibility issues with certain Snort rules or preprocessors.

Distinctly placed among network monitoring tools, Zeek (*https://zeek.org*) functions primarily as an NSM tool rather than operating as a signature or anomaly-based IDS like Snort or Suricata. Its main role is to analyze network traffic, generating comprehensive logs, events, and scripts (*https://oreil.ly/sO8n2*) that offer an in-depth view of your network activity. Zeek's scripting capabilities are a significant part of its "secret sauce"; they allow for complex analyses (such as packet entropy analysis), making it a formidable tool for deep network insights.

Although Zeek doesn't inherently perform detection or alerting tasks, its versatility allows it to be integrated with other tools, like Snort or Suricata, to add those vital capabilities. This way, Zeek can be used to complement and enhance the detection abilities of your network security setup.

One of Zeek's standout features is its cluster architecture (*https://oreil.ly/RgBHR*). This structure allows for workload distribution across multiple nodes, each running an independent instance of the tool. This not only enhances performance but also significantly boosts scalability, making Zeek highly adept at scaling across networks.

While Zeek requires a different approach compared to Snort or Suricata, it offers a uniquely versatile and granular view of network traffic. This, coupled with its comprehensive network analysis capabilities, makes it an invaluable tool in the right situations. Adding Zeek to your security arsenal offers a highly customizable alternative for network traffic monitoring and understanding, further fortifying your network defenses.

The learning curve for each tool may vary depending on your background, experience, and specific use case. When it comes to customization, Zeek's scripting language is a game changer: it empowers users to craft their own logic and functionality for network analysis. Snort and Suricata also offer their own rule languages, enabling the creation of custom signatures and detection rules.

Snort, Suricata, and Zeek are powerful NIDS tools that can help protect your network from potential threats. They each have their strengths and weaknesses, so it's worth taking the time to test them out in your own environment to see which one fits best. After all, a well-chosen NIDS is like a faithful guard dog (or guard pig in the case of Snort), helping to keep your network safe.

Host-Based IDSs

A host-based intrusion detection system (HIDS) is a dedicated software application that vigilantly monitors a specific host or device within a network. Because it's installed directly onto the device it is assigned to monitor, it can keep a close eye on a variety of activities specific to that host. This setup contrasts with a network-based IDS, which observes traffic across the entire network from key monitoring points.

Deploying a HIDS on individual hosts offers unique benefits but also presents potential challenges. Let's imagine how this might compare with a network-based approach in practice. Imagine yourself as Mando, the head of security at a cutting-edge tech startup. Among your team is Matt, a passionate software developer known for their late-night coding sessions. One evening, they're deep into their latest project when they realize they need a specific open source tool. Matt quickly finds it online and installs it on their workstation, not realizing that the site they downloaded it from isn't the official source.

Unbeknownst to them, the downloaded package carries a concealed malware payload. Once installed, it starts subtly altering system files and sending small, encrypted packets of data to an external IP address. Your company has a solid NIDS in place, which is excellent for overseeing traffic, but it can't decrypt these data packets or recognize their unusual destination due to its limited purview.

This is where your HIDS, installed on Matt's workstation, springs into action. It identifies the changes in system files and sends out an alert. It also takes note of the unfamiliar outbound connections, particularly at the late hour, and flags them as anomalous. Alerted by your HIDS, you quickly investigate the issue, remove the malware, and stop the data leak, all before your morning coffee. This story illustrates how a HIDS can provide visibility into host-level activities and catch threats that might slip past a NIDS.

Now, let's briefly consider EDR. An EDR solution is a cybersecurity tool that provides real-time monitoring and response to potential threats at the endpoint level. It not only detects malicious activities but also helps with response and remediation steps. This might include isolating the affected endpoint from the network to prevent the spread of malware or automatically launching countermeasures to neutralize the threat.

In our example, an EDR solution would have detected malicious activity on Matt's workstation, just like the HIDS. However, it could also have immediately isolated his machine from the network, stopping any outbound data transfer. Then, depending on its configuration, it could have either alerted you to the issue for manual intervention or automatically initiated the malware removal process.

In cybersecurity, new acronyms seem to pop up as quickly as the innovations they represent. This can sometimes blur the boundaries between terms like HIDS, EDR, MDR, and XDR (see "EDR/XDR/MDR/All the "Rs"" on page 66 for a refresher). However, rather than getting entangled in the web of acronyms, it's more useful to focus on the specific features and capabilities of these systems. After all, the name or category of a tool doesn't matter as much as what it can do for you. So, our aim in this section is to shed some light on the potential capabilities you might expect from various types of HIDS solutions. (Remember, it's all about what these systems can do to protect your assets, regardless of what acronym they go by.)

Popular open source applications for host-based intrusion detection include OSSEC (*https://www.ossec.net*) and osquery (*https://www.osquery.io*). However, if you're looking for something more advanced, commercial solutions like LimaCharlie (*https://limacharlie.io*) offer capabilities that go a step further.

OSSEC is a prime example of a flexible open source HIDS solution. This powerful software, which can be deployed on various operating systems such as Windows, Linux, and macOS, offers meticulous monitoring of host behaviors. Its focus areas include file integrity, log analysis, and rootkit detection.

As of this writing, Atomicorp (*https://atomicorp.com*) offers a commercial variant of OSSEC known as Atomic OSSEC. This expanded version broadens the feature set, introducing active response capabilities similar to those found in other solutions like LimaCharlie. These capabilities further the XDR functions, illustrating how different tools can overlap and cause some confusion.

Examining the file integrity feature of OSSEC, we find a thorough system at work. OSSEC uses a secure hash algorithm (SHA) to create a cryptographic hash for each crucial system file. This hash is stored in a database and serves as a benchmark for future comparisons. If any of these files undergo changes, OSSEC detects the discrepancy by comparing the current checksum with the stored one, providing a real-time overview of system changes. Huzzah!

osquery, another valuable tool, utilizes a different approach. It lets you interact with your infrastructure as if it were a database, enabling you to write SQL-based queries to investigate your system's state. Whether you're interested in running processes, loaded kernel modules, open network connections, browser plug-ins, hardware events, or file hashes, osquery offers a unified approach to collecting and monitoring this data. One of the things that makes it so powerful is that you can run a single simple SQL query and get back the real-time state of all enrolled endpoints across your fleet. osquery also scales really well.

The realm of HIDS also encompasses specialized tools known as *honeypots*. Acting as decoys, honeypots are designed to attract attackers by creating environments that appear to be legitimate components of your network. However, these environments are, in fact, isolated and closely monitored. As honeypots don't perform any real network function apart from acting as traps, any interaction with them is deemed suspicious.

Several notable open source honeypot tools exist that could be useful additions to your security measures. Cowrie (*https://oreil.ly/yS8ms*), for example, emulates an interactive SSH and Telnet server. For database-related vulnerabilities, you might consider MysqlPot (*https://oreil.ly/DrUKJ*) and the NoSQL-Honeypot-Framework (NoPo) (*https://oreil.ly/fB1Zf*). For Postgres databases, check out Sticky Elephant (*https://oreil.ly/jCJHH*). Thinkst Canary also has its OpenCanary (*https://oreil.ly/t27uk*) project, which will mimic an array of network-accessible services for attackers to interact with (such as a fake SMB or FTP server).

All these honeypots meticulously log all interactions, granting you invaluable insights into the tactics attackers might use. The point we're trying to make by talking about so many different solutions is that if you use a piece of technology within your environment, chances are there's a honeypot version of it that you can integrate into your overall security strategy.

The value of incorporating honeypots lies in their remarkably high signal-to-noise ratio when alerting. After all, why would there be any interaction with a honeypot service on your network, unless it's triggered by a vulnerability scan (which you can allow-list from alerting)? Alerts from honeypots are of extremely high fidelity and should be considered as part of your host intrusion detection monitoring plan.

By strategically combining the monitoring capabilities of HIDSs, such as those provided by OSSEC and osquery, with the proactive trap-setting approach of honeypots, you can significantly increase your host-level security. This combined approach ensures threats are effectively identified and neutralized.

IPSs

An IPS functions similarly to a NIDS, but with an enhanced level of involvement. Rather than merely monitoring network traffic, an IPS is strategically placed inline within the network. Its placement allows it to actively intercept and block connections it determines to be malicious or against established policy, acting like a traffic cop.

Unlike a traditional firewall, which uses IP addresses and ports for filtering, an IPS's decision to block or allow traffic is determined by matching signatures to the traffic. This offers a more detailed level of scrutiny, helping to identify potential threats based on their behavior or pattern rather than just the source or destination of the traffic.

Some IPS solutions, however, function more like an IDS and aren't inline. These solutions try to disrupt connections by injecting reset packets into TCP streams. This approach avoids the need for an inline device but offers a less stringent block, as it can potentially be circumvented by someone who knows the technique.

As mentioned earlier, Snort is a popular open source IDS/IPS. When its "active response" mode is enabled, Snort can respond in various ways when a signature match is triggered, with the actions dictated by the rule options specified in Snort's configuration file. For example, it can send TCP Reset (RST) packets, ICMP (Internet Control Message Protocol) unreachable packets, or even custom HTML pages to block the connection. Another popular free solution is Security Onion. Security Onion combines Suricata, Zeek, the Elastic Stack, and many others into a comprehensive platform for threat hunting, NSM, and log management.

In addition to open source solutions, several commercial IPS solutions are available in the market. These solutions often provide features beyond those available in open source options and can cater to a wide range of business requirements and environments.

NGFWs

Next-generation firewalls (NGFWs) are a step forward in network security technology. They incorporate the traditional packet filtering capabilities of a classic firewall but supplement this functionality with more advanced features to provide a deeper level of security.

One critical feature that separates NGFWs from traditional firewalls is the integration of intrusion prevention capabilities. The integrated IPS functionality allows an

NGFW to analyze traffic at a granular level, much like a standalone IPS, and block detected threats in real time. The embedded IPS can utilize signature-based detection, protocol anomaly–based detection, and heuristic detection techniques to identify threats. This amalgamation of firewall and IPS functionalities provides enhanced security by permitting legitimate traffic and blocking malicious traffic based on the behavior of the traffic, not just IP addresses and ports.

Furthermore, NGFWs often include other security features that align more with the host-based detection approach. These may include application control, user identity tracking, and even sandboxing capabilities for unknown files. Some NGFWs also have SSL/TLS inspection capabilities to analyze encrypted traffic, which is an area where traditional NIDS and IPS solutions may struggle.

While NGFWs provide extensive security coverage and ease of management by combining multiple security functionalities into a single device, they are not a one-size-fits-all solution. Depending on the organization's size, network architecture, and specific security requirements, a combination of NGFWs, standalone NIDSs, standalone IPSs, and host-based detection systems may provide the most comprehensive security posture.

As of the current writing, the market is ripe with popular NGFW solutions from notable vendors like Cisco, Check Point, Palo Alto Networks, Fortinet, SonicWall, and Sophos. However, keep in mind that the landscape of NGFW providers will continue to evolve over time. During the process of selecting an NGFW solution, it's crucial to take into account factors such as the scale of your organization, the necessary throughput when all security features are operational, and the specific security capabilities your organization requires. Lastly, always ask for a proof of concept demonstration before making a purchase decision.

IDSs and IPSs in the Cloud

The need for effective security measures within cloud environments continues to grow. Traditional IDSs and IPSs play a crucial role in securing on-premises networks. However, their role and implementation can vary substantially in a cloud environment.

The elasticity, scalability, and distributed nature of the cloud require a more tailored approach to intrusion detection and prevention. Cloud IDS/IPS solutions need to integrate seamlessly with cloud native constructs and adapt to the dynamic environment. They should be capable of scaling with your cloud workloads, providing real-time visibility into network traffic, and effectively responding to potential threats. Understanding the nuances of cloud-based intrusion detection and prevention is key to maintaining robust security in the modern cloud era.

What do we mean by this? Consider the case of a microservices-based application (*https://oreil.ly/tY8cS*) running in a Kubernetes cluster, where each microservice is a container that can be created, destroyed, or replaced at any time based on demand or deployment strategies. This architecture is ephemeral in nature; containers are transient, making traditional IDS and IPS strategies less effective.

In a traditional monolithic on-prem application/architecture, an IDS or IPS would monitor traffic on a relatively static set of hosts, devices, or network segments. However, in the case of a Kubernetes-based application, the landscape is constantly changing as new containers are spawned, old ones are destroyed, and services move around based on scaling needs or failures in the system.

In such scenarios, a traditional IDS/IPS solution will struggle to keep pace with the rapidly changing environment. The IDS/IPS would need to continuously update its monitoring focus to accommodate the shifting landscape, and this dynamic context could lead to blind spots or ineffective threat detection.

Instead, a cloud native IDS/IPS solution is needed, which can seamlessly integrate with the Kubernetes orchestration system. Such a solution will understand the Kubernetes API and lifecycle events, enabling it to automatically adapt to changes in the network architecture and scale alongside the application. Moreover, it should also be able to interpret container-specific protocols and patterns and understand the multitenant nature of Kubernetes to ensure efficient and accurate threat detection and prevention.

Importantly, none of the services mentioned here operate like an actual network IDS, as described earlier in this chapter. To gain that capability in the cloud, consider deploying a purpose-built virtual machine with a virtual network tap that directs traffic to that IDS VM.

AWS

AWS has its own built-in IDS/IPS solution, Amazon GuardDuty (*https://oreil.ly/KLPQe*), which is a threat detection service that continuously monitors for malicious or unauthorized activity (you saw an example of how to configure this service to send email alerts when it detects a security event in Chapter 14). GuardDuty uses machine learning, anomaly detection, and integrated threat intelligence to accurately identify threats. For example, if an EC2 instance starts behaving in an unusual way, like talking to known bitcoin mining addresses, GuardDuty will raise the alarm, alerting you of the potential security issue. GuardDuty is also one of the best tools you can use to identify IAM role abuse and anomalies. For a complete list of finding types, consult the GuardDuty documentation (*https://oreil.ly/wwzcZ*).

AWS also supports third-party IDS/IPS tools like Alert Logic (*https://www.alert logic.com*) and Trend Micro's Deep Security (*https://oreil.ly/r0vHd*), offering flexibility based on your requirements. For instance, if you're already using Deep Security in your on-prem environment, you can extend that protection to your AWS cloud without needing to learn a new tool.

Don't forget, when working with AWS three main types of log sources should be on your radar. First, there's AWS CloudTrail. This handy tool records all the actions happening in your AWS account from an API standpoint, like when you're provisioning or making user changes, as well as when making changes to AWS services. Then you have VPC Flow Logs. These logs are your go-to for raw traffic data, as they capture all traffic moving into and out of your AWS account's VPCs. And finally, let's not forget Amazon EventBridge (also discussed in Chapter 14). This service is a bit of a catch-all, capturing and routing the majority of other log sources in AWS.

Azure

In the Microsoft Azure ecosystem, a few components play significant roles in intrusion detection/prevention and managing log sources. Microsoft Defender for Cloud (*https://oreil.ly/g5rFB*) is the starting point, providing a broad view of your security posture. This service operates like an IDS/IPS, alerting you to potential threats and providing tools for investigation and remediation. It also integrates with Azure Sentinel (*https://oreil.ly/N-kAe*), a powerful SIEM that leverages Kusto Query Language (KQL) (*https://oreil.ly/ItNYl*) and uses AI and machine learning to automate threat responses and analyze suspicious activities.

While each component has its strengths, the IDS/IPS functionality of Microsoft Defender shines, offering signature-based and threat intelligence–based attack detection and prevention capabilities. Defender prioritizes security posture management, highlighting areas for improvement and offering tailored recommendations. Azure Sentinel can feed off of Defender's data for deeper analysis and response abilities.

Azure uses three types of logs (*https://oreil.ly/Wo-nU*) for security and operations. Azure resource logs show you what's happening within resources like virtual machines or databases, but you need to specify where to send these logs for review: either Azure Monitor Logs, Azure Event Hubs, or Azure Storage. Azure AD (now Entra ID, but see our earlier note about this name change) logs record sign-in activity and changes, helping you keep track of user behavior and spot potential issues. Finally, Azure Monitor Logs pull together data from across Azure and non-Azure resources, providing a comprehensive overview of your system's activity.

GCP

Google Cloud Platform (GCP) offers Event Threat Detection (ETD) (*https://oreil.ly/0mzQn*) for effective intrusion detection and prevention. ETD monitors your Cloud Logging data, detecting potentially harmful activities, creating detailed findings about the threats and their potential targets, and recommending mitigating actions. These findings are accessible in the Security Command Center, or you can use Cloud Pub/Sub to transfer them to other security applications.

When it comes to monitoring, GCP provides several types of logs (*https://oreil.ly/J1dte*). Cloud Audit Logs, part of Cloud Logging, records all administrative activities. Cloud Logging itself collects, stores, and analyzes logs from various sources, helping you to troubleshoot issues, identify security incidents, and gather metrics. You also have third-party logs from services such as firewalls or IDSs within GCP, application-specific logs, network traffic logs, and Security Command Center findings generated from ETD's monitoring of Cloud Logging data. It's crucial to understand what each type of log offers and to choose those that best fulfill your monitoring and security requirements.

Working with IDSs and IPSs

When you start running an IDS or IPS with its default settings, you may find it generates more alerts than you can manage. An overload of alerts can lead to alert fatigue, where you become desensitized and might overlook or ignore important alerts. This has happened even in big, mature security operations teams, and it's a situation you want to avoid.

To manage this issue, it's important to reflect on why you're using an IDS or IPS. Whether you're trying to intercept incoming threats to your web server, monitor unauthorized usage of messaging apps by employees, or detect malware activity, understanding your goals helps in pruning unnecessary alerts.

The bulk of the alert volume usually comes from two sources: false positives and high-frequency events. False positives are alerts generated for threats that don't exist, while high-frequency events are routine occurrences that trigger alerts. By reducing these two types of alerts, you can better manage the volume of incidents that need investigating, making your data more useful and manageable.

Managing False Positives

Keeping logs and alerts that no one reviews is hardly beneficial, except for the purposes of maintaining a historical record. It's more effective to focus on key items, setting alerts for those and acting on them, rather than to try to track everything and end up ignoring most of it.

Addressing false positives is critical for avoiding alert fatigue. It can be accomplished in several ways. The simplest method is to remove the signatures causing these alerts. This immediately stops the false positives, but the downside is that you lose visibility of whatever the alerts were initially set to monitor, which could be a significant loss.

If your IDS/IPS allows you to create custom rules or modify existing ones, you might be able to refine the rules to eliminate the false positives without missing the initial events. The adjustment to make depends on the rule in question. Some examples of rule improvement include setting a specific offset for the pattern-matching part of the rule, establishing particular ports or IP addresses for the signature, or adding additional exclusion parameters to filter out false positives. One way to do this may be by adjusting the severity level to something like "informational" and logging the event to your SIEM so that you can still go back and have that data available if something more interesting happens.

If you have enough time and scripting skills, you can filter alerts prone to false positives into a separate log. This way, they can be stored for historical purposes and summarized in a daily report. This approach prevents responders from being overwhelmed by alerts, but it also means these alerts won't be discarded entirely.

Non-false positive alerts that occur frequently can also fill up log files and contribute to alert fatigue. Remember that just because a signature is being triggered correctly doesn't mean you need to know about it every time. For instance, if your system is entirely FreeBSD-based, alerts about attempted Solaris-specific exploits might be correctly triggered, but they won't impact your system. Filtering out such noncritical alerts can help you streamline your monitoring.

Finally, bear in mind that tuning out false positives is a continuous and iterative process, not a one-time task.

Writing Your Own Signatures

Snort, described earlier in this chapter, uses a simple, flexible signature language that enables network administrators to create or import custom rules for detecting and averting network attacks. Snort rules consist of a header and several options that specify the action, attack pattern, and message, among other things. You can find detailed information in Snort's comprehensive documentation (*https://oreil.ly/vuhhB*).

Before we dive in, here are a few basic examples of Snort rules that you can use to build some understanding and gain some familiarity:

- Alert for any UDP traffic from any source to port 53 (commonly used for DNS queries):

```
alert udp any any -> any 53 (msg:"DNS Request Detected"; sid:1000001;)
```

- Alert for any traffic from a specific IP address (in our case 192.168.1.100 as the source):

```
alert ip 192.168.1.100 any -> any any
(msg:"Traffic from specific IP detected"; sid:1000002;)
```

- Alert for any FTP traffic containing the string "PASS" (indicating a password is being sent):

```
alert tcp any any -> any 21 (content:"PASS"; msg:"FTP password detected";
sid:1000003;)
```

You can also use Snort rules from external sources, such as the CISA alerts (*https://oreil.ly/VCxrp*) or Cyvatar cheat sheets (*https://oreil.ly/fKs_9*).

When creating a signature, start with a minimal rule first. A simple signature might look like this:

```
alert tcp any any -> any 443 (msg:"Test Rule"; sid:1000004; rev:6;)
```

This rule will match TCP packets with destination port 443, regardless of the source or destination IP address. The msg parameter specifies what will be logged in the log files, the sid is the unique ID of the rule, and rev represents the revision number, which helps track changes to the rule in subsequent versions of the signature files.

However, to improve the accuracy and reduce the risk of false positives, you need to capture a unique portion of the data. To do this, you use the content argument, which allows you to search for hex and ASCII values within packets. For hex values, you wrap the representation in pipes (|):

```
alert tcp any any -> any 443 (msg:"Test Rule"; content:"|c0 14 c0 0a
c0 22 c0 21 00 39 00 38|"; sid:1000004; rev:66;)
```

That rule might be sufficient, but to further minimize the risk of false positives you can use the offset parameter to specify the exact location from the start of the packet to search for the content. It's like telling the system to skip a certain number of bytes from the start of the payload before it begins its search. If you set offset: 40, as in this example, the system will bypass the first 40 bytes of the payload and start searching from the 41st byte:

```
alert tcp any any -> any 443 (msg:"Test Rule"; content:"|c0 14 c0 0a c0 22
c0 21 00 39 00 38|"; offset: 40; sid:1000004; rev:666;)
```

This can be useful when you're looking for specific content that you know, based on the protocol or pattern of the traffic, will appear at a certain position within the payload. By using `offset`, you can narrow down the scope of your search and reduce the likelihood of the rule matching traffic it shouldn't, which in turn reduces the number of false positives.

Since tools like Snort and Suricata maintain state information, they know the direction of the data flow. So, you can use the `flow` parameter to further focus the analysis on only packets flowing from the client to the server. Finally, you can use the `refer ence` field to provide a reference URL for further information (you know, in case you get hit by a bus and someone else needs to review the signatures you've crafted):

```
alert tcp any any -> any 443 (msg:"Unicorn Test Rule"; flow:to_server;
reference:url,https://tinyurl.com/tdishandbookv2; content:"|c0 14 c0 0a c0 22
c0 21 00 39 00 38|"; offset: 44; sid:1000004; rev:4;)
```

The examples we included in this section are not exhaustive and do not cover all the options available in the Snort signature language. So, in this case, it's important to go read the manual. You can repeat this process with other options to create specific rule sets for various types of traffic on your network. In our experience, this pairs really well with conducting atomic red team testing or testing against captured PCAP files from a malware sandbox—which you could easily do with a command like the following, where the `-r` parameter reads in a provided PCAP network capture:

```
snort -c snort.conf -r malware.pcap
```

IDS/IPS Positioning

When dealing with network-based devices, the physical positioning of the device within the network infrastructure will significantly influence the traffic it is capable of inspecting and the nature of the attacks it can prevent.

The prevailing strategy involves placing these devices at crucial choke points within the network. This typically includes the internet connection, along with any other wide area network (WAN) links that might connect different office locations and data centers. This setup ensures that traffic traversing these key links is thoroughly analyzed. As a result, it effectively captures events that concern the majority of network administrators. It's important to remember, however, that this setup will not monitor traffic that does not flow across these links. The significance of this will depend on your network topology and the types of traffic you wish to be alerted about.

Consider these examples:

1. The first potential setup involves placing the IDS/IPS at the point where traffic flows between the corporate network and the internet. This positioning allows for the capture of all inbound and outbound internet traffic, theoretically capturing incoming attacks sourced from the internet as well as unwanted connections leaving the environment, like data exfiltration attempts. However, this setup will not provide visibility into the internal network traffic (i.e., LAN ←→ LAN traffic entirely within the corporate network).

2. A second approach positions the IDS/IPS such that it captures traffic between the internal LAN and the internet, as well as traffic between the internal LAN and the demilitarized zone (DMZ). This placement provides some visibility into both internal and internet traffic, but it doesn't allow scrutiny of the traffic flow between the DMZ and the internet.

3. In a third approach, the IDS/IPS is positioned to monitor only the traffic that begins or ends on the internal LAN. While this setup doesn't offer visibility into external traffic flows, it ensures a comprehensive view of all internal traffic, like the communication between workstations and internal servers. For expansive environments with hundreds of VLANs, monitoring can be a formidable task. However, this challenge is foundational to microsegmentation and can be a valuable security investment for those with the necessary resources and budget.

 When discussing microsegmentation, it's worth considering that a traditional IDS/IPS setup with a tap might not always align with your security objectives. In many cases, implementing an NGFW could be a more effective strategy for the organization. This approach is evident in the practices of numerous businesses that have successfully incorporated microsegmentation into their network structures.

For further reading, be sure to check out the SANS whitepaper on network IDS and IPS deployment strategies (*https://oreil.ly/4knE6*) by Nicholas Pappas.

Encrypted Protocols

One final issue to consider is that network-based IDSs and IPSs focus on data as it travels across the network. Since they do not have access to data at either endpoint, they're blind to the content of encrypted communications without the necessary keying material for decryption.

This inability to view the content of encrypted communications means that many attacks will go undetected. Take, for example, an exploit aimed at a vulnerable module in WordPress. Assuming the site is only accessible via TLS, as the exploit is concealed within an encrypted connection, an IDS or IPS will miss it. These systems can only identify threats apparent in the unencrypted parts of the communications, such as the HeartBleed vulnerability (*https://heartbleed.com*) (this vulnerability was not within the encrypted payload but was exposed in the unencrypted handshake of TLS connections—i.e., the heartbeat).

Signatures based on data like IP addresses and port numbers will still function. However, to lessen the effects of encryption on threat detection, there are emerging tools and techniques that you can use. For example, many modern firewalls have built-in capabilities to decrypt SSL/TLS traffic, providing visibility into encrypted data flows. These NGFWs can analyze traffic for threats but may also introduce performance overheads, cause issues with certain websites or applications, and potentially pose legal or privacy concerns.

The visibility of IDSs and IPSs into encrypted data flows is heavily influenced by the unique configuration of your network and the deployment of your IDS/IPS tools. Systems like Snort and Suricata, although unable to independently decrypt SSL/TLS traffic, can scrutinize such traffic using JA3 hashes (*https://oreil.ly/R4z7V*) or by integrating with a proxy (or reverse proxy) that can decrypt SSL/TLS traffic. However, if these systems precede the proxy in the packet chain, they may be unable to access the decrypted traffic.

Some NGFWs have inherent capabilities for SSL/TLS traffic decryption, although their usage incurs performance overheads that you need to be aware of before you incorporate them into your environment and may raise legal concerns. Despite these challenges, these firewalls can offer invaluable insights into encrypted data traffic.

Conclusion

IDS and IPS solutions form a crucial part of any comprehensive information security program. Selecting the right vendor, determining the optimal device placement, and configuring the system appropriately are all critical security decisions. However, it's equally important to ensure that logs are meticulously collected and that there are defined runbooks in place to action any generated alerts. Unexamined data collection achieves little to nothing.

It's also important to remember that these are not an all-encompassing solutions. Their detection capabilities are restricted to traffic with a preestablished signature, and they are largely ineffective against encrypted protocols. The tools described here should be integrated as a component of a broader security strategy rather than being relied upon as standalone solutions.

CHAPTER 22
Logging and Monitoring

Most operating systems, applications, and hardware devices produce some kind of event log. Many people consider logs to be simply a historical record that can be used to retrospectively debug issues such as why an email wasn't delivered, why a web server isn't running, or how long a server had been complaining about a failing disk before it exploded and somebody actually looked at the logs. Logs can, however, be used much more proactively from a security perspective, providing not only retrospective insights but also much more in-depth views into the environment.

The same can be said of other types of monitoring, too. Companies generally have a better handle on monitoring than logging. For example, telemetry data on disk, memory, CPU, and network interface usage can be used for capacity planning and to provide preemptive information regarding potential issues. This sort of data can also be used to provide additional insights into events that might be happening within the environment.

In this chapter, you will learn what to log, where to log it, and what to do with those logs to gain the best advantage you can from the information that you already have.

Security Information and Event Management

In the past, centralized log aggregation may have simply been handled by a Unix host with a large amount of storage running syslogd and collecting the logs for the environment into its own */var/log/* directory. However, now we have security information and event management (SIEM) platforms that perform this role and much more.

A SIEM not only collects logs but also takes those logs and other security-related documentation and correlates or compares them for analysis. This correlation activity allows more intelligent security-related alerts and reports to be created and helps identify trends. Correlation logic should be the backbone of every SIEM solution, and it's much more effective when used over a range of log sources. For example, an organization can correlate various security events like unusual port activity on routers and firewalls, suspicious DNS activity, malicious process activity, signature matches from a web application firewall and IDS/IPS, and signatures/behaviors recognized by antivirus or endpoint solutions to detect a potential threat.

A traditional SIEM can be set up in one of several different configurations: software installed on local servers, a hardware appliance, a virtual appliance, a cloud-based service, or even a combination of these. Often, a SIEM is put in place and expected to automatically work, detecting all possible malicious activity in an enterprise. While many do come preconfigured with various alerts, dashboards, and reports, they still need to be customized. When a SIEM is added to any environment it must be continuously trained and configured on what exactly to look for. Every environment is completely unique and, as such, should have a properly configured and tuned SIEM tailor-fit to it. Not only will this be one of the most customized pieces of a security architecture, but this tuning will often require a significant amount of time, and it's an ongoing process. As the network changes, new software is added, new threats are realized, or new behavior is seen, the SIEM must continue to be updated and tuned.

Why Use a SIEM

Operating systems of any kind and appliances or devices with an underlying OS tend to have some kind of log repository. On Windows, this is the Event Viewer, and on Unix platforms (and many appliances) it's typically the */var/log/* directory, with the contents coming either directly from the filesystem or via syslog. For cloud services, logs are commonly ingested via an API connection over the internet. Other than the cloud API connection, the common theme of the log flow is that the logs are stored on the host from whence they originated (in the cloud, well...they're still in the cloud). In the case of a compromise this leaves the logs exposed and a single point of failure, as the evidence that you wish to examine is being protected by the very host that you can no longer trust. What's more, they're distributed in potentially hundreds of places. The solution to this problem is to collect and aggregate logs in a central location. Centralized logging, such as that provided by a SIEM, offers a key benefit: the logs are no longer stored on the host that created them. This means that in the event of a compromise, hardware failure, or malicious action by a rogue member of staff, the logs will remain intact and, if properly configured, in a state where they cannot be tampered with.

Scope of Coverage

In addition to centralized logging, a SIEM will provide essential security and operational alerting, dashboards, and reports. As we'll cover in this chapter, properly configuring a traditional SIEM is a process that can take a large amount of time, energy, and knowledge. How do you know where to start?

The scope of what to log can be a contentious issue. There are two main schools of thought on this:

Everything

This generally stems from the point of view that what is required is not known until it is needed, so it's a good idea to store everything and search and filter later. This does indeed provide access to all the possible data that may be required, but it also creates more of a challenge when it comes to storage, indexing, and in some cases transmitting the data. If a commercial solution is used, licensing may also depend on volume.

Only what you need

Rather unsurprisingly, this approach is the polar opposite; technology resources are way less utilized in this scenario, but there is a risk that something will be missed. The idea here is that when you're getting a new system of log collection and correlation up and running, it's best to start slowly with what you know you need and then build upon that. This is definitely not a bad way to start ingesting logs if the majority of the configuration is in-house.

Sadly, in reality, the major factor driving what you log will probably be cost. If this is the case in your organization, it is best to consume logs more aggressively from high-value systems, high-risk systems, and those facing external networks and make savings in areas that are of lesser importance from a security perspective. Tying specific log ingestion to a standards framework, as covered later in this chapter, will help you focus on what data will be important from a security perspective.

If both the staff and the organization are new to the idea and implementation of a SIEM, it is recommended to begin with systems that are already delivering security logs, such as IPS/IDS and endpoint protection solutions. This will offer the ability for the team to become familiar with the software and configuration options while combining several applications into one log management system. After processes and procedures have been established, other logs (such as Windows logs, DNS logs, logs from honeypots, and application and database logs) can be added for a deeper look into the infrastructure.

Designing the SIEM

Before you implement a SIEM, it's best to have a broad understanding of not only what should and should not happen on the network, but also what the major pain points of the organization are that it will attempt to address. Steps to take prior to implementation include:

1. Define the coverage scope. Many organizations put a SIEM in place to cover a compliance requirement. This may drive which sections of the network are initially focused on. Other areas may be left out of scope altogether, such as a segmented guest network.

2. Establish threat scenarios/use cases. As discussed in Chapter 1, use cases are where you go through an attack virtually, walking through each stage or level step by step. It's possible to tie the levels of the attack to a framework such as MITRE ATT&CK (*https://attack.mitre.org*) or the Cyber Kill Chain (*https://oreil.ly/csb9r*). When this approach is used, individual detection and alerting configurations can be used to counteract an attack at different stages in the intrusion attempt.

3. Determine the applicability of alerts. During design and as a possible step in the creation of an overall risk profile, different threats should be prioritized. Walk through the threats that have been identified and alerts that come as standard with the SIEM to prioritize what makes sense for the specific network it will be placed on. For example, a match on a PCI data alert won't be something to be categorized as critical if there is no PCI data present on the network.

4. Perform a proof of concept. Just because there are active rules and alerts on a SIEM doesn't necessarily mean they will capture what you think they will. Testing the detections will not only help strengthen internal security but will also build the purple team's skillset (for more on purple teaming, see Chapter 20). If there is an alert created for detecting port scans, don't only attempt to trigger it, but also attempt to get around it, looking for potential gaps in the alerting. A third-party red team exercise or penetration test can further help you determine whether the platform is working as intended. The engagement should test the detections and also either help with retesting anything that wasn't detected or provide the internal team with instructions about how to retest.

5. Create a Record of Authority (ROA) document defining where logs will be stored and the retention period for each log. An ROA is often a compliance requirement, to ensure the data is kept for a certain period of time.

Log Analysis and Enrichment

Once logs are stored in some sort of central repository, it's time to start performing analysis. Ideally, you'll monitor and analyze your logs and raise alerts in real time (or as near real time as possible) for events, or combinations of events, that are worthy of further investigation. Depending on the SIEM you're using, it may be difficult to jump directly to this stage. Many higher-end tools come preconfigured with at least a default set of alert rules, some of which are integrated with threat intelligence feeds; for others, you may need to spend some time running ad hoc queries in order to see what works and what doesn't.

It's common to discover that your SIEM isn't displaying events and information that you would assume are logged by default. This is in part because, for Windows operating systems in particular, the default configurations may be lacking, so you may need to take some actions to enrich the logging (such as using Sysmon and Group Policy, described in the following subsections). Once the rules have been tuned to provide an acceptable level of false positives and false negatives, you can set up real-time alerting. Keep in mind that the goal is not to produce an exhaustive list of all events—if that were the case, people would be employed just to tail logs all day. We'll talk more about log types to focus on and producing alerts that are useful and appropriate to your environment in "Alert Examples and Log Sources to Focus On" on page 293.

Sysmon

Sysmon (System Monitor) is part of the Sysinternals Suite, now owned by Microsoft. It's one of the most commonly used add-ons for Windows logging.

With Sysmon, you can detect malicious activity by tracking code behavior and network traffic as well as creating detections based on the malicious activity. It enriches the standard Windows logs by enabling higher-level monitoring of events such as process creations, network connections, and changes to the filesystem.

Installing Sysmon

Sysmon is extremely easy to install and deploy. The following steps will turn on an incredible amount of logging:

1. Download (*https://oreil.ly/F-JJq*) Sysmon (or the entire Sysinternals Suite).
2. Choose a configuration for your deployment:
   a. SwiftonSecurity (*https://oreil.ly/wVH4O*): Good starting point, stable, performant, less frequently updated.
   b. Modular (*https://oreil.ly/ZGmQd*): More advanced configuration options, ties attacks to MITRE ATT&CK framework, more frequently updated.
3. Download your chosen configuration and save it as *config.xml* in *C:\windows*.
4. Install Sysmon by opening up a command prompt as administrator and typing the following command:

   ```
   sysmon64.exe "accept eula" c:\windows\config.xml
   ```

> *Sysmon.exe* is for 32-bit systems only. *Sysmon64.exe* is for 64-bit systems only.

Detecting common threats with Sysmon events

There are several extremely helpful Windows Event IDs that Sysmon generates to help detect threats that are common in many different enterprises. A full list of Event IDs that Sysmon can generate is available on the download page. A few examples of the more useful events generated for security purposes are listed here:

Event ID 1: Process creation

Not only will Sysmon show what processes are being run, but it will also show a lot of information about the executable or binary itself. It provides hashes for all of the binaries that are run on the system and indicates whether they are signed or not, making it easy to see if malicious code is attempting to mimic legitimate programs such as PowerShell or other built-in Microsoft tools. Figure 22-1 shows the event created when the Registry Editor program is run.

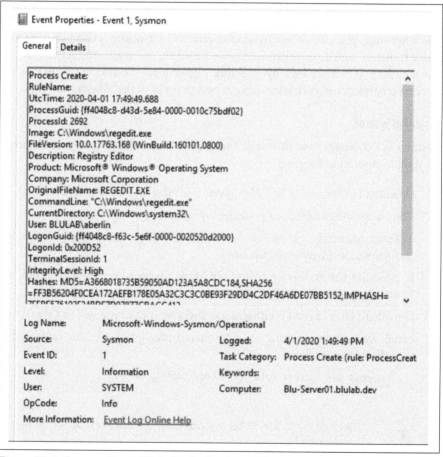

Figure 22-1. Sysmon Event ID 1, for the Registry Editor program

In certain cases (when you are unable to have an allow list–only environment), you can use events such as these to alert when processes are run, if they are signed by the appropriate vendor, or if they are spawning processes that they shouldn't be (such as MS Word spawning PowerShell).

Event ID 3: Network connection detected

These events can be useful in detecting command and control traffic (which may indicate that attackers are sending commands that steal data, spread malware, etc.), as well as giving visibility into what applications are accessing certain internet resources. In the example shown in Figure 22-2, we can see where *Setup.exe* has been run and by whom, as well as that it is reaching out to download additional content from a cloud provider.

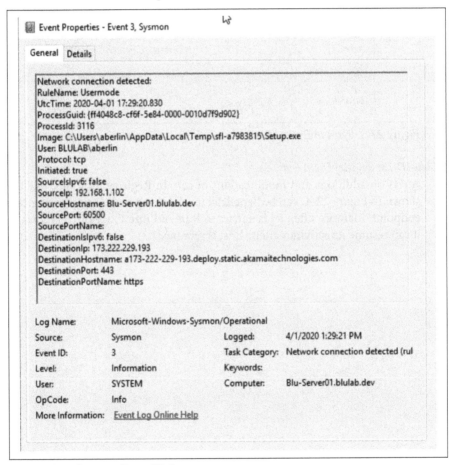

Figure 22-2. Sysmon Event ID 3

Event ID 4: Sysmon service state changed

One potential action an attacker or malicious user could take is to disable the Sysmon service, if they have the privileges to do so. Figure 22-3 shows an example of this event.

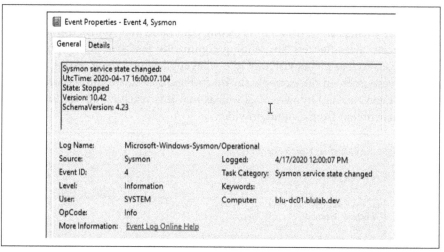

Figure 22-3. Sysmon Event ID 4

Event ID 13: RegistryEvent (value set)

Alerts on additions and modifications of certain Registry locations, like the one shown in Figure 22-4, can be beneficial for detecting malicious persistence on an endpoint. Malware often adds entries to Run and Run Once on Windows so that it can resume its activities after a host is rebooted.

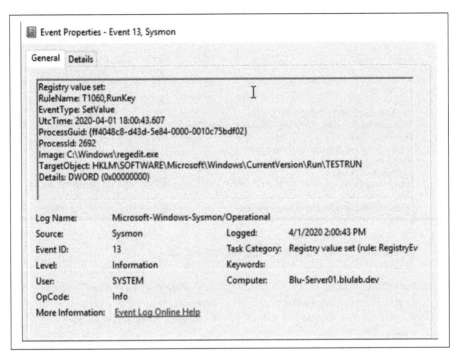

Figure 22-4. Sysmon Event 13

Event ID 22: DNSEvent

There are several benefits to logging DNS traffic, such as identifying malicious remote access tools, security misconfigurations, and command and control traffic. Using Sysmon to enable DNS logging at the host level is one of the best ways to track DNS resolutions in a Windows environment (see Figure 22-5).

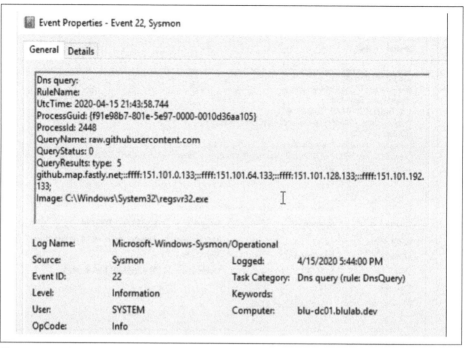

Figure 22-5. Sysmon Event ID 22

If you need to access the Sysmon events locally as opposed to viewing them in a SIEM, you will find them in the Event Viewer under Applications and Services Logs→Microsoft→Windows→Sysmon.

Group Policy

When locally hosted Windows environments comprise the bulk of an infrastructure design, Group Policy is invaluable to system administrators. This is the central place to configure settings across the Windows domain, and logging is no exception. However, by default, Windows is not configured to log a decent amount of the necessary security-related Windows Event IDs. For example, in order to detect authentication attacks such as password spraying and brute force attacks, the domain needs to be configured to log failed authentication attempts.

The ability to configure advanced auditing was introduced in Windows Server 2008 R2. There are a few different ways to select the correct settings as far as security logging is concerned. Beyond manually figuring it out yourself, if you'd like to take a step-by-step approach you can take a look at Malware Archeology's Windows Logging Cheat Sheet (*https://oreil.ly/-b0-b*). Another option is to use Logmira (*https://oreil.ly/4klit*), a GPO backup with preconfigured logging settings that can be imported into the Group Policy Management Console.

Alert Examples and Log Sources to Focus On

Creating alerts based on different log types can be a very useful way of discovering unusual activity within your environment. Of course, context is key, and tailoring alerts to your specific environment will yield the most relevant results.

This section details some specific examples to illustrate the sorts of alerts that can be easily generated via log analysis, in addition to collecting alerts from tools like IPSs/IDSs, endpoint solutions, and web application firewalls. Remember, the aim of alerting on threats and suspicious behavior is not to produce an exhaustive list of all events. If too many alerts are generated, they risk being lost in the noise or simply ignored by analysts (a phenomenon commonly known as alert fatigue). Keep alerts to only those that should be acted upon, and keep the alerts useful and actionable.

Authentication Systems

Authentication systems are an obvious starting point for analysis, as usage of user credentials is typically well understood. When analyzing the contents of authentication logs within the context of the environment, there are several tests that can yield immediate results:

- Repeated login failures above a set threshold could be a sign of a brute force attack or misconfigured clients (or simply a user who can't remember their password).

- Certain types of authentication are inherently insecure, such as logins over HTTP or Telnet that are transmitted in clear text over the network. Alerting on clear text authentication can assist in removing it completely from your environment.

Application Logs

Most server applications, including email servers, web servers, and other (probably) internet-facing services, generate logs of one type or another. These logs can provide useful insight into adversaries performing attacks against these hosts or performing reconnaissance. For example:

- Too many 4XX responses from a web server can indicate failed attempts at exploitation. 4XX codes are responses such as "not found" and "access denied," and as such are a common byproduct of people attempting (and failing) to call vulnerable scripts. A high frequency of 4XX errors may indicate an attack or scan in progress.

- Too many hits on one specific URL, or many different URLs on one web server, could indicate that something is being brute-forced or enumerated. Of course, repeated calls to the same URL could be normal depending on the website setup, so it's important to consider the context of the environment in order to determine if this concern is applicable.

- Connects and disconnects with no transaction on multiple types of servers in your environment can be an indication that someone is probing the network. This can be caused by simple port scanning, scraping protocol banners, probing TLS stacks, and other types of reconnaissance.

- New services, processes, and ports should not be unplanned configuration changes, especially on servers. Identifying a baseline per host and maintaining a list of unwanted or unapproved services, processes, and ports can be useful for detecting malicious program installations or activity.

Cloud Services

Moving to cloud infrastructure means adapting to a new security landscape—one that involves third-party services managing substantial parts of the environment. This shift doesn't imply a decrease in the need for thorough logging and monitoring, however; if anything, it's the opposite. Even when systems are handled by external providers, it's important to maintain active control over the security and operation of your data.

In Chapter 14, we talked about the shared responsibility model. With this model, both the cloud provider and the customer have specific duties to ensure the overall security of the cloud environment, and it's critical to understand who is responsible for what (hint: when it comes to security, with the exception of the physical infrastructure, it's almost always yours).

A good way to think about anything that happens in the cloud is that there's typically an API call that happens, which is logged somewhere. This log, if you've correctly captured it, can tell you exactly what happened in your cloud environment for any given action or change. Think of it like a flight data recorder. Cloud logs contain a *ton* of useful information about your applications, virtual machines, databases, and other cloud services you use. They are critical for understanding the events occurring within your environment and are indispensable for ensuring the security and integrity of your data.

AWS

As mentioned in Chapter 21, with AWS there are three main sources of logs that are relevant for threat detection. First up is CloudTrail, which records all activities within your AWS environment. Each action generates an event that gets logged (like creating an S3 bucket or provisioning a new EC2 instance), and these logs capture critical details such as the identity of the API caller, the time of the API call, the source IP address of the API caller, and so on. From a logging perspective, if you have these logs flowing into your SIEM, you can detect events that you care about and take corrective action. Such events might include overprovisioning IAM users, deploying public S3 buckets, or not adhering to tagging schema.

Next up are VPC Flow Logs, which contain metadata about all traffic moving into and out of your AWS account's VPCs. Finally, EventBridge serves as a serverless event bus; it's a sort of catch-all, capable of capturing and routing most other log sources in AWS.

AWS also has its own built-in threat detection solution, Amazon GuardDuty, which monitors for malicious or unauthorized activity using machine learning, anomaly detection, and integrated threat intelligence. It's not free, but in our opinion, it's worth the cost.

Azure

Azure Monitor (*https://oreil.ly/1T29A*) collects and analyzes telemetry data from your cloud and on-premises environments, aiding in understanding application performance and proactively identifying issues affecting your applications and the resources they depend on. In addition, Azure offers Microsoft Defender for Cloud, a cloud workload protection platform that can alert you to potential threats and provides investigation and remediation tools.

For Azure logs, focus on Azure activity logs (*https://oreil.ly/U-vry*), which show control plane events on Azure resources such as virtual machines or databases. Azure AD logs (these are different from on-premises AD logs) can record sign-in activity and changes, aiding in user behavior tracking. In addition to these log types, Microsoft also provides Azure resource logs (*https://oreil.ly/R5Izx*), which can include data plane operations like network flows or data access.

GCP

Google Cloud Platform (GCP) offers a set of tools for security logging. A key tool is Cloud Logging (*https://oreil.ly/QlL0K*), which collects and stores logs from GCP services and applications, including audit logs (*https://oreil.ly/mCZJn*). It also allows you to analyze these logs and set up alerts, helping improve security measures. Additional services like Log Analytics and Log Router help you understand log data and direct logs to different locations (like a SIEM) for further analysis.

As mentioned in the previous chapter, for threat detection GCP has a service called Event Threat Detection (ETD) (*https://oreil.ly/25Ezh*); like Amazon GuardDuty, it scans your logs for potential threats and sends alerts through Cloud Logging or Pub/Sub. To use these tools effectively, they need to be configured properly, updated regularly, and managed by a trained team. As the user, it's your job to make sure your cloud environment is secure. This means ongoing learning and adaptation are crucial to get the most out of GCP's security logging tools.

Databases

Many times, databases are a place where much of the juicy information resides—the customer records, transaction data, patient information, and other important data that if lost or breached would result in chaos. There are a large number of different monitoring and alerting options, depending on what data is housed in a database and what type of software the database is built on. Here are a few points to keep in mind:

- Log access or attempted access to sensitive data by users and applications accessing (or attempting to access) servers that are not associated with them. This can provide a detailed look into where data is moving to and from.

- In addition to access, there are other activities that should be closely logged and monitored. Queries, the copying and deletion of databases and tables, and all activities by privileged users are examples of these. Alerts can be created for any activity outside of the normal baseline to monitor for data exfiltration or malicious access.

- Other authentication-related activities, such as multiple unsuccessful login attempts or a user performing privilege escalation, may point to malicious behavior. Unusually large numbers of queries may also point to an attempted brute-force attack.

DNS

Detailed logging of DNS queries and responses can be beneficial, for many reasons. The first and most obvious purpose is to aid in incident response. DNS logs can be very helpful for tracking down malicious behavior, especially on endpoints in a DHCP pool. If an alert is received with a specific IP address, that IP address may not be on the same endpoint by the time someone ends up investigating. This can slow down the investigation, giving the malicious program or attacker more time to hide themselves or spread to other machines.

DNS logs are also useful for identifying other compromised hosts, downloads from malicious websites, and whether malware is using domain generation algorithms (DGAs) to mask malicious behavior and evade detection.

If you're using Windows OSs, Sysmon (discussed earlier in this chapter) is definitely your best bet when it comes to logging this type of traffic.

Endpoint Protection Solutions

Endpoint solutions (EDR, XDR, etc.) are security software solutions that address endpoint security issues, securing and protecting endpoints against malware, attacks, and inadvertent data leakage resulting from human error. They are not based solely on signatures, as earlier antivirus programs were, but on a combination of signatures, hashes, and identifiable actions and behaviors that can be identified as malicious. Like with many other technologies, any endpoint solution must be tuned on its own first for any effectiveness to carry over to a logging solution.

IDSs/IPSs

IDS/IPS solutions, discussed in depth in the previous chapter, are commonly incorporated in the earliest stages of security alerting. They are fairly easy to configure and often have hundreds or thousands of signatures or rule sets enabled by default, which you can tune to monitor your specific traffic effectively. When you first start using these tools, you will likely receive a huge number of notifications about activities that you were not aware of in your environment but that are not really problematic (i.e., false positives). To avoid alert fatigue, you'll need to do some tuning to get the number of false positives to an acceptable level. It's common practice to enable notifications on all high and critical alerts that aren't automatically blocked and use other less critical signatures as informational during investigations.

Operating Systems

Collecting endpoint operating system logs is an absolute must for any type of advanced detection and monitoring. Both Windows- and Unix-based systems produce large volumes of local logs that can be beneficial in many ways:

- Baselining any operating system in an enterprise environment can be fairly difficult; however, once this is completed, new processes can be tracked and alerted on. This can be simplified with a good-quality endpoint solution and standard settings.

- For Windows OSs, Sysmon (discussed earlier in this chapter) is a very valuable and free tool that can be added to enhance logging and map activity back to components such as the MITRE ATT&CK framework.

- On Linux, software such as osquery or OSSEC can offer additional logging and detection capabilities, such as the file integrity monitoring that is required for PCI DSS environments.

- Command-line logging is an extremely powerful way to see in depth what is being run on endpoints. For Windows, it can be used to alert on PowerShell scripts like Bloodhound or Mimikatz being run, and on Linux you can monitor for things like permission changes or scripts running.

Proxy and Firewall Logs

Firewalls, proxies, and other systems that provide per-connection logging can be very useful indeed, particularly in discovering unexpected outbound traffic and other anomalies that could indicate a threat from an insider or an intrusion that is already in progress:

- Outbound connections to unexpected services can be an indicator of data exfiltration, lateral movement, or a member of staff who hasn't read the acceptable use guide properly. Connections to cloud-based file storage, instant messaging platforms, email services, and other systems can often be identified by hostnames and IP addresses. Context is necessary, but if these connections are not expected, they are probably worthy of further investigation.

- Matching IP addresses or hostnames on block lists is a little contentious, because block lists are generally not complete or up-to-date. However, you should monitor for and block connections to known command and control infrastructure. There are publicly available lists of known C&C servers that can be used for blocking at the firewall for both egress and ingress, as well as SIEM alerting.

- Connections of unexpected length or bandwidth can be an indicator that something unusual is happening. For example, running sshd on port 443 can fool many proxies and firewalls; however, an average HTTPS session does not last for six hours, and even a site that is left open for long periods typically uses multiple smaller connections. The SSH connection to a nonstandard port would quite possibly appear to be long in duration and low bandwidth.

User Accounts, Groups, and Permissions

Most changes to user accounts, groups, and permissions are not active parts of malicious activity or attacks, as normally an attacker has bypassed the need to change the account or service they already have control over. However, knowing that risky behavior is happening in an environment can help avoid insecure practices:

- Default accounts should be used only when necessary, as they are considered shared accounts. Alerting on the use of these accounts when not approved can point to activity of an unknown origin. If default accounts must be used in an environment, they should be put in a highly scrutinized and controlled group.

- Changes to the Domain Admins, Enterprise Admins, or other privileged groups in Active Directory should be rare. While attacks don't often rely on malicious additions to such groups, it is still vital to alert on such changes for auditing reasons.

- Creation of local users or addition of users to local administrative groups should be monitored as well, especially in an environment where IAM is centralized. Having local administrative access can lead to gaining access to the domain.

Testing and Continuing Configuration

As mentioned earlier in this chapter, testing the validity of your SIEM's components is extremely important. It's never a good sign when an incident happens or a penetration test report comes back and there are zero detection alerts from the SIEM. There are several processes that you can implement to assist in ensuring that alerting is working properly:

Test on your own
> Internal testing is always a great idea! Having a professional offensive security firm test your defenses and detections is generally something that can only be done on an infrequent basis. Using your own internal resources to conduct spot checks of certain elements of your alerting systems will give you greater confidence than having a comprehensive test done once a year and hoping things will keep working as intended in between.

Script the tests
> Create scripts with scheduled tasks that can be run on a regular basis. For example, the DomainPasswordSpray (*https://oreil.ly/GeeV9*) PowerShell script can be run against an environment using a bogus list of users and passwords. It should trigger a password spraying event after a certain threshold, and using fake users means you won't lock out any legitimate accounts. The team over at Red Canary has an amazing tool called Atomic Red Team (*https://oreil.ly/Lmon7*) that can be used to automate many different attack patterns.

Conduct tabletop exercises
> While running through tabletop exercises, use them as an opportunity to validate that specific alerting is present as well as add any potential new detections that arise during the exercise.

Perform full audits
> Audit the environment for proper logging by asking a handful of important questions:
> 1. How many endpoints should be logging in the environment?
> 2. Has the amount of logs vastly increased/decreased since the last check?
> 3. Are all ingress/egress network points accounted for?
> 4. Has any new software been implemented that could be logging to the SIEM?

Aligning with Detection Frameworks, Compliance Mandates, and Use Cases

When crafting detection playbooks to ensure the greatest number of legitimate and purposeful alerts, it is sometimes helpful to align with a security framework as well as general use cases based on the common threats that your organization might face. These frameworks can be a great resource for detection ideas and real-life examples of attacks seen in the wild.

MITRE ATT&CK

MITRE ATT&CK (*https://attack.mitre.org*) is a free, globally accessible knowledge base of adversary tactics and techniques based on real-world observations that is commonly used as the foundation for the development of specific threat models and methodologies in the private sector, in government, and in the cybersecurity product and service community.

The framework is broken down into more than a dozen specific sections, all focusing on different areas of an attack. While it wouldn't be wise to alert on all of these (e.g., systems rebooting, vulnerability scans from the internet), it provides a great list of common attack vectors to map detections and reports to. There are a variety of ways to use the framework, including Structured Threat Information Expression (STIX) format and the ATT&CK Navigator (Figure 22-6), which can be helpful for visualizing coverage.

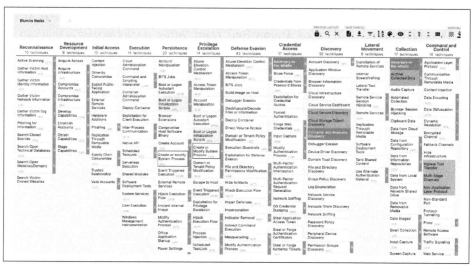

Figure 22-6. The MITRE ATT&CK Navigator (https://oreil.ly/wTNG6)

Sigma

Sigma (*https://oreil.ly/-eOEg*) is a generic, open signature format that allows you to describe relevant log events in a straightforward manner. The rule format is very flexible, easy to write, and applicable to any type of log file. Its main goal is to provide a structured form in which researchers or analysts can describe their detection methods and make them shareable with others.

Using this rule format, especially at the start of your detection engineering program, has the added benefit of making it much easier to move between SIEM vendors or software platforms. As it's a standard format that can be used across platforms, there are a large number of publicly available Sigma rules that have already been written, so you don't have to start from scratch when creating detections. These publicly available rules provide a great baseline for what should be alerted on as well as an easy way to index and document what could be applied in your environment. Figure 22-7 shows an example of a Sigma rule for detecting a webshell with Sysmon.

```
Code   Blame   38 lines (38 loc) · 1.06 KB                                          Raw

 1    title: Webshell Detection With Command Line Keywords
 2    id: bed2a484-9348-4143-8a8a-b801c979301c
 3    description: Detects certain command line parameters often used during reconnaissance activity via web shells
 4    author: Florian Roth
 5    reference:
 6        - https://www.fireeye.com/blog/threat-research/2013/08/breaking-down-the-china-chopper-web-shell-part-ii.html
 7    date: 2017/01/01
 8    modified: 2019/10/26
 9    tags:
10        - attack.privilege_escalation
11        - attack.persistence
12        - attack.t1100
13    logsource:
14        category: process_creation
15        product: windows
16    detection:
17        selection:
18            ParentImage:
19                - '*\apache*'
20                - '*\tomcat*'
21                - '*\w3wp.exe'
22                - '*\php-cgi.exe'
23                - '*\nginx.exe'
24                - '*\httpd.exe'
25            CommandLine:
26                - '*whoami*'
27                - '*net user *'
28                - '*ping -n *'
29                - '*systeminfo'
30                - '*&cd&echo*'
31                - '*cd /d*'  # https://www.computerhope.com/cdhlp.htm
32        condition: selection
33    fields:
34        - CommandLine
35        - ParentCommandLine
36    falsepositives:
37        - unknown
38    level: high
```

Figure 22-7. An example Sigma rule (https://oreil.ly/AKKqE)

Compliance

Aligning any SIEM implementation with a compliance standard tends to leave people more frustrated than confident. However, when selecting a SIEM provider (or building your own), it's a good idea to keep any compliance standards in mind.

Use Case Analysis

With multiple log types across the entire enterprise collected into a single repository, new areas for analysis become possible. Use cases—otherwise known as threat models—should be built around the major risks previously identified using this analysis. Some of the more common areas to focus on are access control, perimeter defenses, intrusion detection, malware, application defenses, and resource integrity.

Creating and tuning use cases should be viewed as an ongoing project, because the threat landscape is ever-changing. There are always new threats to model and new indicators to monitor for. For example, here are some use cases you might want to consider:

Brute-force attack
> It is incredibly trivial to install and run password brute forcing and cracking software. Correlating logs for detection of this requires both success and failure audits to be captured—as users may legitimately enter wrong passwords, it's important to test both successful and failed authentication to see the difference in the logging.

Data exfiltration
> Data exfiltration by an inside threat actor can be one of the more difficult attacks to detect. Start by logging which resources are being accessed by whom and when. Identify critical resources and users, develop a baseline to identify threshold limits, and monitor user activity during and after business hours. It would be useless to alert on all data exfiltration (very little gain for a huge amount of effort); the key is determining what constitutes the highest risk. More than likely, the recipe for Coca-Cola isn't sitting in a text file on a shared drive—at least, we hope not!

Business email compromise (BEC)
> This is one of the most common initial vectors of attack. When an attacker gains access to a user's mailbox, they have the keys to get more information from other employees and potentially even exfiltrate information via email. Are you able to detect when someone is forwarding email outside of your organization, or if an inbox rule has been created to forward anything with "wire transfer" mentioned? These are common avenues of attack after someone has maliciously gained access to an account.

Ransomware

Dealing with ransomware is one of the most common struggles enterprises face today. When asked, "What keeps you up at night?" many sysadmins will answer, "Getting hit with ransomware." That makes creating a use case for this scenario a good idea. There are a large number of different detection mechanisms that can be used at each stage of the ransomware attack chain, from initial compromise (e.g., via credential stuffing) to encoded PowerShell commands being run, all the way to endpoint files being encrypted.

Conclusion

Correctly consolidated logs are one of the most powerful detection tools available to us. However, it can take a significant amount of time and capital to make effective use of them. With a solid, steady design planned around relevant risks, log correlation and a SIEM can greatly decrease the time it takes to detect and mitigate security issues in your environment.

CHAPTER 23

The Extra Mile

Congratulations! You've made it to the last chapter! Here's a cookie:

```
document.cookie = "username=LastChapter; expires=OnReceipt 12:00:00 UTC";
```

After reading this book, you should be ready to provide the sound building blocks of an information security program. You should also be fully equipped to handle the common insecure practices that we've seen in so many environments. But the learning doesn't stop here! Here, in the extra mile, we'll give you some additional tidbits of information and some great resources for you to go check out that will make your defenses that much stronger.

Email Servers

Running and installing an email server is a large time and technology commitment. Bulk spam and phishing are major concerns. Modern spam filters claim to block 99.99% of spam and phishing emails, but to give you an idea of the scale of the problem, it is estimated that nearly half of all emails sent worldwide are spam (*https:// oreil.ly/NgKOu*).

You'll also need to watch out for commonly misconfigured server settings. Many email servers currently on the internet are misconfigured, which contributes in part to the amount of spam being sent. In addition, misconfigurations may delay or even prevent an organization's mail from being delivered—certain configurations will land the IP address or domain of the mail server on a block list, which organizations can subscribe to for enhancing filtering efforts. There are some common configuration checks that should be performed on mail servers being hosted in your environment. MXToolbox (*http://www.mxtoolbox.com*) provides a large list of different tests that can be performed for this purpose.

For a mail server on the internet, here are some of the things you'll want to think about:

Open mail relay

Having a mail server set up as an open relay allows anyone who can access it on port 25 to send mail through it as anyone they want. Mail servers should be configured to only relay messages for the domains that they are associated with.

Server hello

A mail server hello (aka HELO/EHLO) is the command an SMTP server sends to identify itself during a message exchange. While having an incorrect hello does not impact the server's ability to send or receive mail, it should identify the sending server in such a way that it can be used to pinpoint servers with problems, such as leaking spam or incorrectly formatted emails. An example of a correct mail server hello is HELO mx.batsareawesome.com; settings such as localhost or 74.122.238.160 (the public mail server IP address) are against RFC 2821 (*https://www.ietf.org/rfc/rfc2821.txt*) and best practice.

Reverse DNS

Another technique spam filtering tools use is looking at reverse DNS (rDNS) or pointer (PTR) records on an IP address attempting to deliver mail. A generic rDNS record is common when the device sending mail has no control over changing it to a correct setting. For example, a residential IP address through a local DSL provider will have a record of something like dsl-nor-65-88-244-120.ambtel.net for the IP address 65.88.244.120. This is a generic rDNS that is autogenerated for the majority of public IP addresses dynamically assigned by ISPs. When you're operating a mail server, it's more than likely that the IP address will be a static address that will need to be configured to have an rDNS record to match that of the server. Unless your organization owns and controls its own public IP addressing space, you'll need to contact your ISP or other upstream provider and ask them to make the change on their name server to match the hostname and corresponding record of the sending server (instead of using an individual's account, such as an alias of *mail.batsareawesome.com*).

Email aliases and group nesting

While not necessarily a direct security issue, making use of email aliases and group nesting (groups within groups) is a good habit to get into. For example, Aaron is the lead security engineer. They have all licensing information and alerting sent to their mailbox and use rules to disperse them throughout the different teams. When Aaron leaves, their account becomes corrupted somehow, or something else happens to it, and it becomes a large task to reset everything to go to a new person. Instead, an alias of *high-ids-alerts@lintile.com* could be set up containing both the security operations center (SOC) group and the SecEngineer group, which would automatically disperse the alerts to where they need to go regardless of whether Aaron stays with the company.

Another example would be for licensing information. Often, management and engineers need to have working knowledge of license expiration and renewals. For example, the company BHaFSec could use a specific alias account such as *licensing@bhafsec.com* for everything to do with SSL and software licensing, containing the Exec and SecEngineer groups. Such setups greatly reduce the likelihood of miscommunication.

Outsourcing

Outsourcing your email server is not a crime. Given all the effort involved in keeping an email server running, filtering spam, configuring everything correctly (e.g., not acting as an open relay), and any number of other issues, it may well suit your organization to simply outsource the day-to-day management of your email. Google and Microsoft 365, for example, both offer managed services whereby user administration is the only task left. Both organizations have large, capable security teams, which could free you up to pursue other more important tasks.

DNS Servers

DNS is a main building block of the internet and technology in general. There are several security considerations (*https://www.sans.org/white-papers/1069*) to keep in mind when designing your DNS infrastructure. Paying attention to these can help you defend against vulnerabilities such as DNS spoofing, DNS ID hacking, and DNS cache poisoning. DNS spoofing occurs when a malicious server answers DNS requests that were intended for another server. DNS queries contain a specific ID that the attacker must have to successfully spoof the server, so spoofing can only be completed with the addition of ID hacking. DNS cache poisoning is another form of DNS spoofing, consisting of making a DNS server cache false information. Usually this consists of a record that maps a domain name to the wrong IP address. All of these attacks have the goal of forcing connections to a malicious service or server.

The following steps can be taken to prevent and safeguard against attacks on DNS servers and infrastructure:

Restrict recursive queries.

Recursion is the process a DNS server uses to resolve names for which it is not authoritative. If the server doesn't contain a zone file that is authoritative for the domain in the query, it will forward the connection to other DNS servers using this process. The problem is that DNS servers that perform recursion are more vulnerable to DoS attacks. Because of this, you should disable recursion on the DNS servers in your organization that will only answer queries for which they are authoritative (typically, this means queries for your internal resources).

Segregate internal and external DNS servers.

Restrict the possible queries and the possible hosts that are allowed to query to the minimum. Not every network device needs to be able to resolve addresses on the internet. In most cases, the only machines that need to be able to resolve external addresses are gateway devices, such as a web proxy server. The majority of devices can be configured to use internal DNS servers that do not perform recursion for public names.

Restrict DNS zone transfers to only trusted name servers.

By issuing a specific request (a query of type AXFR), the entirety of the DNS server database can be obtained. While this isn't a significant security threat, it does give an attacker an upper hand by giving them access to internal information and a list of subdomains and settings. You should restrict this type of query to only trusted name servers.

Implement passive DNS.

A passive DNS server (as illustrated in Figure 23-1) will cache DNS information, queries, and errors resulting from the server-to-server communication between your main DNS server and other DNS servers on the internet. It can store this data in a centralized database for analysis. For example, you might use this information to develop security measures such as new domain alerting (a good percentage of brand-new domains are spun up solely for the purpose of distributing malware).

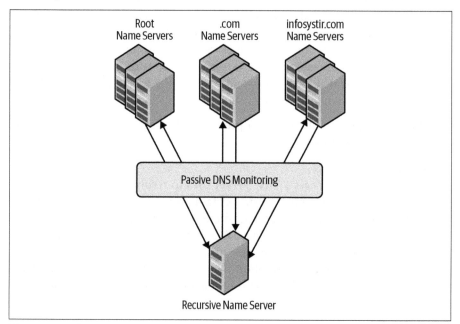

Figure 23-1. Passive DNS monitoring

Implement a DNS sinkhole.

A DNS sinkhole server (like Pi-hole (*https://pi-hole.net*)) works by spoofing the authoritative DNS server for known bad domains to combat malware and viruses, as shown in Figure 23-2. It then returns a false address that is nonroutable, ensuring the client is not able to connect to the malicious site. Malicious domains can be identified through the malware analysis process, open source sites that provide details on malicious IP addresses, and phishing emails. Sinkhole servers make use of Response Policy Zone (RPZ) DNS records.

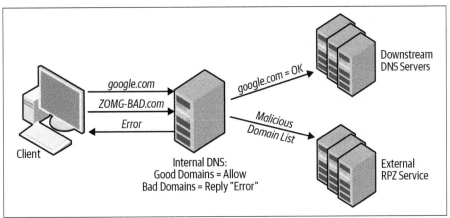

Figure 23-2. Sinkhole DNS

Do not implement DNSSEC.

The DNS Security Extensions (DNSSEC) are a set of extensions to DNS that provide the resolvers with data origin authentication. We recommend that you do not implement this. It has extremely high risks for the small amount of extra security that may be gained; not only is there a risk of taking down all of your DNS infrastructure, but the larger DNSSEC packets can provide attackers with a reliable source of DDoS amplification.

Security Through Obscurity

Security through obscurity is the term used for "hiding" assets, services, or procedures in nonstandard ways. When used as the basis of a security program it is useless, but there are some methods that can be implemented as an added measure.

Do:

- Set up services on nonstandard ports. For example, instead of a web administrative logon listening on port 443, change it to 4043, or set the FTP server to listen on port 2222.

- Rename the local Administrator account to something else that makes sense for your organization.
- Reconfigure service banners not to report the server OS type and version.

Don't:

- Block Shodan's scanners/crawlers or other internet scanners from accessing public IP addresses. Just because a single service won't be indexing the data doesn't mean malicious people aren't going to find it—and as we demonstrated in Chapter 20, you can use Shodan's services to assist in finding security gaps.
- Label datacenters and equipment closets something super obvious like "Network Data Center."
- Put any device or service on an internet-facing connection without having it tested for vulnerabilities.

Useful Resources

Finally, we'll finish with a list of books, blogs, podcasts, and websites that we find useful, to provide you with some ideas for where to go to learn more.

Books

- Of course, this one, but you already have it, so go you!!!
- *Blue Team Handbook: Incident Response Edition* (*http://www.blueteamhand book.com*) by Don Murdoch (CreateSpace)
- *Building an Information Security Awareness Program: Defending Against Social Engineering and Technical Threats* by Bill Gardner and Valerie Thomas (Syngress)
- *Complete Guide to Shodan* (*https://leanpub.com/shodan*) by John Matherly (Leanpub)
- *Designing and Building a Security Operations Center* by David Nathans (Syngress)
- *Hacking Exposed Industrial Control Systems: ICS and SCADA Security Secrets & Solutions* by Clint Bodungen, Bryan Singer, Aaron Shbeeb, Kyle Wilhoit, and Stephen Hilt (McGraw Hill)
- *How to Develop and Implement a Security Master Plan* by Timothy Giles (Auerbach)

Blogs

- ASEC (*https://asec.ahnlab.com*)
- DFIR Report (*https://thedfirreport.com*)
- Internet Storm Center (*https://isc.sans.edu*)
- Krebs on Security (*https://krebsonsecurity.com*)
- Mandiant (*https://www.mandiant.com/resources/blog*)
- Pentestlab.blog (*https://pentestlab.blog*)
- Schneier on Security (*https://www.schneier.com*)
- SpecterOps (*https://posts.specterops.io*)
- SpiderLabs Blog (*https://www.trustwave.com/Resources/SpiderLabs-Blog*)
- TrustedSec (*https://trustedsec.com/blog*)
- Unsupervised Learning (*https://danielmiessler.com*)

Podcasts

- 7 Minute Security (*https://7minsec.com/projects/projects-podcast*)
- Brakeing Down Security (*http://www.brakeingsecurity.com*)
- Cloud Security Podcast (*https://cloud.withgoogle.com/cloudsecurity/podcast*) by Google
- CyberWire Daily (*https://thecyberwire.com/podcasts*)
- Darknet Diaries (*https://darknetdiaries.com*)
- Defensive Security (*http://www.defensivesecurity.org*)
- Detection: Challenging Paradigms (*https://www.dcppodcast.com*)
- Malicious Life (*https://malicious.life*)
- Microsoft Threat Intelligence Podcast (*https://oreil.ly/jqrE7*)
- NCSC Cyber Series (*https://oreil.ly/HkTxJ*)
- Risky Business (*http://risky.biz*)
- Threat Vector by Unit42 (*https://oreil.ly/rAXT2*)
- TrustedSec (*https://www.trustedsec.com/podcasts*)

Websites

- Allinfosecnews (*https://allinfosecnews.com*)
- Awesome Annual Security Reports (*https://oreil.ly/llG-9*)
- CISA (*https://www.cisa.gov*)
- CTFtime (*http://ctftime.org*) (list of upcoming CTFs)
- Dark Reading (*http://www.darkreading.com*)
- Digital Forensics Investigative Questions (*https://dfiq.org*)
- Explainshell (*https://explainshell.com*)
- Hacker News (*https://thehackernews.com*)
- IR Playbooks (*https://github.com/msraju/Incident-Response-Playbooks*)
- MalwareBazaar (*https://bazaar.abuse.ch*)
- Malware of the Day (*https://oreil.ly/S9V9s*)
- MultiRBL (*http://multirbl.valli.org*) (multi-block-list mail server checker)
- NIST National Vulnerability Database (*https://nvd.nist.gov*)
- OSINT Framework (*http://osintframework.com*)
- pentest-bookmarks (*https://oreil.ly/Lndnd*) (motherload security link dump)
- RegExr (*https://regexr.com*) (help with learning/validating regular expressions)
- SpeedOf.Me (*http://speedof.me*) (non-Flash, non-Java internet speed test)
- TinyEye (*http://www.tineye.com*) reverse image search
- Ultimate Windows Security (*https://www.ultimatewindowssecurity.com*)
- Unprotect Project (*https://unprotect.it*)
- US Government Configuration Baseline (*https://usgcb.nist.gov*)
- VirusTotal (*https://www.virustotal.com*)

User Education Templates

Live Phishing Education Slides

This template (or one like it created by you and your team!) can be used when auto-directing users after a live phishing campaign, as well as for normal instruction.

You've Been Hacked!

But it's OK...and it was only a quiz (the real test is from an attacker). (Click the arrows for more info!)

What Just Happened, and Why?

- Did you know: real attackers are making these same attempts all the time against our network?
- We'd rather help ourselves become stronger before the attackers can help themselves to our patients' data.
- No matter how many advanced technical hurdles internet security puts in place, the best defense is always an alert member of the team (you!).
- Classroom is theory—treating that first patient wasn't. It's better to practice when it's safe.

Social Engineering 101(0101)

Computers are black and white, on or off; humans aren't, so unfortunately we present a better target to attackers:

- RSA (security company) hacked in 2011 via email (*https://oreil.ly/5o-sZ*)
- HBGary (security company) hacked in 2011 via reused passwords and email (*https://oreil.ly/c9Xjr*)
- Google/Adobe—hacked, operation Aurora 2010 (*https://oreil.ly/sWD8Z*)

So It's OK That You Were Exploited (This Time)

- If people who work for computer technology companies—some of which specialize in security—fall for attacks, it's to be expected that you would fall for similar attacks as well.
- We get better with practice; this is an opportunity for that practice.

No Blame, No Shames, Just...

- You work for a healthcare organization where listening and trusting people is a priority! That's good!
- ...but social engineering plays on your good nature and trust by building rapport ("I love our patients, too!"), making a request ("Password, please!"), and often faking urgency ("The CEO/CIO/CNO all want this done now!").

A Few Strategies for Next Time

- If you aren't expecting an email from someone (even if you know them), don't click the links or open the attachment.
- If you think it might be work related, reply to the person and ask for more specifics.
- If a website is asking for personal information (like your password), and you don't recognize the site, call the IT help desk.

Because There Will Be a Next Time

- If the site looks correct, make sure that it is a secure site (*https://* in the URL bar, look for the lock).

If Something Feels Funny

- You just logged in, and you went immediately back to the login page.
- The site doesn't use HTTPS but requests a password.
- You received an email from someone you don't know or about a package you didn't send.
- A document that claims to have payroll information in it.
- A greeting card as an attachment.

If Something Looks Funny

- You open an attachment and you get a weird error, or the document doesn't contain what it said it would.
- You are prompted to turn on macros or install a driver update, or a new version of Flash player.
- The website looks like ours, but the website address (URL) in the address bar looks different.
- You find a USB thumb drive or a CD/DVD lying around.

If Something Sounds Funny

- You get a call from "IT," and they ask for your username and password or say they are working on a problem you have *not* reported.
- A call from a new vendor who wants to know who our current vendor for *xyz* is (so that they can call back and pose as being from that company).
- A request from the "fire marshal" to look at the extension cords under your computer desk (should be with facilities).
- You find a USB thumb drive or a CD/DVD lying around.

Feels, Looks, or Sounds Funny—Call the IT Help Desk

- If it is something normal, they can help you.
- If it is not, they'll escalate the issue so that we can take swift, appropriate action and warn other users.

What If I Already Clicked the Link or Opened the Attachment?

- No blame, no shame, but please—CALL NOW!
- The sooner your IT team knows, the sooner they can help you and prevent the issue from going farther.

What If I Didn't Click the Link or Attachment?

- If you think it looks suspicious, better safe than sorry.
- Your IT team still needs to know about the possible threat to our patients' protected health information (PHI).
- Other users might not be as discerning.
- The attacker might come back with something better next time.

Your IT Team Is Here for You!

- Would you like a one-on-one session to talk about any of this information?
- Do you lead a team who could benefit from this material?
- If so, please contact the help desk at x1111 and let us know!

Phishing Program Rules

Some explanation and rules of the phishing program will help your users get excited and involved in the rewards program.

Phishing is the act of attempting to acquire information such as usernames, passwords, and credit card details (and sometimes, indirectly, money) by masquerading as a trustworthy entity in an electronic communication.

The IT team would like to present a new contest called "Something Smells Phishy!"

We'll be putting on our hacker hats and trying to get you to fall for our security tests. While we won't be trying to gather your credit card details, there are currently real hackers out in the world trying to get every bit of information they can.

They are the real bad guys and the whole point behind this campaign. Expect to see more training and key points to remember:

1. Don't click links in emails.
2. Don't open attachments that you aren't expecting.
3. Never give your username/password to anyone.
4. If it smells phishy REPORT IT!

All of this is a training exercise, and the more you learn, the safer we all are and the more chances you have to win some awesome prizes! Each time you report a legitimate phishing attempt (either from us or a real attacker) your name gets entered into the phish bowl for the following prizes!

Things that should be reported:

1. Suspicious emails trying to get your information (usernames, passwords, what software we use, banking info, etc.).
2. Suspicious emails with attachments that you didn't expect.
3. People attempting to access your computer that you haven't authorized.

Index

Ruby, 239
Rust, 239
SDLC (software development lifecycle), 243
secure coding, 240-241
testing
dynamic, 242
peer review, 242
static, 241
CodeQL, 162
Committee of Sponsoring Organizations of the
Treadway Commission (COSO), 2, 86
Common Vulnerability Scoring System (CVSS),
234
communication
incident response, 63-64
policies, 48
company-wide teams, 41
Compatible Time-Sharing System (CTSS), 174
compliance, 81
CCM (Cloud Control Matrix), 86
CIS (Center for Internet Security) and, 85
COBIT (Control Objectives for Information
and Related Technologies), 86
COSO (Committee of Sponsoring Organizations of the Treadway Commission),
86
documentation and, 50
FERPA (Family Educational Rights and Privacy Act), 82
financial industries, 88
frameworks, 85-87
GLBA (Gramm-Leach-Bliley Act), 82-84
governmental agencies, 88-89
healthcare industry, 89-90
HIPAA (Health Insurance Portability and
Accountability Act), 84
ISO-270000 series, 86-87
MITRE ATT&CK, 87
NIST CSF (Cybersecurity Framework), 87
PCI DSS (Payment Card Industry Data
Security Standard), 84
policies and, 44
risk management and, 6
SOX (Sarbanes-Oxley) Act, 85
compliance officer, 82
confidentiality, integrity, and vulnerability
(CIA) triad, 71
configuration management
DR (disaster recovery) and, 80

misconfigurations, 152-153
written configuration standards, 145
consistency
documentation and, 50
policies, 43
continuous improvement, 7
contractors, physical security, 96
Control Objectives for Information and Related
Technologies (COBIT), 86
COSO (Committee of Sponsoring Organizations of the Treadway Commission), 2, 86
credential management, 161-162
credential stuffing attacks, 137
credit cards, 84
criticality, inventory schema and, 26
CSA (Cloud Security Alliance), 4
CSF (Cybersecurity Framework), 1
CTSS (Compatible Time-Sharing System), 174
CVSS (Common Vulnerability Scoring System),
234
Cybersecurity Framework (CSF), 1
Cybersecurity Maturity Model Certification
(CMMC), 89

D

data at rest
DR (disaster recovery) and, 79
encryption, 141
data center physical security, 94-95
data classification, 22
system creation, 22-24
university advancement example, 24-25
data in transit
DR (disaster recovery) and, 79
encryption, 142
data labeling, 28
data leakage, databases, 139-140
data storage
large enterprises, 22
midmarket enterprises, 21
small businesses, 20-21
database management system (DBMS), 135
databases
authentication, 143-144
authorization, 144
cloud databases, 134
configuration, 145
encryption, 141-143

firewalls, 146
hardening, 145-146
insider threats, 140
logging and, 296
management in the cloud, 146
Marriott Breach case study, 135, 136
Microsoft Access, 135
NoSQL, 134
patches, 145
RDBMS and, 134
relational databases, 134
self-managed, 134
serverless, 134
SQL injection, 138-139
unauthorized access
brute force attacks, 137
credential stuffing attacks, 137
data leakage, 139-140
dictionary attacks, 138
DBMS (database management system), 135
DDoS amplification, 210
decommissioning, asset management lifecycle, 34
decryption, 128
defense evasion, 140
demilitarized zone (DMZ), 214
Department of Defense (DoD) compliance, 89
deployment, asset management lifecycle, 34
desktop firewalls, 125-126
detection playbook, 162
development (see code development)
devices
endpoints, 130
hardening
firmware, 198-199
software patches, 198-199
DHCP (Dynamic Host Configuration Protocol), 35
diceware passphrases, 176-177
dictionary attacks, 138
digital linear tape (DLT) drives, 73
Digital Ocean, 153
directory information, 82
disaster recovery (see DR)
disk images, incident response and, 67-68
distribution of knowledge, policies and, 43, 50
DLT (digital linear tape) drives, 73
DMZ (demilitarized zone), 214
DNS (Domain Name System)

rDNS, 306
DNS logs, 296
DNS servers, 307-309
documentation, 17, 19
document contents, 53-54
hierarchy, 49
incident response and, 64, 65
physical security, 92
policies
language, 44
statements, 44
policy documents, 45-46
communication, 48
storage, 48
topics, 46-48
procedures, 52-53
standards, 50-52
DoD (Department of Defense) compliance, 89
Domain DNS Zone Master, 104
Domain Naming Master, 104
domains, AD DS (Active Directory Domain Services), 103-105
DR (disaster recovery)
alternate systems, 75
backups
failover, 78
physical, 73
cloud native strategies, 75-76
configuration management and, 80
data at rest and, 79
data in transit and, 79
datacenter loss, 77
dependencies, 77
hardware failure, 77
high-availability systems, 74
patching and, 80
physical access and, 78
physical security and, 80
ransomware, 77
RPO (recovery point objectives), 72
warm standby and, 74
RTO (recovery time objectives), 72-73
warm standby and, 74
scenarios, 77-78
scope, 71
system function reassignment, 75
testing, 79
user access and, 80

versus BCP (business continuity planning), 71

warm standby, 73-74

dumpster diving, 247

Dungeons & Dragons analogy, 22

duties, segmentation, 223-225

Dynamic Host Configuration Protocol (DHCP), 35

dynamic testing of code, 242

E

EAP (Extensible Authentication Protocol), 188

Ebbinghaus forgetting curve, 56

EC2 (Elastic Compute Cloud), 151

ECC (elliptic-curve cryptography), 177

EDA (event-driven architecture), 160

EDR (endpoint detection and response), 66, 266

(see also XDR/EDR platforms)

educational records, 82

egress filtering, 207-208

Elastic Compute Cloud (EC2), 151

electronic protected health information (ePHI), 84

elliptic-curve cryptography (ECC), 177

email notifications, 164-166

alerts, EventBridge, 167-169

GuardDuty, 166

testing, 169-171

email servers, 305-307

encrypted protocols, network hardening and, 202-203

encryption

AES (Advanced Encryption Standard), 177

data at rest, 141, 146

data in transit, 142, 146

databases, 142-143

decryption, 128

ECC (elliptic curve cryptography), 177

full-disk, 126-127

IDSs (intrusion detection systems), 280

IPSs (intrusion prevention systems), 280

MySQL database, Operation Lockdown, 147-148

performance and, 142

post-quantum, 178

quantum-hardened, 178

recommendations, 179

RSA (Rivest-Shamir-Adleman) algorithms, 177

SSL/TLS protocols and, 142

TDE (transparent data encryption), 142

endpoint detection and response (EDR), 66, 266

(see also XDR/EDR platforms)

endpoints, 3, 121

centralization and, 131

devices, 130

hardening

desktop firewalls, 125-126

disabling services, 124-125

encryption, full-disk, 126-127

Ivanti Endpoint Manager Mobile, 258

logging and, 296

patching, 122

macOS, 122-123

third-party updates, 124

Unix desktops, 123

Windows Update service, 122

protection tools, 128

visibility, 129

ePHI (electronic protected health information), 84

ETD (Event Threat Detection), 276

event-driven architecture (EDA), 160

EventBridge, 167-169

evil twin attacks, 211

executive champions, asset management and, 41

executive sign-off, policy documents, 45

executive teams, 2

extended detection and response (XDR), 66

(see also XDR/EDR platforms)

Extensible Authentication Protocol (EAP), 188

F

failover, 78

Family Educational Rights and Privacy Act (FERPA), 82

Federal Information Security Management Act (FISMA), 89

FedRAMP (Federal Risk and Authorization Management Program), 89

FERPA (Family Educational Rights and Privacy Act), 82

FGPPs (fine-grained password policies), 183

promiscuous mode, 268
proxy logs, 298
Puppet, 123
purple teaming, 245, 260-262
Python, 239

Q

quantum-hardened encryption protocols, 178

R

RADIUS (Remote Authentication Dial In User
    Service), 187-189
rainbow tables, 176
RAM, incident response and, 68
ransomware, 4
    recovery, 77
    use case, 10-12
RAS (Remote Access Server), 188
RDBMS (relational database management sys-
    tem)
    Microsoft SQL Server, 134
    MySQL, 134
    PostgreSQL, 134
rDNS (reverse DNS), 306
RDS (Relational Database Service), 134
recovery point objectives (see RPO)
recursion, 307
regulated industries, compliance, 88-90
regulatory compliance, 6
    documentation and, 50
    policies and, 44
relational database management systems (see
    RDBMSs)
relational databases, 134
Relative ID (RID) Master, 104
release, SDLC (software development lifecycle),
    244
remediation
    prioritizing, 234-235
    XDR/EDR platforms, 67
Remote Access Server (RAS), 188
Remote Authentication Dial In User Service
    (RADIUS), 187-189
remote exploits, 4
remote offices, physical security, 95
replication, cloud native DR, 76
requirements, SDLC (software development
    lifecycle), 243

resources, 310
RFID (radio frequency identification) keys, 97
RID (Relative ID) Master, 104
risk acceptance, 5, 236
risk assessment, 2-5
    inventory schema, 26-28
risk avoidance, 5
risk management, 6-9
Risk Management Framework (RMF), 2
risk remediation, 5
risk transfer, 5
Rivest-Shamir-Adleman (RSA) algorithms, 177
RMF (Risk Management Framework), 2
rogue access points, 211
roles and responsibilities
    policy documents, 45
    segmentation, 223-225
routers, 204-205
RPO (recovery point objectives), 72
    high-availability systems, 74
    warm standby and, 74
RSA (Rivest-Shamir-Adleman) algorithms, 177
RTO (recovery time objectives), 72-73
    dependencies and, 77
    high-availability systems, 74
    warm standby and, 74
Ruby, 239
Rust, 239

S

SaaS (software as a service), 150
salting, 179
Sarbanes-Oxley (SOX) Act, 85
SCCM (System Center Configuration Man-
    ager), 101
Schema Master, 104
SCIM (System for Cross-Domain Identity
    Management), 155
scope
    policy documents, 46
    risk assessment and, 4
    vulnerability assessment tools, 231
screen lock, 128
SDLC (software development lifecycle), 243
SDN (software-defined networking), 222
SDP (software-defined perimeter), 203
Search Processing Language (SPL), 154
secrets management, 161-162

repetition, 56
success rate tracking, 60

V

vendors, 3
video surveillance, 92-93
virtual LANs (see VLANs)
virtual private networks (VPNs), 219-220
visitors, physical security, 95
VLANs (virtual LANs), 205
    logical segmentation and, 216-217
VPC Flow Logs, 295
VPN attacks, 211
VPNs (virtual private networks), 219-220
vulnerabilities
    remediation prioritization, 234-235
    risk acceptance, 236
    severity rating, 234
vulnerability assessment, 227
    tools, 230-232
vulnerability management, 28, 227
    program initialization, 232-234
    software, 35
vulnerability scans, 228-230

W

war room, incident response and, 63
warm standby, disaster recovery and, 73-74
WEP (Wired Equivalent Privacy), 207
Wi-Fi Protect Access (WPA), 207
Windows Management Interface (WMI), 35
Windows Server Update Services (WSUS), 101,
    122

Wired Equivalent Privacy (WEP), 207
wireless network attacks, 211-212
wireless protocols
    4G/5G cellular networks, 206
    Bluetooth, 206
    NFC (Near-Field Communication), 206
    WEP (Wired Equivalent Privacy), 207
    WPA (Wi-Fi Protect Access), 207
    WPA2, 207
    WPA3, 207
    Zigbee, 206
Wireshark, 69
WMI (Windows Management Interface), 35
workspace physical security, 92
WPA (Wi-Fi Protect Access), 207
WPA2, 207
WPA3, 207
WSUS (Windows Server Update Services), 101,
    122

X

XDR (extended detection and response), 66
XDR/EDR platforms, 66-67

Y

YAML, 153

Z

Zeek, 68, 268
zero trust network access (ZTNA), 203
Zigbee, 206

About the Authors

Amanda Berlin is a highly accomplished network defender and public speaker. She is a principal detection and product manager for Blumira, leading an R&D team dedicated to lowering time to detection and improving the overall security landscape. She has spent over a decade in different areas of technology and sectors providing infrastructure support, triage, and design. Amanda has been involved in implementing a secure PCI process and HIPAA compliance as well as building a comprehensive phishing and awards-based user education program. Amanda serves as the founder and CEO of Mental Health Hackers, a nonprofit dedicated to providing education and guidance to tech workers around mental health topics. Amanda is also the co-host of the "Brakeing Down Security" podcast. On X, she's @InfoSystir.

Lee Brotherston is the founding security engineer at OpsHelm. Having spent nearly two decades in information security, Lee has worked as an internal security resource across many verticals, including finance, telecommunications, hospitality, entertainment, and government, in roles ranging from engineer to IT security manager.

William F. Reyor III, based in Connecticut, is a seasoned threat researcher and director of security at Modus Create. He has a wealth of experience across various technology sectors, providing critical cybersecurity support and innovative solutions. His notable career trajectory includes key roles at prominent organizations (such as The Walt Disney Company and Raytheon Technologies) and Chief Information Security Officer at Fairfield University. His work primarily revolves around investigating threat actor activities, developing automated threat detections, and streamlining incident responses. Additionally, William has made significant contributions to the cybersecurity community as one of the lead organizers for Security BSides Connecticut since 2011.

Colophon

The animal on the cover of *Defensive Security Handbook* is a Malayan porcupine (*Hystrix brachyura*), which is a species of rodent native to South and Southeast Asia. This porcupine can be found in Nepal through northeast India, central and southern China, Myanmar, Thailand, Vietnam, peninsular Malaysia, and throughout Borneo. It's also found on the island of Penang, Malaysia.

The Malayan porcupine's body is large, stout, and covered with sharp, rigid quills, which are modified hair. Quills on the upper body are rough and black with white or yellow stripes. The porcupines' short, stocky legs are covered in brown hairs; they have four claws on the front legs and five on the hind legs. Young porcupines have soft quills that become hard as they enter adulthood.

Malayan porcupines often live in forest habitats or open areas near forests. They inhabit dens near rocky areas by digging into the ground, where they live in small groups. They can also live in burrows connected by a network of trails or in a hole in tree bark or roots. The Malayan porcupine can give birth to two litters of two to three young annually; its gestation period is 110 days. They forage at night and typically feed on roots, tubers, bark, and fallen fruit, and sometimes on carrion and insects. During the day, they rest singly or in pairs. They can live up to 27 years.

Many of the animals on O'Reilly covers are endangered; all of them are important to the world.

The cover illustration is by Karen Montgomery, based on an image from *Beeton's Dictionary*. The series design is by Edie Freedman, Ellie Volckhausen, and Karen Montgomery. The cover fonts are Gilroy Semibold and Guardian Sans. The text font is Adobe Minion Pro; the heading font is Adobe Myriad Condensed; and the code font is Dalton Maag's Ubuntu Mono.

O'REILLY®

Learn from experts.
Become one yourself.

Books | Live online courses
Instant answers | Virtual events
Videos | Interactive learning

Get started at oreilly.com.

©2023 O'Reilly Media, Inc. O'Reilly is a registered trademark of O'Reilly Media, Inc. | 175_7_v0.1875

Milton Keynes UK
Ingram Content Group UK Ltd.
UKHW050428310824
447623UK00003B/6

9 781098 127244